THE GREAT NORTHEAST BREWERY TOUR

TAP INTO THE BEST CRAFT BREWERIES IN NEW ENGLAND AND THE MID-ATLANTIC

BEN KEENE

PHOTOGRAPHY BY BETHANY BANDERA

First published in 2014 by Voyageur Press, an imprint of Quarto Publishing Group USA Inc., 400 First Avenue North, Suite 400, Minneapolis, MN 55401 USA

The information in this book is true and complete to the best of our knowledge. All recommendations are made without any guarantee on the part of the author or Publisher, who also disclaims any liability incurred in connection with the use of this data or specific details.

We recognize, further, that some words, model names, and designations mentioned herein are the property of the trademark holder. We use them for identification purposes only. This is not an official publication.

Voyageur Press titles are also available at discounts in bulk quantity for industrial or sales-promotional use. For details write to Special Sales Manager at Quarto Publishing Group USA Inc., 400 First Avenue North, Suite 400, Minneapolis, MN 55401 USA.

To find out more about our books, visit us online at www.voyageurpress.com.

ISBN: 978-0-7603-4448-4

Library of Congress Cataloging-in-Publication Data

Keene, Ben, 1978-
    The great northeast brewery tour : tap into the best craft breweries in New England and the Mid-Atlantic / Ben Keene ; photography, Bethany Bandera.
        pages cm
     Summary: "A full-color illustrated travel guide to notable craft breweries of the northeast and mid-Atlantic states"-- Provided by publisher.
    ISBN 978-0-7603-4448-4 (pbk.)
    1. Microbreweries--Northeastern States. 2. Microbreweries--Middle Atlantic States. I. Title.
    TP573.U6K44 2014
    663'.420974--dc23
                       2013024671

Acquisitions Editor: Grace Labatt
Design Manager: James Kegley
Cover Design: Gavin Duffy
Layout: Kim Winscher

Printed in China

To Ali, my first and favorite beer touring companion.

This book is for you.

TABLE OF CONTENTS

FOREWORD

Back in the day, when I was a college student in Boston in the early 1980s, we had no beer. And we had neither bread nor cheese, but we didn't know that. We thought we had all of these things—surely we drank something called "beer," didn't we? And did we not peel the cheese from between the panes of plastic? But here's the strange secret—we didn't really *like* beer. In those days the legal drinking age was eighteen, and like many college students, we drank whatever we could afford. When beer was "good," it tasted like fizzy water at best, and when it was "bad," it brought a swampy new meaning to the word.

A word we never applied to beer was "beautiful." I discovered "beautiful" while living in London after graduating from film school. When I wasn't stage-managing rock bands, I was at the pub, learning some of the most important lessons of my life. Real beer could be beautiful, fascinating, transporting, even magical. And it mattered a lot where you drank your beer and with whom you drank it. As I traveled through Europe, I reveled in wonderful beer in almost every country, but when I returned home to the States, I found the same barren beer shelves and taps that I'd left behind. The only answer lay in my own pot, a six-gallon glass jar, bags of barley malt, cans of elixirs, little packets of living powders, and a quest for beauty. It's taken decades, but out of thousands of pots in thousands of kitchens, the American craft beer movement emerged, and what a wonderment it is to behold.

Today, thirty years later, "beautiful" resides in the American beer glass, we have real bread and real cheese to accompany it, and we have brilliant places to drink it. This is a book about some of those places, places you want to know about, places you should end up. Within several hours' drive of my home in Brooklyn, there are more than 60 million people, and some of these people have created dozens of great places to enjoy beer. Our guide is Ben Keene, and Mr. Keene knows his beer. More importantly, he is a map enthusiast and a Master of Creative Wandering, a skill that he now brings to bear on our behalf. *The Great Northeast Brewery Tour* wheedles its way in a suitably relaxed manner through some of the finest breweries of the northeastern United States, tells us the stories of the people who built them, tastes some of their excellent beers, and then wanders off to check out all sorts of cool things nearby. Out of all of these meanderings rises something more than mere entertainment. To say that this book shows us beer enthusiasts "a design for living" may sound all too grand, but read it and I think you might agree.

I have a few questions. When the sun begins to set on the gorgeous beaches at Sandy Hook, New Jersey, where might you go? Do you know your way to The Chubby Pickle? Have you had the tasty, summery Boat Beer from Carton

Brewing? While driving though rural Maine, will you find your way to Baxter Brewing? Might you ride the ten-mile bicycle loop around Lake Auburn? In *The Great Northeast Brewery Tour*, you will find a lot more than breweries and their beers—you'll find people that you want to meet and days that you want to have. You'll find that many Northeastern breweries have themselves become beautiful. Many Northeastern craft breweries were once well-loved but grubby affairs cobbled together out of dented old dairy tanks and rolls of duct tape. Today, the beauty isn't just in the beer—here you'll find handsome spaces where you can happily bring not only friends, but your whole family. Breweries have once again taken their rightful places at the centers of their communities, and if that isn't beautiful, I don't know what is. Get this book, turn off your computer, walk out the door, and wander off into the great Northeast. There are people out there waiting to brew a pint for you and to have a pint with you. Go. Live a little. No, actually, *live a lot*.

— Garrett Oliver, Brooklyn, New York

PREFACE

Ask any brewer or student of America's beverage history and you'll hear a similar refrain: The craft beer movement as we know it started on the West Coast. Some people will correctly point to Jack McAuliffe and his New Albion Brewing Company in California's wine country as the pioneer whose ales launched a thousand breweries. The year was 1976. Ken Grossman of Sierra Nevada soon followed, launching his now iconic brand and setting off a domino effect of sorts that spread from coast to coast. Then in 1981, William S. Newman founded the first microbrewery in the East, but like McAuliffe, he only managed to stay in business for six short years.

Today, the United States has more than 2,400 breweries scattered across its fifty states, more than at any other time since the 1880s. And while California and the Pacific Northwest continue to innovate and push the envelope, the Northeast, which includes several beer companies that opened their doors in the 1980s, has seen a remarkable amount of change, too. New York alone has more than one hundred companies brewing beer within its borders, and even the tiny District of Columbia now has upward of ten breweries and brewpubs. In fact, by the time you finish reading this book, another enterprising individual will probably have received federal approval for the next hot brewery.

After lagging behind its western counterparts for so long, the Northeast—where the first European brewers established themselves in the seventeenth century—has surged forward in the last decade, adding breweries at a surprising clip, from the White Mountains to the Potomac River. But it's not only sheer numbers that make this news impressive. These breweries (and their beers, of course) are also noteworthy for their diversity, creativity, and dedication. From urban brewpubs with no distribution and brewery hotels with rooms for sleeping off an indulgent evening, to rural farmhouse breweries and larger established breweries with familiar names and logos, these businesses represent a wide range of people, products, and goals. Some of them, like the Alchemist and Fiddlehead in Vermont, choose to focus on a single beer, working to perfect a recipe and offering limited runs of anything else. Others, like Marshall Wharf in Maine and Bluejacket in D.C., seem intent on trying nearly everything, from low-alcohol session beers to challenging sours that might throw your taste buds for a loop. You'll find small breweries that concentrate on British styles (Norwich), bigger breweries that have earned fame for hoppy American styles (Flying Dog), and even a few places that seem willing to toss just about anything into a beer, from licorice root and cayenne pepper to bread fruit and grape must (Dogfish Head). So when you hear people describe the United States as the most exciting brewing nation in the world (hang out at enough breweries and you will), know that they aren't exaggerating.

I grew up outside of Washington, D.C., spent more than a decade in New York, and currently live in Massachusetts. A Belgian neighbor and a bottle of Chimay first opened my eyes to the possibilities of beer, and for the better part of my adult life, I've watched the Northeastern beer scene grow and mature. I set out to write this book to convey my enthusiasm for some of the breweries that I'm especially fond of. This book isn't intended to be a tasting guide though—I haven't tried every beer made in each of the states I visited, nor will my favorites necessarily match your own. Besides, dozens of of books and websites already rate and review thousands upon thousands of beers. Neither was I trying to write the definitive brewery reference. The sheer number of them meant I never stood much of a chance of ending up with a comprehensive volume; I could have easily included twice as many. My goal is to stimulate curiosity and encourage exploration. I have, however, found many breweries that now number among my favorites. Visit them, compare them, and find yours.

From the beginning, I envisioned this book as a visual record, a snapshot of the craft beer landscape at a particular point in time. Hopefully I've provided a context for Bethany's beautiful images, and hopefully you'll view them as another storyline that complements my own. To me, beer is much more than liquid in a glass. It's about people, places, and, increasingly, terroir. It's a drink for all occasions that can satisfy with its simplicity or dazzle with its sophistication. Throughout the Northeast, craft brewers are experimenting with local ingredients, from wheat and barley to fruits and honey, and in a few cases, native yeast. As wood aging has become more popular, some of these breweries are also turning to local wineries and distilleries for barrels. Plus, in the last handful of years, small-scale hop farming and malting have begun to return to the region. The future looks promising.

As much as possible, I tried to cast a wide geographic net, aiming to encourage beer travelers to venture west from the coast, to explore beyond the I-95 corridor. When you visit the places in this book, you'll almost inevitably end up chatting with someone else making their first trip (or their weekly growler run) to the same brewery. Even if you're the shy type, introduce yourself—beer people tend to be a friendly lot. During the course of your conversation, you'll probably learn about at least one other brewery nearby, one that you could probably squeeze into your schedule or at least remember for the next time. At the Brooklyn Brewery someone might mention SingleCut Beersmiths in Astoria, Queens; in Chelsea, Massachusetts at Mystic Brewery you could learn about Night Shift Brewing in nearby Everett. And in Philadelphia, a beer-loving city if there ever was one, you'll likely hear mention of Victory, Yards, and the Nodding Head. Remember these names and seek them out. This book is intended to be a compass pointing the way, not a GPS plotting an unwavering route.

In the end, I didn't want to write another book full of technical explanations and beer minutiae. I find the flavor profiling categories developed by Greg Engert of D.C.'s Bluejacket appealing and uncomplicated. Rather than the 33 pages of style guidelines published by the Brewers Association in 2013, Engert groups beers according to seven characteristics: malt, roast, smoke, crisp, hop, fruit and spice, and tart and funky. Clear and to the point, in many ways these categories make sense even if you haven't spent as much time thinking about beer as someone like Engert has. When I surveyed the existing literature on craft beer, I saw a need for a book that, like many a beer, is approachable—a book that doesn't necessarily require a vast knowledge of the subject or its jargon. I understood that The Great Northeast Brewery Tour would be subjective, but hopefully I've shown the depth and breadth of craft brewing in a single part of a large country, a dynamic region with a rich cultural and culinary history and brewers producing exceptional, unusual, and memorable beers.

Thomas Hooker Brewery
BLOOMFIELD

Relic Brewing
PLAINVILLE

New England Brewing
WOODBRIDGE

Two Roads Brewing
STRATFORD

CONNECTICUT

NEW ENGLAND BREWING

YEAR FOUNDED: 1989

OWNERS:
Rob Leonard and Matt Westfall

ANNUAL PRODUCTION:
3,000-3,500 barrels

YEAR-ROUND & SEASONAL BEERS: Sea Hag IPA, Elm City Lager, Atlantic Amber, Ghandi Bot Double IPA, Imperial Stout Trooper, Fuzzy Baby Ducks IPA, Friar's Quad, 668 Neighbor of the Beast, Ghost Pigeon Porter, Scrumtrulescent Saison, Premeditated Murder Barleywine, Coriolis, Gold Stock Ale, Wet Willy Scotch Ale

LOCAL FLAVOR: Observant visitors might notice the likeness of a legendary singer scattered around the brewery. At last count there were nine pieces of Elvis art.

It's hard not to like a company with a sense of humor. So when a brewery calls their American IPA Fuzzy Baby Ducks and dubs their Scotch Ale Wet Willy, you'd have to be a stoic not to crack a smile. When brewer Rob Leonard, the current co-owner of New England Brewing, bought the name and beer recipes from his employers in 2001 though, things were serious. As in seriously troubled. After some initial success in the '90s, the small South Norwalk business had hit a rough patch, and Leonard found himself with a brand in need of rebuilding. Taking the four products in New England Brewing's range with him to Woodbridge and deciding it was time for a little reinvention, he opted to focus on beers he liked to drink. Of course quality obviously counts, but Leonard thought beer should be fun, too. So he "fired" the flagship beer, Atlantic Amber, tweaked the barleywine, renaming it Premeditated Murder, and brought in Matt Westfall, a younger head brewer who has helped New England experiment with barrel aging and new hop varieties.

Sample these additions and more by visiting the brewery, tucked away on a side street just outside of New Haven. Prepare to be greeted at the door by Eli, a black Labrador retriever who may or may not be authorized to check IDs. Tastes are always free and growler fills run between $10 and $20, depending on the beer. Quirky T-shirts featuring label art cost $15. There's no fancy taproom here, just the corner of a working brewery that serves as a tasting bar and growler-filling station. Chat with other visitors, pose for a picture with "Forky" the forklift, ask about the brewing process, or just drink your beer and bob your head along to The Clash's *Combat Rock* or whatever album happens to be in rotation.

CONTACT

7 Selden Street
Woodbridge, CT 06525
203-387-2222
www.newenglandbrewing.com
@NewEnglandBrew

TASTING ROOM HOURS:

Mon-Fri, Noon-6pm;
Sat, 11am-3pm

LODGING:

The Study at Yale
1157 Chapel Street
New Haven, CT 06511
203-503-3900
www.studyhotels.com

Get to know the brewery by starting off with Elm City Lager (5% ABV), a pale gold, hoppy pilsner that remains a favorite for the two brewers. Next, move on to Sea Hag IPA (6.2% ABV), a medium-bodied example of the style that gets its mildly spicy character and zesty citrus quality from a combination of European Noble hops and American Cascade hops. The slightly bitter aftertaste tends to linger pleasantly. On the other hand, if the darker end of the beer spectrum is your thing, ask for a splash of chocolaty Ghost Pigeon Porter (5.8% ABV). This beer confidently walks the line between sweet and bitter, melding sugary molasses flavors with the snappy bite of anise or black licorice. Playing around with a few of their bigger beers, Leonard and Westfall have aged their 8.8% ABV Double IPA in tequila barrels to transform Ghandi Bot into Zapata Bot and filled a number of chardonnay barrels with their 9% ABV Belgian pale strong ale to create Chardonneighbor of the Beast.

To try a pint of New England beer with a meal, head into downtown New Haven where a number of taverns have one of their ales on rotation. At Prime 16 Taphouse & Burgers (203-782-1616; www.prime16.com), the bright, biting, and draft-only Gold Stock (6.5% ABV) mingles well with the salmon burger. Just around the corner is the Cask Republic (475-238-8335; www.thecaskrepublic.com), a self-described neighborhood restaurant that frequently hosts beer dinners.

Four short miles from the brewery, Yale University, founded in 1701, is a pleasant place to admire three centuries of architecture. One highlight is certainly the Yale Peabody Museum of Natural History (203-432-5050; www.peabody.yale.edu). West Rock Ridge State Park (203-287-5658; www.ct.gov/deep) is the best place to go for views of the harbor and Long Island Sound. A bit farther from downtown, Lighthouse Point Park (203-946-8019; www.cityofnewhaven.com/Parks) and nearby Fort Hale Park are both worth seeking out for a picnic, a quick dip in the Sound, or bird-watching in the spring and fall. 🍺

RELIC
BREWING COMPANY

YEAR FOUNDED: 2012

FOUNDER:
Mark Sigman

ANNUAL PRODUCTION:
250-350 barrels

YEAR-ROUND & SEASONAL BEERS: Blackheart, HBC 342, Clockwork, Antiquity, Prologue, Shipwright, Queen Anne's Revenge, Stella, Fool's Gold Alt, Houndstooth, Whiting Street, Witching Hour, Fieldhand, Fortnight, Transatlantic, Ryddle, The Falconess, One Foot in the Grave

LOCAL FLAVOR: With a background in marketing, Sigman tapped some of the graphic artists he's worked with in the past to design labels for Relic.

Before beer, Mark Sigman was addicted to travel. From Thailand to Mongolia, and Turkey to Jordan, he spent years working seasonal jobs in order to be able to take long trips abroad. Along the way, he also did a fair amount of culinary exploration, tasting anything and everything from East African millet beer to the ur-beers of Germany and the Czech Republic. A move to Jackson Hole, Wyoming, introduced him to craft beer, and like so many brewers before him, once his eyes had been opened to its diversity of styles and flavors, he wanted to learn how to make his own. After eighteen years as a homebrewer, Sigman finally decided to open a beer business in his home state, dubbing it Relic after the artifacts and antiquities he admired on his international journeys.

The Relic's tasting room is an unfussy space, with two small windows, exposed pipes running across the ceiling, and a handful of contemporary paintings and illustrations on the walls—the work of local artists that Sigman chooses on a monthly basis. Drop in to sample beer, check out the artwork, and trade stories about adventures abroad. Samples of Relic beers on tap are free, while 22-ounce bottles range from $6 to $9 and growler fills start at $10. You can also purchase T-shirts and tulip glasses emblazoned with the Relic logo, an imperial pint glass flanked by a pair of heraldic lions.

Fittingly, Sigman decided his first beer would be an old ale, a sweet and malty British style that historically had a low level of bitterness and a trace of sour acidity. He called it Antiquity (8.3% AV). One of the things that makes Relic a fun place to visit is the surprise factor: you don't necessarily know what they will be pouring until you get there. Brewing with several different yeast strains and occasionally incorporating out of the ordinary ingredients like Valencia oranges and lavender, Sigman clearly enjoys challenging expectations about beer. Rye ales have become more popular in recent years, but Relic offers a hoppy rye lager called Prologue (5.6% ABV) instead. Whiting Street (5.6% ABV), a pre-Prohibition beer made with flaked corn, is fermented with both ale and lager yeast. Which isn't to say he neglects hopheads. Quite the opposite. Yellow-orange in color, Clockwork (5% ABV), a sessionable IPA with a fresh, fragrant aroma, is full of bittersweet lime flavor and finishes with an herbal aftertaste. And Fortnight (7.2% ABV) is a

CONTACT

95B Whiting Street
Plainville, CT 06062
860-255-4252
www.relicbeer.com
@RelicBrewing

TASTING ROOM HOURS:

Fri, 4-7pm; and
Sat, Noon-3pm

LODGING:

The Connecticut River Valley Inn
2195 Main Street
Glastonbury, CT 06033
860-633-7374
www.connecticutrivervalleyinn.com

more assertive IPA with brown sugar pushing its boozy presence higher and several American hop varieties giving it a citric bitterness.

Several area restaurants feature Sigman's beers with regularity. J. Timothy's Tavern (860-747-6813; www.jtimothys.com) in Plainville is one such establishment, and their dinner menu includes numerous entrees well suited for a beer pairing. Assuming you make it to dessert, skip the cordial and try the bread pudding with a glass of Queen Anne's Revenge porter (7.75% ABV). Within walking distance of the brewery, 50 West (860-351-5066; www.50westct.com) serves lunch and dinner and proudly devotes one of its six draft lines to Relic. Order a house specialty like the New England mac and cheese with sweet peas and smoked ham and then hope to see Fool's Gold Alt (7% ABV) on the drink list. A few miles away in Bristol, Barley Vine (860-589-0239; www.barleyvinect.com) is another gastropub with beer-friendly comfort food.

The Connecticut River Valley contains dozens of attractions that can round out a trip to the Constitution State. Just north of Relic in Hartford, the Mark Twain House and Museum (860-247-0998; www.marktwainhouse.org) preserves the legacy of Samuel Clemens. If you're looking for an activity that's a little less quiet, the New Britain Rock Cats (860-224-8383; www.rockcats.com) play their home games just east of Plainville. Also, the Mount Southington Ski Area has fourteen short trails, seven lifts, a rental shop, and a small restaurant. 🍶

THOMAS HOOKER BREWERY

YEAR FOUNDED: 1996

FOUNDER:
Curt Cameron

ANNUAL PRODUCTION:
12,000 barrels

YEAR-ROUND & SEASONAL BEERS: American Pale Ale, Blonde Ale, Hop Meadow IPA, Imperial Porter, Irish Red, Liberator Dopplebock, Munich Style Golden Lager, Old Marley Barleywine, Chocolate Truffle Stout, Watermelon Ale, Octoberfest, Nor'Easter Lager

LOCAL FLAVOR: Thomas Hooker, a Puritan minister who immigrated to New England in 1633, founded Hartford with a hundred members of his congregation from Cambridge, Massachusetts. History is unclear on whether or not he liked beer.

The company known today as the Thomas Hooker Brewery actually started off in Hartford as a brewpub called the Trout Brook Brewing Company. And as one of the brewpub's most popular beers, Thomas Hooker Ale eventually seemed like a pretty good name for a Connecticut company that at times couldn't decide if it wanted to be a restaurant or a brewery. In 2003, the new name became official, and in 2007, Cameron, who had previously found success in the Silicon Valley and then running a pair of area liquor stores, moved brewing operations west to Bloomfield where he grew production tenfold in a matter of five years. Along the way, the self-described serial entrepreneur also discovered a passion for craft beer; in 2009 he decided to plant 200 hop plants on his property in New Hartford, west of the brewery. Several years later, those flowers ended up in a barrel-aged saison. With business booming in Bloomfield, Cameron is now close to moving back to Hartford into an even larger space with a restaurant and beer garden.

Inside the current space, a few cushy old couches, a number of old coffee tables littered with beer magazines, two flat-screen TVs, and an XBox all make it clear that this is a place to relax with other beer pilgrims. It's a casual, comfortable environment that's completely lacking in pretense. A panel exhibit by the Connecticut Historical Society shares biographical information about Thomas Hooker, highlights the state's brewing history, the role of taverns in colonial times, and Prohibition while the rest of the décor consists of framed awards, tongue-in-cheek Hooker Beer posters, and a small collection of bottles and growlers lined up near the ceiling. In the brewhouse behind the tasting room proper, a large cartoony mural brightens the space. New growlers will set you back $11 (more if you want to fill it with porter or dopplebock), while refills run $8 for 64 ounces of fresh beer. At the brewery's Friday night open houses, a $10 donation is requested for a tour, tasting, and souvenir glass. A local nonprofit, the Village for Families and Children, also receives a portion of the proceeds.

Thomas Hooker produces a straightforward lineup of approachable beers, from a Munich-style golden lager to their rich, dark Imperial Porter, but it's their seasonal releases that have been some of their most popular. Watermelon Ale (5.1% ABV) went over well from the moment it was first released, offering a crisp, light body, and a thirst-quenching touch of melon perfectly suited for the heat of summer. Meanwhile, the full-bodied, deep, dark brown Chocolate Truffle Stout (7.1% ABV) is for dessert lovers. Cocoa powder and cocoa nibs from Munson's, the state's largest chocolatier, as well as six different types of malt and roasted barley give this beer its identity: a silky sweetness and a full body. Add their award-winning Octoberfest Lager (5.7% ABV) to that seasonal list, and you have a tough choice to make about what time of year to visit. Lined up alongside its siblings in a tasting flight, the delicate nature of the straw yellow, medium-bodied Blonde Ale causes it to get lost in the mix a bit, while the chewy, smooth, and malty Irish Red (5.5% ABV) and the barrel-aged Old Marley Barleywine (10% ABV) assert themselves as beers to be remembered. More recently, Hooker has taken another step into the flavorful world of barrel aging, releasing a saison as the first in their Connecticut Barrel Series in 2013. Brewed with peppercorn and Saaz hops from Cameron's hop farm, it spent time in oak barrels from Jonathan Edwards Vineyard in North Stonington and Hopkins Vineyard in Warren.

When hunger strikes, make your way to Harry's Bishop Corner (860-236-0400; www.harrysbc.com) for pizza Napoletana that's consistently rated as one of the best in the Hartford area. Subtle and smooth with a mild level of bitterness obtained from a Czech hop variety called Saaz, Hooker's Blonde Ale (4.6% ABV) would be equally delicious with a classic Margherita pie or a specialty pizza such as the white clam with fresh wild-caught clam, garlic, lemon juice, and a generous drizzle of extra virgin olive oil. There's also a good chance you'll find Blonde Ale at Plan B (860-231-1199; www.planbburger.com), a popular burger bar chain that offers their patties more than twenty different ways. Meanwhile, at Max's Oyster Bar (860-236-6299; www.maxrestaurantgroup.com/oyster) in

West Hartford, one tap line is devoted to a single beer all the time: Brewtus Maximus (5.96% ABV). Brewed by Thomas Hooker especially for the Max Restaurant Group, this straightforward and approachable pale ale is only available at locations of this Connecticut family of restaurants. The versatility of Brewtus makes it a suitable partner for everything from the crab cake with black garlic aioli and peppadew sweet peppers to the crispy striped bass with clams, saffron potatoes, and tomato.

Before or after a tour of Hooker, outdoor enthusiasts will want to allow time for a hike down the road at Talcott Mountain State Park (860-242-1158; www.ct.gov/deep). In 1914 Gilbert F. Heublein, a food and beverage tycoon who briefly owned Minnesota's Hamm Brewing Company, built a lavish Bavarian-style summer home complete with an impressive tower at the summit of the mountain. Climb Heublein Tower's 110 stairs on a clear day, and you'll be able to see Hartford, the Long Island Sound, and Mount

CONTACT

16 Tobey Road
Bloomfield, CT 06002
860-242-3111
www.hookerbeer.com
@hookerbeer

TASTING ROOM HOURS:

Fri, 5-8pm (first and third Friday
each month); Sat, Noon-5pm

LODGING:

Simsbury 1820 House
731 Hopmeadow Street
Simsbury, CT 06070
860-658-7658
www.simsbury1820house.com
www.connecticutrivervalleyinn.com

Monadnock in New Hampshire from your manmade aerie more than a thousand feet above sea level. When temperatures dip below freezing at the end of the year and through the winter months, the Winding Trails Cross Country Ski Center (860-677-8458; www.windingtrails.org) is a great place to enjoy a snowy afternoon. Rolling terrain crisscrossed by twelve miles of groomed trails, a hill for snow tubing, and a pond for ice skating make Winding Trails an easy choice for anyone who enjoys outdoor activities. Thirsty for some evening entertainment? Head to the Bushnell Center for the Performing Arts (860-987-5900; www.bushnell.org) in Hartford for Broadway and off-Broadway tours, jazz, blues, cabaret and comedy performances, and world music concerts.

TWO ROADS
BREWING COMPANY

YEAR FOUNDED: 2012

FOUNDERS:
Brad Hittle, Phil Markowski,
Clement Pellani, Peter Doering

ANNUAL PRODUCTION:
4,000-5,000 barrels
(plus contracted beers)

**YEAR-ROUND &
SEASONAL BEERS:** Ol' Factory
Pils, Road to Ruin Double IPA, Workers
Comp Saison, Honeyspot Road White
IPA, Igor's Dream Russian Imperial Stout,
Henry's Farm Double Bock, No Limits
Hefeweizen, Hizzoner Maibock, Pumpkin
Ale, Octoberfest, Holiday Ale

LOCAL FLAVOR: The Baird Machine
Company built the building that houses the
brewery today and once made rivets and
buttons for Levi Strauss & Company.

When the label reads "the road less traveled," you might expect a few wrong turns on the way to Two Roads. Luckily, this ambitious Connecticut brewery is less than half a mile from Interstate 95. The six-acre lot and an imposing, century-old brick factory building make Two Roads hard to miss, too. As it turns out, the Robert Frost–inspired mantra refers to the beers themselves, not the address. When the four founders decided to do something about the state's lack of native craft beer, they also decided to brew classic styles in unique ways, and to do it with an eye on the environment— repurposing an old building and installing systems to be as energy efficient as possible.

The result is a modern brewery that exudes industrial charm. Enter from the parking lot and climb a creaky wood staircase to reach the second–floor tasting room and retail shop. On the way you'll pass black and white photos of the old machine shop as well as several shots of early Sikorsky helicopter models (the company is headquartered in Stratford). A large central bar with sixteen taps and two growler stations dominates the space. On weekends, join a tour (first come, first served) or sidle up to the bar to sample the available beers ($2 for four tasters, $5 for a pint, $6 for special releases). Round, waist-high tables made from old cable spools dot the room if the bar gets too crowded, and from May to September an outdoor beer garden offers a third area to relax with your beer. A retrofitted 1966 Airstream houses the tap system for the beer garden. Plus from New York, it's a short train ride to Stratford and then a bus ride away.

Brewmaster Phil Markowski made his mark at Long Island's Southampton Publick House where he won more than twenty awards for his recipes, many of which were designed in the tradition of Belgian farmhouse ales. Start by sampling Worker's

Comp Saison (4.8% ABV), an effervescent pour with lemongrass and tropical fruit aromas and the subtly spicy aftertaste of clove and toasted cinnamon stick. Meanwhile, his white IPA, Honeyspot Road (6% ABV), named for the nearest highway exit, is a hazy yellow beer with a creamier mouthfeel due to the addition of wheat. Lemon curd and bananas foster spring to mind with each flavorful sip. The aroma might remind you of a hoppy Belgian wit, but the bite definitely says IPA. Given the proximity of Igor Sikorsky Memorial Airport and the National Helicopter Museum, it's little surprise the Two Roads crew chose to call their barrel-aged Russian imperial stout Igor's Dream (10.9% ABV). Meanwhile, the brewery had fun naming their double IPA, a beer with aromas of sawdust and orange spice, a bitter backbone, and a sturdy malt profile, calling it Road to Ruin (7.2% ABV).

For a laid-back atmosphere outside of the Two Roads tasting room, check out Dive Bar & Restaurant (203-933-3483; www.divebarandrestaurant.com) or Barnum Publick House (203-690-1044; www.barnumpublickhouse.com) just south of Stratford. Of course if you're having a good time and don't want to give up your seat at the bar, Fat Sammy's Pizzeria (203-870-6422; www.fatsammyspizza.com) delivers to the brewery.

In Bridgeport, cruises of Black Rock Harbor leave from Captain's Cove Seaport on weekends between May and September. To relax on the shores of the Long Island Sound, make your way to Short Beach Park in Stratford or Seaside Park in Bridgeport (860-424-3034; www.lisrc.uconn.edu/coastalaccess/index.asp). For years, the Barnum Museum (203-331-1104; www.barnum-museum.org) in Bridgeport attracted tourists fascinated by the life of P. T. Barnum. Tornado damage to the building forced it to close for repairs, however, and only the modern wing remains open on a limited schedule. Fortunately there's more to this city than beaches and historic architecture. Plan ahead and you can see the minor league Bridgeport Bluefish (203-345-4800; www.blueportbluefish.com) at one of their home games at the Ballpark at Harbor Yard. 🍾

CONTACT

1700 Stratford Avenue
Stratford, CT 06615
203-335-2010
www.tworoadsbrewing.com
@2RoadsBrewing

TASTING ROOM HOURS:

Tue-Fri, 3-8pm; Sat, Noon-8pm;
Sun, Noon-5pm
(Tours on Fri at 5pm;
Sat at 1, 3, & 5pm;
and Sun at 1 & 3pm)

LODGING:

Delamar Southport
275 Old Post Road
Southport, CT 06890
203-259-2800
www.delamarsouthport.com

GREENVILLE
Twin Lakes
Brewiwng
Co.

Dogfish Head
Craft Brewery
MILTON

GEORGETOWN
16 Mile Brewing Co.

DELAWARE

16 MILE
BREWING COMPANY

YEAR FOUNDED: 2009

FOUNDERS:
Chad Campbell and Brett McCrea

ANNUAL PRODUCTION:
4,000 barrels

**YEAR-ROUND &
SEASONAL BEERS:** Amber Sun Ale, Old Court Ale, Blues' Golden Ale, Inlet India Pale Ale, Responders Ale, Harvest Ale, Oyster Stout

LOCAL FLAVOR: Established as a new seat of government for Sussex County in 1791, Georgetown was intended to be 16 miles from anywhere in the county.

About halfway between the Maryland state line and coastal Lewes, the small community of Georgetown, Delaware, slows eastbound traffic with its town circle. A mile south, not far from the first permanent courthouse in Sussex County, 16 Mile Brewing Company has crafted malt-forward, low-alcohol, English-style ales for the past five years, steadily building a local following of beer aficionados. Sitting on just over eight acres, an old agricultural barn built in the early 1900s serves as the brewhouse, now filled with kegs and fermenters instead of livestock and farming tools. Owners Chad Campbell and Brett McCrea both grew up in Delaware and attended Washington College in Maryland but didn't meet until later in adulthood. Before beer ignited a new passion in each of the partners, Brett worked in counter-terrorism while Chad had a career in real estate and teaching. These days, the two occupy themselves at the brewery that sits on land owned by Brett's family—mashing in grain, operating the forklift, cleaning equipment, and leading the occasional tour. The hours at 16 Mile might not be any shorter than their previous occupations, but both have embraced the quieter lifestyle.

Spacious and bright, the tasting room at 16 Mile is a pleasant place to lose an hour or two on a road trip across the Eastern Shore. In the winter, a fireplace keeps things warm while a pair of flat-screen televisions often tuned to ESPN mean you won't miss the latest from the world of sport. The vibe is English pub meets American tavern, with an antique musket hanging at one end of the room and a large, antique-looking map of the DelMarVa peninsula just to the left of the long bar. The owners explain that they designed the public space with the intention of encouraging everyone who turns up to meet and mingle. On busy days, wait for your growler fill by challenging another visitor to a game of darts or bring a Frisbee and step outside to toss it around on the lawn. A five-ounce sample of a single beer is $2, six samples are $10, and a flight of all eight beers on tap costs $12. Growlers meanwhile, run $15–$20, depending on the ale you plan to bring home. Live music on the weekends and an annual event on Delaware Day in December when they roll out a draft trailer are two more good reasons to visit.

As a fan of cask ale and quaffable English styles, McCrea will say that they see promise in session ales. With a few exceptions, 16 Mile doesn't go for hop bombs or boundary-pushing boozers. Both Blues' Golden (5.9% ABV), a straw-yellow, clean-finishing beer with a sweet cornflake aroma and Responders Ale (4.1% ABV), a crisp, golden, and slightly dry beer, are light-bodied beverages designed to go down easy. The Fallen Firefighters Foundation also benefits from a portion of the sales proceeds from Responders Ale. More complex beers in their lineup include vaguely roasty Amber Sun (6.1% ABV) and Inlet IPA (6.1% ABV) with its orange-brown hue, malty nose, snappy hop bite, and herbal finish.

An ongoing collaboration series has allowed 16 Mile to branch out while enabling them to raise money for local charities. Recent releases have included Delaware Oyster Stout (6.2% ABV) brewed with cherrywood smoked malt and a hundred fresh Delaware Bay oysters, and Post-Apocalyptic Porter (6.5% ABV), a chocolate chili beer. Hazy brown from the addition of cocoa powder with a citric nose, an earthy flavor, and a kiss of spicy heat, this is one of their most complex beers to date.

Georgetown has a limited number of drinking and dining options, but The Brick Hotel & Restaurant (302-856-1836; www.brickhotelrestaurant.com) usually has bottles of Old Court Ale (6.1% ABV) and Blues' Golden. Try the latter with the Fish of the Moment over rice pilaf with a side of summer squash. Flavorful and not especially high in alcohol, this slightly sweet golden ale will satisfy without outshining your entrée. On Thursdays, local beers are discounted during happy hour at the Brick. For other restaurants with extensive beer lists, make the drive to the coast. On the ground floor of the Rodney Hotel in Lewes, the Rose & Crown (302-827-4475; www.roseandcrownlewes.com) has held beer dinners with 16 Mile in the past and braises the short rib used in their 16 Mile Sliders in beer from Georgetown. Should you turn up there with an appetite, start with the beer-battered calamari—accented with chives and slices of jalapeno—and then order the Rose & Crown Shepherd's Pie. Filled with savory duck confit and topped with nutty parmesan, it wants to be paired with a rich pint of Harvest Ale (6.1% ABV). You'll also find Old Court at Rehoboth's Jam Bistro (302-226-JAMM; www.jambistro.com).

When you've had enough to eat and drink, get a taste of the First State's history during a free tour of the Zwaanendael Museum (302-645-1148; www.history.delaware.gov/museums/zm/zm_main.shtml) in Lewes. Distributed across two floors of a brick building modeled after a similar structure in the Dutch town of Hoorn, the museum includes exhibits on Swanendael, Delaware's first settlement, and the state's role in the War of 1812. Lighthouse lovers, meanwhile, have two attractions in the area: the nineteenth-century Fenwick Island light and the Lightship Overfalls (302-644-8050; www.overfalls.org), one of seventeen in the country that happens to be docked in Lewes. To spend a little time in the sun, simply head east. The Dewey, Rehoboth, and Lewes Beaches (as well as their respective boardwalks) are all less than twenty miles away. The state's flat landscape also makes it friendly to cyclists of all levels. Rent a bike at Lewes Cycle Sports (302-645-4544; www.oceancycles.com) and go for a ride around Cape Henlopen State Park, or if you're feeling energetic, take it to Rehoboth and back. 🍾

CONTACT

413 South Bedford Street
Georgetown, DE 19947
302-253-8816
www.16milebrewery.com
@16mile

TASTING ROOM HOURS:

Tue-Wed, Noon-5pm;
Thu, Noon-7pm; Fri, Noon-10pm;
Sat, 11am-9pm; Sun, 11am-7pm
(Tours Thu-Sat on the hour)

LODGING:

The Brick Hotel on the Circle
Eighteen The Circle
Georgetown, DE 19947
302-855-5800
www.thebrickhotel.com

DOGFISH HEAD
CRAFT BREWERY

YEAR FOUNDED: 1995

FOUNDER:
Sam Calagione

ANNUAL PRODUCTION:
200,000 barrels

**YEAR-ROUND &
SEASONAL BEERS:** 60 Minute IPA, 90 Minute IPA, Burton Baton, Immort Ale, India Brown Ale, Midas Touch, Namaste, Palo Santo Marron, Raison D-Etre, Shelter Pale Ale, Sixty One, Aprihop, Chicory Stout, Festina Peche, Punkin Ale, Tweason'ale

LOCAL FLAVOR: William Shipley started Delaware's first brewery in the eighteenth century at the foot of Wilmington's Quaker Hill. When Sam Calagione opened his brewpub more than two centuries later, there hadn't been a brewery in the state for forty years.

There are cool, cutting-edge breweries that constantly push the limits of beer, there are popular breweries with a fan base that laps up every drop they can make, and then there's Dogfish Head. From rather humble beginnings brewing twelve-gallon batches of Shelter Pale Ale about half a mile from the ocean at Dogfish Head Brewings & Eats in Rehoboth Beach, this company has grown to become one of the largest craft beer producers in the country. Along the way, they've pioneered continual hop additions, collaborated with musicians, re-created ancient fermented beverages with the help of a biomolecular archaeologist, and dosed an IPA with Syrah grape must to produce a beer-wine hybrid. To think it all started with an English major who fell in love with Sierra Nevada Celebration Ale. For a brewer with nearly twenty years of experience in the industry, Dogfish founder Sam Calagione has also somehow found time for a handful of other jobs: author, TV personality, rapper. In spite of these diversions though, he's always come back to beer, beginning with his first, a homebrewed cherry ale. When he opened the brewpub—named for a landform in Maine—Delaware was one of nine states without a brewery; today, with Calagione's help it's become a magnet for beer seekers eager to try his "off-centered ales" straight from the source.

Since graduating from brewpub to production brewery, Dogfish seems to keep growing; each of the large fermentation tanks visible outside the old vegetable cannery they moved into in 2002 can hold 25,000 gallons of beer. Tours start in the gift shop and include four samples, often something new and different that the brewery has recently introduced. For those

with kids, they also have Beach Beer Soda on tap. As you walk through the sprawling facility, you'll learn more about Calagione and the vibrating football game toy that led to the creation of 90 Minute IPA. You'll also have the chance to see one of the two largest wooden tanks in the country—10,000 gallon cylinders built from dense Paraguayan palo santo timber and constructed without nails, screws, or glue. You'll hear all sorts of trivia from your guide, including the fact that when Calagione and his friends started hand corking the first bottles of Dogfish beer, it would take all day to finish one hundred cases of beer. With the high-tech automated system they have now, they can do the same amount in about ten minutes. Stock up on swag at the end of your tour if you wish (they don't do growlers), but don't leave without getting your photo next to their steampunk tree house out front; it's the perfect quirky souvenir from Milton.

Dogfish made its mark with India pale ales, and their 90 Minute IPA (9% ABV) continues to impress drinkers with its pungent drinkability and notes of citrus, pine, and brandy. Chicory Stout (5.2% ABV) was another beer first introduced to the world at the brewpub, and its combination of roasted chicory, organic coffee, St. John's wort,

licorice root, and oatmeal make it an extremely interesting and complex example of a stout. Newer releases such as 61 (6.5% ABV) seem to defy categorization, too. This beer begins with their best-selling 60 Minute IPA and then things get strange. To produce the desired peppery, fruity, and tannic qualities of wine, the brewers add Syrah grape must from California. Other Dogfish beers with unusual ingredients include the oak-aged Immort Ale (11% ABV), brewed with vanilla, peat-smoked barley, and maple syrup from Calagione's farm in Massachusetts, and Namaste (5% ABV), a zippy witbier made with lemongrass. Punkin (7% ABV) meanwhile, is their take on the popular pumpkin ale; its deep copper color recalls fall foliage while the nose throws off aromas of cinnamon, allspice, brown sugar, alcohol, and cooked pumpkin. A medium-bodied beer, Punkin starts off sweet, evolves into a flavor that combines nutty malts and squash, and finishes with a welcome touch of hop bitterness.

Naturally, the first place to go for a Dogfish Head is the modest little Rehoboth Beach brewpub where it all started. The only problem is that during the summer months there's usually a line to get in. A long one. Fortunately, tracking down one of Sam's beers isn't difficult to do in Delaware. Roughly half a mile from Dogfish Head Brewing & Eats, a(MUSE.), a restaurant with a quirky name and inspired dishes (302-227-7107; www.amuse-rehoboth.com) serves contemporary American fare, interesting cocktails, and Indian Brown Ale (7.2% ABV). A six- or an eleven-course tasting menu might give you the best sense of chef/owner Hari Cameron's approach to food, but the late night menu offers the most bang for your buck. Have an Indian Brown with pickled veggies on toast with mustard and crème fraiche, an order of potato soup with mushroom, onion, and pine nuts, add a farm egg sandwich with smoked collard greens on sourdough, and finish with the Beach Bomber: chocolate ice cream, gingerbread, marshmallow, and graham cracker sand. Which is not to say that Brewing & Eats (302-226-2739; www.dogfish.com/restaurant) is a disappointment for those who wait. From rosemary parmesan fries and 60 Minute IPA truffle mustard to Raison D'Etre braised short ribs (using beef from Calagione's farm) and Chicory Stout bacon chocolate cheesecake, this is a joint that takes beer and food where others fear to tread.

When the sun is shining, southern Delaware is a great place to go to get out on the water. From wind surfing and sailboats to stand–up paddleboarding and kayaks, the First State will certainly be attractive to the amphibious beer tourist. Book a spot with Ecobay Kayak Adventures (302-841-2722; www.ecobaykayak.com) in Ocean View to join a wildlife spotting trip or a leisurely sunset paddle on Indian River Bay. In Milton, self-starters can also rent canoes from Wilson's Sunshine Marina (302-684-3425; www.miltonde.com/milton/sunshinemarina/marina.html), put in at Memorial Park, and follow the Broadkill River Canoe Trail. To the east of Dogfish, The Nature Conservancy maintains the Edward H. McCabe Preserve (302-684-3425; www.nature.org), 143 acres of forest and wetland that's home to more than one hundred species of waterfowl, raptors, and songbirds. Park in the lot on Route 257 (Round Pole Bridge Road) and follow the marked hiking trail into the preserve. If you're not in a hurry to get somewhere in particular, you might decide to leave your car parked at the brewery and stroll down Chestnut Street into the center of Milton. The highlight for foodies is undoubtedly King's Ice Cream (302-684-8900; www.kings-icecream.com), a family business that also happens to have created two flavors (Amber Caramel and Harvest Hazelnut) using wort from 16 Mile Brewing. 🍺

CONTACT

#6 Cannery Village Center
Milton, DE 19968
302-684-1000
www.dogfish.com
@dogfishbeer

TASTING ROOM HOURS:

Tue-Sat, 11am-5pm
(Tours every 45 minutes)

LODGING:

Homestead at Rehoboth B&B
35060 Warrington Road
Dewey Beach, DE 19971
302-226-7625
www.homesteadrehoboth.com

TWIN LAKES BREWING COMPANY

YEAR FOUNDED: 2006

FOUNDERS:
Sam Hobbs and Matt Day

ANNUAL PRODUCTION:
3,000-4,000 barrels

**YEAR-ROUND &
SEASONAL BEERS:** Greenville
Pale Ale, Winterthur Wheat, Tweeds
Tavern Stout, Route 52 Pilsner,
Oktoberfest, Caesar Rodney Golden Ale,
Three Monks, Jubilicious

LOCAL FLAVOR: A natural spring
on the Hobbs Farm is known as the
Washington Well because his troops used
it during the Battle of Brandywine Creek
in 1777.

To be perfectly honest, for all of their picturesque appeal, Greenville's Twin Lakes are probably more accurately described as ponds, little bodies of water on the Hobbs family farm where the community has gone to ice skate for generation after generation. Allegedly, Joe Biden brought his first date here many years ago. It hasn't been intensively farmed in quite some time, but the land has remained essentially rural, with a few homes scattered around the 252-acre property today. In 2001, Sam Hobbs and his friend Matt Day decided they could do something with the old tractor barn and set to work conceptualizing a business they describe as a hundred-mile brewery. Their thinking was simple and straightforward: good beer, like corn, or tomatoes, or other farm stand produce, should be fresh and local. With that in mind, they also looked to area landmarks as well as state history when naming their beers. Winterthur Wheat takes its name from the DuPont mansion turned museum just up the road, while Caesar Rodney Golden Ale acknowledges the local patriot who rode roughly eighty miles through the night to cast the deciding vote in the Declaration of Independence on July 2, 1776.

Before it became the Twin Lakes taproom, the second-floor space over the barn served as a studio for Hobbs's uncle, an accomplished painter. Even now it has a certain mismatched, lived-in charm, with cushy chairs and couches arranged around a fireplace and worn Oriental rugs covering the floor. A collection of ceramic growlers sculpted by Paul Romanick, a potter from Newark, Delaware, occupy a shelf on another wall. The bar itself is tiny, but the environment is big and welcoming. A large wall of windows fills the room with natural light, and an outdoor deck almost doubles visitor capacity on busy weekends during the warmer months. Summer, a yellow Labrador retriever, might wander in and out, and a couple of locals will almost always be there, telling stories, sharing news, and sipping beer. Tours ($22) are rather informal, and include lots of details about local history as well as a tasting, and often a nibble of cheese to go with the beer samples. Afterward, fill up a glass growler to go ($12-$15), or if you're feeling flush and like to cycle in style, pick up a Twin Lakes bike jersey ($75).

You won't find a fruit, coffee, or chocolate beer in the lineup at Twin Lakes; here in the Brandywine Valley brewer Rob Pfeiffer makes beer that tastes like, well, beer. So far, he hasn't brewed an IPA either. No matter though, the Greenville Pale Ale (5.5% ABV) is a fine beer with just enough of a bite to satisfy those who crave that bitter edge in their happy hour beverage. Tangerine orange in color with a floral, citrusy nose courtesy of whole flower Cascade hops, their flagship pours with a beautiful rocky head and goes down exceptionally easy. You can see why they decided to can this beer first—a single serving hardly seems adequate. Greenville Pale is also the only Twin Lakes beer available year–round. Oktoberfest (6% ABV) meanwhile, is brewed for autumn in the style of a

Vienna lager: a subtle use of noble German hops, delicately spicy Tettnanger in this case, a smooth, crisp body, and a clean finish. When winter rolls around again, you'll find Jubilicious (8% ABV) on tap, a rich, reddish, and warming ale for the coldest days of the year made by blending roasted malts with specialty grains.

For the time being, Twin Lakes is happy to limit distribution to one hundred miles. Which means it might be a while before you spot their cans in Manhattan, but it won't take much hunting to track down their beer in Wilmington. The first place to check is the BBC Tavern and Grill (302-655-3785; www.bbctavernandgrill.com) on Kennett Pike. Here you'll reliably find Greenville Pale Ale on tap, alongside other locals like Dogfish, Victory, and 16 Mile. Many of the dishes on their seasonal menu would work with this versatile, medium-bodied ale, including the Asian vegetable stir-fry over jasmine rice with a spicy ginger soy glaze or the fried chicken with cornbread, mashed potatoes,

and haricots verts in a mushroom gravy. Closer to the Pennsylvania state line, Buckley's Tavern (302-656-9776; www.buckleystavern.com) often has Tweeds Tavern Stout (5% ABV), a bold, roasty beer that would perfectly complement a juicy bison burger or a braised lamb shank. Finally, across the street from the Grand Opera House in Wilmington, the Chelsea Tavern (302-482-3333; www.chelseatavern.com) serves food befitting of a gastropub, from bacon-wrapped meatloaf in a pale ale barbecue sauce to steamed mussels with chorizo, shallots, and garlic in a wheat beer broth. Try the latter with a pint of Winterthur Wheat (5.5% ABV), bittered with citrusy Cascade hops.

Tucked behind a stand of trees and surrounded by state parks, country clubs, and the Hoopes Reservoir, Twin Lakes is also close to a handful of tourist attractions that might tempt some travelers to linger in the area. North of the brewery in Pennsylvania, the Brandywine River Museum (610-388-2700; www.brandywinemuseum.org) contains an extensive collection of American art, including landscape painting and portraits, as well as works from well-known illustrators and cartoonists like N. C. Wyeth, Winslow Homer, Maxfield Parrish, Al Hirschfeld, Edward Gorey, Charles Schulz, and Theodor Geisel (Dr. Seuss). Nearby, Longwood Gardens (610-388-1000; www.longwoodgardens.org) contains 11,000 different plant types dispersed across more than a thousand acres. Themed tours, classes and workshops, dining events, and a summer performance series offer even more of an incentive to visit this world famous garden. A few miles from Twin Lakes, Brandywine Creek State Park (302-577-3534; www.destateparks.com/park/brandywine-creek/index.asp) began as a dairy farm owned by the DuPont family and is preserved today as a patchwork of meadows, forest, and freshwater marsh. Bring a picnic lunch or go for a short hike in the summer or fall, rent a canoe for a paddling trip in the spring, or sled in the winter. 🍶

CONTACT

4210 Kennett Pike
Greenville, DE 19807
302-658-1826
www.twinlakes
brewingcompany.com
@twinlakesbrews

TASTING ROOM HOURS:
Wed, 4-7pm; Sat, Noon-4pm
(Tours on the hour)

LODGING:
Inn at Wilmington
300 Rocky Run Parkway
Wilmington, DE 19803
302-479-7900
www.innatwilmington.com

Three Stars
Brewing Co.

DC Brau
Brewing Co.

Bluejacket
Brewing Co.

DISTRICT OF COLUMBIA

DC BRAU
BREWING COMPANY

YEAR FOUNDED: 2011

FOUNDERS:
Brandon Skall and Jeff Hancock

ANNUAL PRODUCTION:
11,000–12,000 barrels

YEAR-ROUND & SEASONAL BEERS: The Public Pale Ale, The Corruption IPA, The Citizen Belgian Ale, Penn Quarter Porter, El Jefe Speaks, Burial at Sea, On the Wings of Armageddon, Hell's Bottom, Stone of Abroath, Middle Name Danger

LOCAL FLAVOR: During the Civil War, the District of Columbia was surrounded by dozens of forts and gun batteries constructed to protect the capital from Confederate forces. One of the eastern defenses, Fort Lincoln, is less than a mile from the brewery.

When Brandon Skall and Jeff Hancock used to run into one another at drum and bass concerts in the 1990s, neither of them could have guessed that they'd end up in business together more than a decade later, let alone the District of Columbia's first production brewery since Prohibition. Yet soon after reacquainting at a house party in 2009, Hancock, who happened to be considering a break from the beer industry, and Skall, who had experience in wine distribution, were talking about starting something new, something fun, a brewery for the nation's capital. They went in feet first, helped to rewrite laws that enable breweries to give out samples and sell growlers, launched on tax day, and ended up with a catchy tagline: Fermentation without Representation. As it turns out, they were on to something. At their launch event at Meridian Pint, a popular beer bar in the District, the line to get in stretched for almost two city blocks and they went through sixteen half-kegs in a matter of hours. They've already expanded multiple times just to meet demand in DC. Today these two music fans can find their beer on tap at the 9:30 Club, one of the city's top concert venues.

Located on Bladensburg Road, several miles east of the National Mall and DC's main attractions, DC Brau isn't much to look at from the outside. Once you find your way to the entrance, though—up a small staircase in the rear of the building—the tasting room is a laid-back place to hang out, talk beer, and wait for a growler fill. Depending on the size of the crowd, they typically run three brewery tours on Saturday afternoons. A Washington Redskins area rug lets you know where the brewery's football loyalties lie, while a maroon-colored Chimay banner hanging from the high ceiling clues visitors in to at least

one of their sources of brewing inspiration. Plunk down on a red vinyl bench in one of the old restaurant booths if you're not in a hurry, and work your way through a tasting flight or survey the selection of T-shirts for sale. If the flat-screen TV above the bar is on, there's a good chance it will be tuned to ESPN, providing a bit of entertainment for sports fans. In addition to their core lineup of beers, the tasting room is often where DC Brau will debut new seasonals; before hurrying off to your next stop, ask about bomber bottles and six-packs that might not yet be available elsewhere.

The first beer to appear in cans printed with the DC Brau logo was The Public (6% ABV), an American pale ale bursting with the smell of grapefruit and pine. A bold take on this style of beer, The Public almost approaches an IPA with its sticky, resinous hop flavor. A medium body and a slightly sweet caramel malt character pull this beer back from the edge, saving it from sliding toward the tongue-punishing end of the bitterness scale. They do brew an IPA called The Corruption (6.5% ABV), as well as a Belgian pale ale that Skall and Hancock will tell you is their crossover beer. Dull orange or light copper in color, The Citizen (7% ABV) is higher in alcohol than its siblings but doesn't come across that way. A taste of this semi-dry beer brings to mind shortbread cookies and lemon pepper. On the other hand, the chocolate brown Penn Square Porter (5.5% ABV) pours like molasses out of the bottle with a firm beige head that resembles cappuccino foam. Sweet yet earthy with aromas of mocha and chocolate liqueur, this full-bodied ale finishes with a slight coffee astringency and a flavor akin to pumpernickel bread. In addition to these selections, DC Brau is now actively souring batches of beer and has also aged limited quantities of their porter and the imperial IPA, On the Wings of Armageddon (9.2% ABV), in whiskey barrels.

A short drive from DC Brau delivers pizza-loving beer drinkers to Menomale (202-248-3946; www.menomale.us), an outpost of authentic Neapolitan-style pies cooked in a hand-built, wood-fired oven. With ten tap lines and an eye toward variety, there's a good chance you'll find them pouring The Public, The Citizen, or The Corruption. If you're lucky enough to find malty, bready Penn Quarter Porter on the beer list, order the Tacchino pizza topped with San Marzano tomatoes, Fior di Latte mozzarella, fresh basil, smoked turkey, mushrooms, grana padano, and extra virgin olive oil, or maybe the Patata topped with creamy potatoes, Italian sausage, black olives, mozzarella, basil, and EVOO. This chocolatey beer would also be a winner with La Bomba, Menomale's pizza dough filled with Nutella and dusted with powdered sugar. Pizza might not be your food of choice though. In that case, Smith Commons (202-396-0038; www.smithcommonsdc.com) on H Street in the Atlas Arts District is worth a visit. Turn up in time for brunch on Sunday and ask for the Smith Biscuits bacon, gravy, and Sriracha. Only instead of a Bloody Mary, go for The Corruption and its wallop of piney, resinous hops. DC Brau launched their IPA here in 2011. The Pig (202-290-2821; www.thepigdc.com) near Logan Circle is another good bet for meaty mains and craft beer on tap.

CONTACT

3178-B Bladensburg Road NE
Washington, DC 20018
202-621-8890
www.dcbrau.com
@dcbrau

TASTING ROOM HOURS:
Sat, Noon-4pm
(Tours at 1, 2, and 3pm)

LODGING:
The Inn at Brookland
3742 12th Street NE
Washington, DC 20017
202-467-6777
www.thedupontcollection.com/
brookland.php

The District, of course has enough museums, monuments, and government buildings to keep a visitor busy for days, if not an entire week. From the White House to the Smithsonian, and the various memorials along the Potomac, it certainly isn't a city that lacks for sights or attractions. To see a different side of the nation's capital though, try a few places that aren't already on every guidebook's Top 10 list. Take the National Building Museum (202-272-2448; www.nbm. org) for instance, a strikingly attractive brick edifice constructed in the late nineteenth century to house the U.S. Pension Bureau. Since 1885, it's also been the venue of choice for first inaugural president's balls. Today it contains a variety of exhibits about architecture, design, and engineering, as well as a small shop and café. Closer to the brewery on DC's northeastern border, Anacostia Park (202-472-3873; www.nps. gov/anac/index.htm) is the nearest place to go for a respite from the city's noise and congestion. And for those who want to do more tasting while they're in town, New Columbia Distillers (202-733-1710; www. greenhatgin.com), just across New York Avenue and walking distance from Gallaudet University, offers free tours and tastings of their Green Hat Gin on Saturdays 1-4pm.

BLUEJACKET BREWING COMPANY

YEAR FOUNDED: 2013

FOUNDERS:
Michael Babin (with Greg Engert, Megan Parisi, and Kyle Bailey)

ANNUAL PRODUCTION:
4,000-5,000 barrels

YEAR-ROUND & SEASONAL BEERS: Gray Jacket, Saison Vespula, Black Berliner Techno Weiss, Sidewalk Saison, Share the Rainbow, Snack Attack, Pretty in Pink, Instigator, Freestyle #10

LOCAL FLAVOR: In 1902, the U.S. Navy published the first edition of the *Bluejacket's Manual*, a manual for new recruits that covers naval life and seamanship.

Compared to other East Coast cities, Washington, D.C., arrived late to the craft beer party. Sure a few bars around the district, notably the Brickskeller (now RFD) have long championed flavorful ales and lagers, but as far as breweries go, this city seemed content with its lone brewpub on New York Avenue. With the addition of the Bluejacket Brewing Company, the nation's capital has a premiere beer destination within sight of the Capitol. Occupying part of a building in the Navy Yard that once served as a boilermaker factory, this multistory boutique brewery and restaurant is designed in the manner that many large breweries were constructed in the past, with a grain mill and mash tun on the upper floors and fermenters, in this case nineteen of them, below, relying on gravity to move everything through the system. When it opened, Bluejacket became the twelfth property in Michael Babin's Neighborhood Restaurant Group and his first foray into fermentation. To see it through to completion, he enlisted Greg Engert, his knowledgeable beer director, and hired Megan Parisi, an accomplished brewer who previously spent eight years at the Cambridge Brewing Company in Massachusetts.

Although it behaves in many ways like a brewpub, Bluejacket does offer daily tours that include a peek at their glassed-in sour room and fifteen-barrel coolship for wild fermented beers. Even without taking the tour, however, it's possible to get a sense of things just by sitting at the bar and looking up: almost all of the brewing equipment is in full view above you. A largely glass exterior also means that stainless-steel tanks and kettles will shine as long as the sun's in the sky. With seating on two levels and outdoors, the restaurant has an upscale beer hall feel with food made from scratch and focused on slow cooking.

Inventive beers, a thoughtful menu, and a stunning physical space made Bluejacket one of the city's most sought-after spots the moment it opened; even with 250 seats, you might find yourself waiting for a seat during busy periods.

When it comes to their beers, Bluejacket aims to create something for every palate and every plate. Each release echoes the flavor profile system at work throughout Neighborhood Restaurant Group: Crisp, Hop, Malt, Roast, Smoke, Fruit & Spice, Tart & Funky. And with five guest taps, fifteen ever-changing tap lines of their own beer, and another five cask ales at all times, they can simultaneously offer hop-forward ales, unfiltered lagers, farmhouse beers, dessert beers, and sours, as well as innovative collaborations with chefs, brewers, writers, mixologists, and vintners. Collaborating with Allagash and Peekskill, Parisi brewed Share the Rainbow (4.8% ABV) with blood oranges and pink peppercorns, partially fermenting it in a coolship with Brettanomyces yeast. Freestyle No. 10 (4% ABV), created with Oxbow, was a rye table seasonal.

The team behind Bluejacket always wanted to do a brewery and a bar, and Chef Kyle Bailey has played a role in the brewing process from the beginning as Engert and Parisi view each beer as a culinary creation. To track down Bluejacket creations elsewhere in the District, the obvious choice is Birch & Barley (202-567-2576; www.birchandbarley.com), a go-to destination for foodies and craft beer devotees alike, or Churchkey, its upstairs neighbor, both a stone's throw from Logan Circle.

A short ten-minute walk from Bluejacket, Nationals Park (202-675-6287; www.nationals.com) is home to the city's MLB team between April and September. On either side of the river of the same name, the Anacostia Riverwalk Trail (202-741-8528; www.anacostiawaterfront.org) snakes along the waterfront for twenty miles from the Navy Yard to Benning Road. Take a walk or pedal for miles. On the north side of I-695, there's the Capitol building, the Library of Congress, the Supreme Court, and the United States Botanic Garden (202-225-8333; www.usbg.gov), a collection of ornamental, medicinal, and endangered plants from all over the world. 🍾

CONTACT
300 Tingey Street
Washington, DC 20003
www.bluejacketdc.com
@bluejacketdc

BREWERY RESTAURANT HOURS:
Open daily for lunch and dinner.

LODGING:
Capitol Skyline Hotel
10 I Street SW
Washington, DC 20024
202-488-7500
www.capitolskyline.com

THREE STARS
BREWING COMPANY

YEAR FOUNDED: 2012

FOUNDERS:
Dave Coleman and Mike McGarvey

ANNUAL PRODUCTION:
2,000 barrels

**YEAR-ROUND &
SEASONAL BEERS:** Sea Change, Peppercorn Saison, Pandemic Porter, Winter Madness, Southern Belle, Two the Dome, Citra and Lemon Peel Saison, Ebony and Ivory

LOCAL FLAVOR: The desire to foster a DC beer community also led the Three Stars partners to open a homebrew shop alongside their brewery on Chillum Place.

Some brewers take a rather impulsive approach to starting a business, launching a company with the beers they themselves want to drink. Friends Dave Coleman and Mike McGarvey came at the industry more methodically however. Coleman, who had studied psychology, had previously been beer director at Big Hunt, a restaurant near Dupont Circle, while McGarvey, with an engineering background, got into homebrewing when he received a kit for his birthday. Once the two discovered a shared passion for great beer, they spent time experimenting and developing recipes, brewing five beers a day on the weekends by starting with a base beer and then modifying it with four different iterations of malt, hops, and/ or yeast. A month later, they'd invite friends over to serve as a tasting panel, rating the results and helping them to understand and improve their products. With time, they saw a market for their ideas, and thought that starting a brewery would enable them to be a part of the community. They also want to give back to DC and hope to partner with a local hunger charity as well as a bakery that can use the thousands of pounds of spent grain they generate on a weekly basis.

Without much starting capital, Coleman and McGarvey put a lot of sweat equity into Three Stars. Before they finally managed to negotiate a ten-year lease with their landlord, the building that now houses their brewhouse and homebrew shop had been used for auto body repair; together with the help of a crew of very dedicated volunteers, they spent many ten- to twelve-hour days renovating and building out the space for their business. Throughout the process, their motto had been not to buy anything new unless absolutely necessary, and not

to pay for labor if they could do it themselves. When it came time to add cold storage for instance, they bid $1.35 for a walk-in cooler at an auction and somehow won with their rock bottom offer. The challenge came when they had to disassemble it, move it to Chillum Place, and put it back together in just three days. Ordinary or even unimpressive from the exterior, Three Stars occupies an enormous footprint with plenty of indoor space for a growing collection of kegs as well as the throngs of fans that turn up on weekends for homebrew supplies, a growler or two of fresh beer ($15-$20), a bite from a food truck like PORC that's often parked out front, or in some cases, all three. Hip-hop beats might be bouncing around the high-ceilinged room as you wait for your beer samples, but if you can make yourself heard, ask one of the founders which beers they're barrel aging in the rear.

Along with an imperial brown ale and a saison, Three Stars officially launched at ChurchKey with Pandemic Porter (9.6% ABV), a full-bodied beer brewed with four types of malt, rolled oats, and wheat. Dark chocolate and the rich flavor of French roast coffee dominate. Fittingly, given that it incorporates toasted pecans, they call their popular imperial brown Southern Belle (8.7% ABV). Drinkable in spite of its alcohol punch, this flavorful beer has a nutty, earthy aroma and a toasty character with just a whisper of sweetness. In the past they've also aged this ale in a cask with vanilla beans and cocoa nibs to create a special release they call Ebony and Ivory. In the future, expect more barrel-aged beers like this one in limited quantities. Their core lineup extends beyond dark and malty, however; these brewers have shown that they've got a few tricks up their sleeves, too. Designed for the sticky dog days of DC's humid summers, Citra and Lemon Peel Saison (5% ABV) is a zippy glass of refreshment with loads of bright citrus flavor

and aroma. Grapefruit and orange notes also sing in Sea Change (6.9% ABV), their American pale ale brewed with floral, citrusy Cascade and Centennial hops.

Some things just taste better together: peanut butter and jelly, burgers and fries, pizza and beer. Visit any one of DC's three Pizzeria Paradiso (202-223-1245; www.eatyourpizza.com) locations and you'll have your proof. Bring a friend or two, check the tap list for Three Stars Peppercorn Saison (6.5% ABV), and order a 12-inch Bottarga pie. Topped with tomato, minced garlic, parsley, parmesan, egg, and Bottarga, a dried fish roe. The somewhat spicy beer with its bitter citrus notes and dry finish should marry nicely with the salty, savory flavors of the pizza. At Meridian Pint (202-588-1075; www.meridianpint.com), the focus is on sustainability, American craft beer, and familiar, not fussy, food. A dish like the fennel-rubbed pork chop with sweet potato gnocchi, spring peas, and smoked pork belly would be fantastic with a pint of Pandemic Porter. Meanwhile, Two the Dome (8% ABV), Coleman and McGarvey's bright, juicy double IPA, could be delicious with mussels steamed in coconut milk with Thai spices, peppers, red onions, and mango. Closer to Rock Creek Park, the three-floor Black Squirrel (202-232-1011; www.blacksquirreldc.com) in Adams Morgan is another gastropub where you stand a chance of finding Three Stars. Don't miss the duck confit spring rolls.

Fortunately for visitors, DC is a city that caters to almost any interest. You could spend days touring the permanent collections at the many cultural institutions in town, or you could hit up breweries by day and entertain yourself with a show at the Kennedy Center, the Folger Shakespeare Library, Arena Stage, or the historic National Theatre (202-628-6161; www.nationaltheatre.org) in the evening. If that doesn't appeal, give in to your inner explorer and check out a 3-D movie or a few of the current exhibits at the National Geographic Museum (202-857-7700; www.events.nationalgeographic.com/events/national-geographic-museum) near Farragut Square. The museum is also a great place to go to see some of the remarkable photojournalism that has appeared in the pages of the society's magazine. Or for a bit of brewing history, visit the Heurich House Museum (202-429-1894; www.heurichhouse.org), an under-the-radar attraction built in the 1890s by Christian Heurich, owner of the Christian Heurich Brewing Company, the largest private employer in the nation's capital at the time. The concrete and steel late-Victorian "Brewmaster's Castle" was also the city's first fireproof home. 🍾

CONTACT

6400 Chillum Place NW
Washington, DC 20011
202-670-0333
www.threestarsbrewing.com
@3starsbrewing

TASTING ROOM HOURS:
Sat, 1-4pm (Tours at 2 & 3pm)

LODGING:
Adam's Inn
1746 Lanier Place NW
Washington, DC 20009
202-745-3600
www.adamsinn.com

all natural soap
made with

BAXTER BREWING CO.

PAMOLA
XTRA
PALE ALE

OXBOW 2011

HOME HEATING SINCE 1911

COMPANYS LEHIGH

Chamber of Commerce INFORMATION

UMERS FUEL CO. | OIL

MARSHALL WHARF
BREWING COMPANY
I LOVE *MW*

Little Max Red Ale 5% $1
Tug Pale Ale 5% $10
Phil Brown Ale 6% $12
Pemaquid Oyster Stout 6%

Marshall Wharf
Brewing Co.
BELFAST

Baxter
Brewing Co.
LEWISTON

Oxbow
Brewing Co.
NEWCASTLE

Rising Tide
Brewing Co.

Allagash
Brewing Co.
PORTLAND

MAINE

ALLAGASH BREWING COMPANY

YEAR FOUNDED: 1995

FOUNDER:
Rob Tod

ANNUAL PRODUCTION:
65,000-70,000 barrels

YEAR-ROUND & SEASONAL BEERS: White, Dubbel, Tripel, Black, Curieux, Four, Odyssey, Confluence, Interlude, Grand Cru, Musette, Fluxus

LOCAL FLAVOR: The wood used to construct the tasting room bar comes from a timber-framed Maine barn built around the time of the American Revolution.

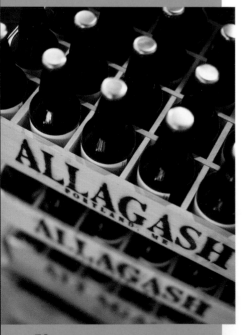

On the door to one of the barrel rooms, a single definition printed in large type essentially sums up the philosophy behind Rob Tod's Allagash Brewing Company. "Innovation," it reads. "Continually pushing the limits of beer and ourselves." Why else would a former geology major who fell in love with Belgian witbier, construct an expensive coolship, a large, shallow vat that cools down unfermented wort and exposes it to bacteria and wild yeast? The answer is that no one in the United States had tried it before, and upon consulting with Cantillon, a family-owned brewery in Brussels, he learned that spring and fall temperatures in the Belgian capital closely resemble those in Portland, Maine. Wanting to change the way people thought about beer, and happy to experiment, Tod, who had started out on his own in a warehouse next to Allagash's current address, went ahead with the project. Many months later, his first sour lambic was ready for bottling.

In spite of its somewhat industrial exterior, Allagash has thoughtfully designed their tasting room, creating a space with a conspicuous degree of New England charm. Posts and beams salvaged from an eighteenth-century barn were used to build the attractive bar and display case, while in the bathroom, oak barrels became vessel sinks. On the walls, at least a dozen medals from the Great American Beer Festival attest to the brewery's success. Tours last about half an hour and delve into the unique processes behind their experimental and Belgian-style ales. In the summer, groups can number up to forty people and fill up quickly, so if you're visiting between June and August, plan ahead and register online before you arrive. Free tastings, once part of the tour experience, are now done separately and include four samples—typically White, one of their uncommon

sours, and two other specialty beers that rotate according to availability. After you've finished with your flight, browse the small gift shop for a T-shirt, wool sweater, hoodie, or beer chalice ($7) to give to that special person in your life. Allagash doesn't currently offer growler fills.

Nearly three-fourths of Allagash's output is White (5% ABV), a cloudy, spicy wheat beer brewed with coriander and Curacao orange peel. Tod introduced the world to his brewery with this crisp, smooth ale, and it continues to attract praise today. After his flagship beer began to catch on, he continued to release Belgian-inspired beers, starting with Dubbel (7% ABV) and then climbing the alcohol ladder to Four (10% ABV), a strong, candy-like and complex quadruple made with four malts, four hops, four sugars, and four yeasts. Another beer like this you will not find. By aging their Triple in Jim Beam barrels, Allagash ended up with the bourbon-tinged Curieux (11% ABV), another product that has quickly grown in demand. But what really sets this brewery apart is their growing range of limited edition barrel-aged and spontaneously fermented ales. Relying on wild yeast and local fruit such as raspberries, they've produced remarkable beers such as the draft-only Respect Your Elderberries (7.9% ABV), as well as Cerise (8.1% ABV), a tart fruit lambic made with a blend of Maine-grown cherries.

Arguably one of the best beer bars on the East Coast, let alone Maine, The Great Lost Bear (207-772-0300; www.greatlostbear.com) also has the distinction of buying and tapping Rob Tod's very first keg in 1995. More than thirty years after opening, it remains a comfortable, unpretentious place to sample beers from across the state and around the world. Expect to find as many as six Allagash beers on tap, including rarities like

Odyssey (10.4% ABV), a dark wheat ale aged on oak. And while they serve many things you'd expect to find at a bar, the Bear does most of them better. The hearty, spicy chili is excellent and can be added to nachos or cheese fries. Also noteworthy is the selection of vegetarian dishes, menu items you'll find under the heading "Carnivores Beware." Closer to the Old Port on the other side of the interstate, Local 188 (207-761-7909; www.local188.com) is an innovative farm-to-table restaurant with ingredients sourced from local foragers, farmers, and fishermen. A Mediterranean-inspired menu includes paella with house-made chorizo sausage as well as a nightly preparation of gnocchi. Try the latter with Allagash's dry, nutty Dubbel (7% ABV). Just across Longfellow Square is LFK (207-899-3277; www.lfkportland.com), a third restaurant with a serious dedication to beer and cocktails. Go for a burger, medium rare, on a pretzel bun.

While Portland is without a doubt an exceptional town for beer, there's more to it than accomplished brewers and award-winning ales. The Portland Museum of Art (207-775-6148; www.portlandmuseum.org) for example, is the state's oldest and largest public art institution with thousands of works of fine and decorative art

from the likes of Winslow Homer, George Bellows, Mary Cassatt, and Claude Monet, as well as Jamie, N. C., and Andrew Wyeth. The PMA also regularly hosts movie screenings, lectures, art classes, and gallery talks. But don't worry if sports sound like a better pairing for your beer vacation than an afternoon in an art museum. Hadlock Field, near the interstate and the city's Amtrak station, is home to the Portland Sea Dogs, a minor league affiliate of the Boston Red Sox. Their five-month season runs from April through Labor Day. Another fun and unique place to spend some time and maybe pick up a souvenir is The Honey Exchange (207-773-9333; www.thehoneyexchange.com) about three miles south of Allagash. Sign up for a Saturday beekeeping class, shop for bee-themed clothing or home goods and food made with honey, or pick up a bottle of Maine mead. 🍾

CONTACT

50 Industrial Way
Portland, Maine 04103
207-878-5385
www.allagash.com
@allagashbrewing

TASTING ROOM HOURS:

Mon-Sat, 10am-5pm
(Tours on the hour)

LODGING:

The Elms Bed & Breakfast
102 Cumberland Street
Westbrook, ME 04092
207-854-4060
www.elmsmaine.com

BAXTER
BREWING COMPANY

YEAR FOUNDED: 2011

FOUNDER:
H. Luke Livingston

ANNUAL PRODUCTION:
28,000-32,000 barrels

**YEAR-ROUND &
SEASONAL BEERS:** Phantom
Punch Winter Stout, Hayride Autumn Ale,
Summer Swelter, Amber Road, Pamola
Xtra Pale Ale, Stowaway IPA

LOCAL FLAVOR: In 1867, one of the
13 Lewiston Mill Rules read: "No person who
drinks intoxicating liquors will knowingly be
employed by the Lewiston Mills."

In 2009, when Luke Livingston decided to give up his beer blog and get serious about his favorite beverage, things happened pretty quickly. He chose a brand name (fortunately, Baxter wasn't taken), wrote a business plan, developed a logo (Pamola, the Abenaki god of thunder with the head of a moose, the feet and wings of an eagle, and a human body), found a site for his brewery across the Androscoggin River from Auburn, the town he grew up in, and in January of 2011, sold his first cans of Pamola Xtra Pale Ale. Twelve months later, Livingston had filled more than 1,650,000 cans with Baxter beer and needed to figure out how to keep up with a growing demand for more. Looking back, picking a name probably seemed like the easy part.

When things on Lincoln Street are less hectic than usual, Livingston might take a break to try one of the rotating beers in the small-batch series—three to four draft offerings usually made just once and available exclusively at the brewery. This could be anything from a smoky, savory German-style rauchbier to a peanut butter porter, a fun American twist on a style that originated in Great Britain. All of the other products brewed here are canned. During a walk through the brick building, visitors will learn about the brewing process, why the company believes in canning, and a bit about the history of the Bates Mill Complex, once the largest employer in the state. After the tour, belly up to the tasting room bar and try some of the other beers ($1 for a four-ounce pour; $3 for a flight of four beers or $4 for a small-batch flight). Baxter also sells salty soft pretzels made by Pretzel Log Gourmet in Monmouth. Future additions could include a seasonal outdoor beer garden.

Following fast on the heels of the smooth, crisp, and snappy Pamola Xtra Pale (4.9% ABV), Baxter debuted Stowaway IPA

(6.9% ABV), a beer for the hop-crazed hordes. Five different varieties turn up in this deep amber-colored drink, providing lots of piney, citrus aroma, plenty of bitterness, and a dry finish that won't quit. Phantom Punch (6.8% ABV), is a bold winter stout that goes easy on the hops in favor of deep, dark roasted barley malt, organic cocoa nibs, and vanilla beans. At the other end of the color spectrum, Summer Swelter (4.9% ABV), a straw-yellow ale brewed with wheat, gives off aromas of lime, lemon, and lemongrass—an effervescent beer you could think of as sunshine in a glass.

Davinci's Eatery (207-782-2088; www.davinciseatery.com) in the mill complex is not only a good bet for a well-prepared Italian meal, it's also a dependable place to find something to drink from the brewery next door. Fuel Restaurant (207-333-3835; www.fuelmaine.com) in downtown Lewiston specializes in French cuisine and also frequently features Baxter beers on their draft list. Get the Cardamom Crème Brûlée with ginger cookies and ask for Hayride Autumn Ale (6.6% ABV) if it's available. She Doesn't Like Guthries (207-376-3344; www.guthriesplace. com), an eco-friendly joint downtown, is a third option for good food paired with something from Baxter or another Maine craft brewery.

One of the biggest annual events in Lewiston/Auburn is the Great Falls Balloon Festival (www.greatfallsballoonfestival.org), a three-day affair attracting thousands to Simard-Payne Memorial Park for entertainment, activities, and balloon launches. Plan ahead and you can purchase a ride in the sky. To see more of the city, rent a bicycle and a helmet from Roy's (207-783-9090; www.roysbike.com) on Farwell Street. Head northwest over Memorial Bridge to complete a ten-mile loop around Lake Auburn, the source of Baxter Brewing's water. On snowy winter days, combine a stop at Baxter with an afternoon on the slopes at nearby Lost Valley (207-784-1561; www.lostvalleyski.com), a small ski resort five miles away. 🍺

CONTACT
70 Lincoln Street
Lewiston, ME 04240
207-333-6769
www.baxterbrewing.com
@baxterbrewing

TASTING ROOM HOURS:
Thu–Sun, Noon–6pm
(Tours at 2pm & 3pm)

LODGING:
The Munroe Inn
123 Pleasant Street
Auburn, ME 04210
207-376-3266
www.themunroeinn.com

MARSHALL WHARF
BREWING COMPANY

YEAR FOUNDED: 2007

FOUNDER:
David Carlson

ANNUAL PRODUCTION:
500-600 barrels

YEAR-ROUND & SEASONAL BEERS: 42 Cream Ale, Ace Hole Pale Ale, Attenuator Doppelbock, Big Twitch IPA, Black Angus, Cant Dog Imperial IPA, Chaos Chaos, Cornholio, Danny McGovern's Oatmeal Stout, Deep Purple, Rauchbier, Docktor Dunklesweizen, Happy Dog Coffee Porter, Illegal Ale-ien, Little Max Red Ale, Little Mayhem, Little Moo Brown Ale, Little Toot, MacFindlay Scotch Ale, Phil Brown Ale, Maxmillian Imperial Red Ale, Old No. 58, Pemaquid Oyster Stout, Pinchy, Sexy Chaos, Scott's Scoville Chili Ale-Ien, Sea Level Stout, Snow Cone Pale Ale, Spicy Ace Hole, T2-R9 Barleywine, Toughcats IPA, Tug Pale Ale, Umlaut Kolsch, Weisse Grip Hefeweizen, Wet Ace Hole, Wet Dog, Wiener, Wrecking Ball Baltic Porter

LOCAL FLAVOR: Known for a time as the Broiler Capital of the World, the city of Belfast used to host an enormous barbecued chicken feast every July.

After spending time out West, David and his wife, Sarah, moved back to Maine with aspirations to open a pub. Beginning with a waterfront lobster pound in Belfast's old granary, they eventually rented and renovated the neighboring 1800s-era boat barn. The look of Three Tides is rough, yet stylish, unassuming and befitting a town with a blue collar history. In 2007, they added the brewery next door, debuting with the drinkable Tug Pale Ale.

With anywhere from four to eight draft lines in the brewery and another seventeen at Three Tides, it's a rare visitor that goes away unhappy. The tasting room won't dazzle every traveler, but those who can look past the cramped space and the funky couches will enjoy the experience that much more. Every beer made on the seven-barrel system by Danny McGovern, formerly of Belfast Bay Brewing, is made with pride. Taste your way through the rotating list of beers on the chalkboard just inside the entrance, or walk next door, order a sampler tray, and depending on the weather, find a seat at the bar inside or on the outdoor deck overlooking a small beer garden built on top of an oyster shell midden. If you plan to be in town during the fall, time your visit with Marshall Wharf's annual Year of Beer and Pemaquid mussel celebration.

Marshall Wharf has gained a reputation for extreme beers, although the bready and light-bodied Little Max Red Ale (4.5% ABV) and malty, peaty Phil Brown Ale (6% ABV) are both meant for quaffing. That said, master brewer McGovern makes a huge Russian imperial stout called Sexy Chaos (11.2% ABV) that will challenge the sobriety of even the most seasoned barflies. Aged on vanilla beans and toasted oak chips, it's a treat for dark beer lovers. Marshall Wharf's lone canned offering, Cant Dog (9.7% ABV), pours a transparent medium amber and produces a generous, creamy head. They call it an imperial pale ale, placing it somewhere between an American IPA and its bigger, brasher

CONTACT
Two Pinchy Lane
Belfast, ME 04915
207-338-1707
www.marshallwharf.com
@marshallwharf

TASTING ROOM HOURS:
Tasting room: Thu-Sat, Noon-7pm;
Brewpub: Tue-Sat, 4pm-Close

LODGING:
The Alden House
63 Church Street
Belfast, Maine 04915
207-338-2151
www.thealdenhouse.com

cousin, the double IPA. Named for the long-hooked tool used by loggers to roll tree trunks, this is a very well balanced, yet high-alcohol beer. Revel in its aromas of mango and tropical fruit, enjoy the honey-like sweetness and soft piney finish, and drink with caution.

With its location on the waterfront, Three Tides' strength is seafood, and what better to wash down half a dozen oysters than a pint of Pemaquid Oyster Stout (6.1% ABV). If raw shellfish aren't your thing, the mushroom caps stuffed with crabmeat or even the caprese salad would go well with the crisp Umlaut Kolsh (4.2% ABV) or the Tug Pale. For more options and a good chance of finding Marshall Wharf on tap, try Nocturnem Draft Haus (207-907-4380; www.nocturnemdrafthaus.com) in Bangor. The char-broiled Angus burger with Trappist cheese and caramelized onions would probably find the smoky Deep Purple Rauchbier (6.2% ABV) very companionable. To the east, in Bar Harbor, the lobster mac and cheese at McKay's Public House (207-288-2002; www.mckayspublichouse.com) deserves a beer than can cut through such a rich dish. Ask if they have Ace Hole Pale Ale (6.1% ABV) when you place your order.

Even with summer traffic clogging Route 1, it's possible to reach Acadia National Park (207-288-3338; www.nps.gov/acad/index.htm), one of the most scenic places on the East Coast, in about ninety minutes. For a closer, smaller slice of nature, look no further than Heritage Park on the Penobscot River, an excellent spot for picnicking in downtown Belfast that hosts a free evening concert series in the summer. A short stroll away, Main Street offers half a dozen small art galleries. For some activity in town, consider a sea kayak tour with Walter Walker Sea Kayak (207-338-6424; www.touringkayaks.com). Book a partial day tour that leaves from Belfast or a longer inn-to-inn trip down the coast.

OXBOW
BREWING COMPANY

YEAR FOUNDED: 2011

FOUNDERS:
Geoff Maslan and Tim Adams

ANNUAL PRODUCTION:
800–1,000 barrels

**YEAR-ROUND &
SEASONAL BEERS:** Farmhouse
Pale Ale, Space Cowboy Country Ale,
Loretta, Sasuga Saison, Saison Noel,
Oxtoberfest, Funkhaus

LOCAL FLAVOR: Before its
conversion into a brewery, the barn on
Oxbow's property was used to store and
repair kayaks.

A sleepy town on the Damariscotta River, Newcastle, Maine, is a good forty-five minutes by car to Augusta, the state's capital. Yet this is where a group of friends decided to start a farmhouse brewery, naming it after a U-shaped bend in a nearby waterway. They like to say they make loud beers from a quiet place. To find out why, step outside of their snug tasting room with a sampler of barrel-aged farmhouse pale ale—the soundtrack is provided by birds and the breeze passing through the branches of hemlock trees—while your taste buds will trip the light fantastic with each successive mouthful of tart, tasty beer.

Geoff Maslan, his wife, Dash, and Tim Adams (who grew up with Dash) founded their brewery after moving to the area in 2009. They tend to think of each beer they brew as an album, and often create concert-like flyers to accompany each new release. Once a year they also host Goods from the Woods, a daylong party with food, DJs, graffiti artists, and special beers they've set aside for the occasion. As with many craft breweries, Oxbow has a strong sense of place—Maslan and Adams have already brewed with local hops and malted grains and plan to grow strawberries, blackberries, cherries, and other fruits on their eighteen-acre property. New growlers cost $5, and fills run from $10 to $15, depending on the beer.

Generally speaking, brewers Adams and Mike Fava concentrate on saisons or farmhouse ales, although they can hardly be called traditionalists. At Oxbow, flavor comes before style adherence. Space Cowboy Country Ale (4% ABV), a year-round offering, might best be described as a cross between an English mild and a Belgian saison with a russet or reddish brown color, an herbal aroma, and a peppery finish. The Saison Noel (10.5% ABV), is something of a bruiser with a deeper brown hue and the alluring smell of dark fruit. In addition to their perennials, Oxbow puts a portion of their beer in wine and bourbon barrels, allowing a wild yeast strain called Brettanomyces and the oak itself to impart additional character. Since the beginning, Oxbow has also experimented with an ongoing project they refer to as the Freestyle Series. The beers released under this label vary as ingredients and friends interested in collaborating become available. So far they've made a smoked chocolate stout and a dry-hopped saison, and last year brewed Freestyle No. 30 (8% ABV) which incorporated Belgian candy sugar and picked up woody notes from time spent on Maine cedar.

For a warm meal made with local ingredients and the possibility of beer on tap from up the road, try the Newcastle Publick House on Main Street (207-563-3434; www.newcastlepublickhouse.com). An entree such as the butter-poached scallops would partner well with Oxbow's Loretta (4% ABV). Continue north on Route 1 to Rockland where chef Keiko Suzuki Steinberger puts a delicious twist on traditional Japanese fare at Suzuki (207-596-7447; www.suzukisushi.com). Almost any of her nigiri or maki rolls would find complementary flavors in Sasuga Saison (4.5% ABV). If they don't already carry this beer, they should.

Water lovers will want to leave time for a trip with Damariscotta River Cruises (917-325-0876; www.damariscottarivercruises.com). Museum-goers, meanwhile, will find a variety of institutions in Rockland, from the fine art collections at the Farnsworth to the maritime artifacts at the Maine Lighthouse Museum (207-594-3301; www.mainelighthousemuseum.org). To see one of the state's historic lighthouses, travel to Owl's Head State Park (207-941-4014; www.maine.gov/doc/parks/index.html) at the southern entrance to Rockland harbor, open to the public several times a week during the summer. If you're more of a culture person, head to Brunswick and check the calendar at Frontier (207-725-5222; www.explorefrontier.com), a cinema and performance space with Oxbow on tap. 🍾

CONTACT

Jones Woods Road
Newcastle, ME 04553
207-315-5962
www.oxbowbeer.com
@oxbowbeer

TASTING ROOM HOURS:
Wed-Fri, 2-7pm; Sat, Noon-5pm

LODGING:
The Tipsy Butler Bed & Breakfast
11 High Street
Newcastle, ME 04553
207-563-3394
www.thetipsybutler.com

RISING TIDE
BREWING COMPANY

YEAR FOUNDED: 2010

FOUNDERS:
Nathan and Heather Sanborn

ANNUAL PRODUCTION:
1,200-1,500 barrels

**YEAR-ROUND &
SEASONAL BEERS:** Atlantis, Calcutta
Cutter, Daymark, Ishmael, Phobos &
Deimos, Spinnaker, Ursa Minor, Zephyr

LOCAL FLAVOR: In 1866, Fourth
of July fireworks caused a massive blaze
that ripped through Portland, destroying
much of the city. After the fire, building
debris was used to expand the East Bayside
neighborhood where Rising Tide is today.

Nathan Sanborn dreamed of one day opening a brewery. While his wife, Heather, commuted from Portland to a law practice in Boston (she's since joined their company full time), Sanborn hatched a plan, called it Rising Tide, and began brewing on a tiny "nano" system that required him to work fourteen-hour days to fill a three-barrel fermenter with wort. In the first year of business, he produced 149 barrels of beer. Their launch was well timed, however, and the couple soon found themselves shopping for a larger facility, eventually moving to a former tractor-trailer maintenance garage in the East Bayside neighborhood.

The tasting room, such as it is (given that the brewery has an open-plan design), faces a little rectangle of green called Kennedy Park. Light streams in through floor-to-ceiling windows at the front of the brewery, wood barrels serve as tables, and a tasting bar tempts visitors with ten taps. On Saturdays a food truck will likely be parked out front, and if it's not too busy, Sanborn or one of the employees might drag out a Rising Tide cornhole board and a few bean bags to give people something to do. Tasting flights with small pours are $3, or for those who prefer to sample their beer in eight-ounce servings, you can pay $2 a glass. Empty growlers cost $6, and can be filled with anything on tap for another $12-$15. Parking is available on site, but Rising Tide is a short mile and a half walk from Portland's Old Port.

Ask them about their approach and the Sanborns will tell you that they want to brew beers that are accessible yet different. Beers like Daymark (5.5% ABV), a crisp pale ale with a floral hop aroma and a spiciness derived from the addition of rye malt, and Ursa Minor (6.7% ABV) an ebony-colored winter wheat beer that is neither American stout nor German dunkle weizen yet expresses characteristics of both, certainly fit the bill. Phobos & Deimos (7.9% ABV) a spring seasonal the color of sandalwood or polished maple wood with an alluring, almost wine-like aroma from Nelson Sauvin hops is another example. Lots of delicate carbonation continues to bring floral smells to the surface of the beer as you drink, while hop flavors of sauvignon blanc grapes, gooseberry pie, and lemongrass go on and on through the somewhat bitter, vinous finish. Their black ale Atlantis (5.3% ABV) also succeeds by avoiding pigeonholing. Pungent hop varieties nudge it in the direction of a black IPA category, but a lower alcohol level and a touch of tannic flavor from cherrywood-smoked malt pushes it back toward a smoked porter.

On Commercial Street, Andy's Old Port Pub (207-874-ANDY; www.andysoldportpub.com) serves warm, filling fare alongside a rotating list of beers from Maine craft brewers like Rising Tide. A few short blocks away, Novare Res Bier Café (207-761-2437; www.novareresbiercafe.com) has attracted a steady stream of pilgrims almost from the moment it opened in 2008. The food menu isn't extensive, but everything is well prepared and small enough to warrant ordering with enthusiasm.

Rent a hybrid or a road bike at Cycle Mania (207-774-2933; www.cyclemania1.com) near Portland's historic Old Port for a pleasant ride through the city. Or book a tour with Summer Feet Cycling (866-857-9544; www.bikeportland-maine.com) to five lighthouses, or better yet, a Bike & Brew trip with a gourmet picnic lunch and stops at three breweries. From sailing adventures to sea kayaking, and whale watching to seal cruises, in Portland there's a boat trip for just about every interest. One option is a twenty-minute ferry ride to Peaks Island on Casco Bay Lines (207-774-7871; www.cascobay-lines.com). Maine's largest city also has after-dark entertainment options, including Portland Stage (207-774-0465; www.portlandstage.org) and the Portland Symphony (207-842-0800; www.portlandsymphony.org).

CONTACT

103 Fox Street
Portland, ME 04101
207-370-BEER
www.risingtidebrewing.com
@risingtidebeer

TASTING ROOM HOURS:

Tue & Thu, 4-7pm;
Fri-Sat, Noon-3pm
(Tours Fri & Sat, 12:30 & 2:30pm)

LODGING:

Wild Iris Inn
273 State Street
Portland, ME 04101
800-600-1557
www.wildirisinn.com

Flying Dog
Brewery
FREDERICK

Milkhouse
Brewery
MT. AIRY

BALTIMORE
The Brewer's Art

Evolution Craft Brewing Co.
SALISBURY

BERLIN
Burley Oak
Brewing Co.

MARYLAND

THE BREWER'S ART

YEAR FOUNDED: 1996

FOUNDERS:
Volker Stewart, Johey Verfaille,
and Greg Santori

ANNUAL PRODUCTION:
1,900 barrels (plus 1,800 off site)

**YEAR-ROUND &
SEASONAL BEERS:** Sublimation,
Green Peppercorn Tripel, Charm City Sour,
Birdhouse Ale, Tiny Tim, Resurrection,
Ozzy, La Pétroleuse, St. Festivus, Zodiac,
Proletary Ale, Monument Ale, Saison
Pécore, Sluggo, Wit Trash, 7 Beauties,
Saison des Mystères, Clamper's Ale

LOCAL FLAVOR: In 1813, Mary
Pickersgill finished sewing the large
American flag that would fly over Fort
McHenry and inspire the "The Star-
Spangled Banner" at the Thomas Peters
Brewing Company on East Lombard Street
near Jones Falls.

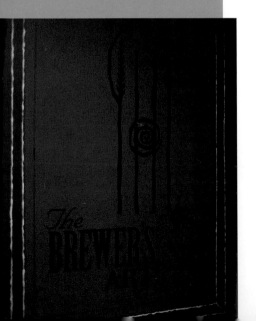

For a business that opened its doors on Friday the Thirteenth, The Brewer's Art has had it pretty good. Although Volker Stewart, a former librarian at the University of Baltimore, is the only one of the three original partners who remains, the quality of both the beer and the menu have held steady over two decades. Built around the turn of the century in the Mount Vernon neighborhood, the townhouse at 1106 North Charles Street functioned as an antiques store before its conversion into an upscale brewpub. From the beginning, the beers here have been heavily influenced by those of Belgium. Greg Santori, the founding brewer, came up with the initial recipes for several of their core offerings, but left The Brewer's Art after a year. Demand and production increased for the next few years, and in 2002 Stewart brought in brewer and college friend Steve Frazier to help tweak the beer recipes as needed, maintain consistency, and grow the business by expanding the brewery's fermentation space. Talented chefs have also come and gone since the days of Johey Verfaille, subtly adapting the menu to their tastes. Tom Creegan, a former manager, is the third current owner.

In spite of the view of the bar through the large picture window, climbing the stairs to The Brewer's Art can feel like entering a private home, or even a museum. Passing through the marbled foyer, you'll enter a lively yet dimly lit space accented by a chandelier and made to look roomier by the presence of a mirror behind the bar. The brewpub actually spreads across two floors of the townhouse, with a small bar and elegant dining room upstairs, and a cavernous rathskeller and second bar below. Ornate interior details like Corinthian columns accompany mismatched furniture, and eclectic art decorates the walls. A huge oil painting of a brewer standing over a steaming kettle hangs above the fireplace. Downstairs, the walls are painted a deep red, and arches and alcoves cast shadows over tables for groups of two and four. As a brewpub, there's no tour to speak of, but if it's not too crowded, you might be able to convince a bartender to give you a taste from one of the six taps before you pay for a full serving. Instead of a full growler, go home with a six-pack of Ozzy or Resurrection in cans.

To describe The Brewer's Art as Belgian-inspired is fair, but only part of the story. Or, to put it another way, their regular lineup is anything but regular. The recipe for their session beer, Zodiac Ale (4.8% ABV), changes with every zodiac sign. Tiny Tim (6.5% ABV), which might be described as a Belgian strong ale, derives its floral and herbal character from buckwheat honey, hibiscus flowers, and rosemary. They've also released a number of different saisons and Grand Cru-style beers made with hibiscus, honeysuckle, lemon balm, cardamom, cinnamon, saffron, hyssop, heather, and calendula flowers. Green Peppercorn Tripel (9% ABV) remains one of their most intriguing creations to date, spicy yet smooth with a delicate sting provided by the combination of pepper and alcohol. And while many of their imaginative ales remain draft-only limited releases, The Brewer's Art started producing selected beers in large-format bottles at

Pennsylvania's Sly Fox in 2007. More recently, they've also begun canning Ozzy (7.25% ABV), a dry and hoppy golden ale with a peppery, almost medicinal aroma, and Resurrection (7% AB), a dubbel that balances dark fruit with bitter hops.

Food is anything but an afterthought at The Brewer's Art, so make an effort to squeeze in more than one meal here during your visit. Starters like chilled English pea soup with a quark and truffle beignet or curried rabbit pâté and pickled baby carrots in a harissa raspberry compote aren't dishes you typically find at a brewpub. As for entrees, you'll have to decide which protein you prefer, but consider the pan-seared Great Lakes walleye with a mélange of spring vegetables and morel mushrooms in crayfish butter. It might be a nice match for a goblet of La Pétroleuse (7% ABV), a malty, golden ale with a yeasty character. Even on a short trip, a place with 102 taps is hard for a beer lover to resist, so give in to the impulse and plan on a pint or two at Max's

Taphouse (410-675-6297; www.maxs.com) in Fells Point. The menu tends to stick to tried and true pub grub, which means satisfying, if somewhat ordinary, options for the beer tourist with an appetite. Try Resurrection with the vegetarian quesadilla: two tortillas filled with portobello mushrooms, artichoke hearts, red onions, wilted spinach, and gorgonzola cheese. Walk back to your hotel if you're worried about calories.

A few blocks south of The Brewer's Art, The Walters Art Museum (410-547-9000; www.thewalters.org) is free and open to the public Wednesday through Sunday. Stroll through their galleries to see art and artifacts from ancient Egypt and ancient Greece, European paintings from the Old Masters, or arms and armor spanning cultures and centuries. With more than a dozen other museums scattered between the harbor and the beltway, Baltimore can entertain visitors for days, assuming you can resist Charm City's other breweries and beer bars. A possible solution to this dilemma is to combine a visit to the National Aquarium (410-576-3800; www.aqua.org) with a stop at the Heavy Seas Alehouse (410-522-0852; www.heavyseasalehouse.com) in the old

Holland Tack Factory building on the edge of Little Italy. Learn about sharks, dolphins, jellyfish, rainforest species, and much more, and then make the short walk east to try a beer cocktail at the alehouse. Of course Baltimore is also home to the Orioles and the Ravens, two teams with adjacent stadiums close to the Babe Ruth Birthplace and Sports Legend Museum (410-727-1539; www.baberuthmuseum.org).

CONTACT

1106 North Charles Street
Baltimore, MD 21201
410-547-6925
www.thebrewersart.com
@brewersart

TASTING ROOM HOURS:

Mon-Sat, 4pm-1:45am; Sun,
5pm-1:45am

LODGING:

868 Park Avenue
Baltimore, MD 21201
443-478-2100
www.brextonhotel.com

BURLEY OAK
BREWING COMPANY

YEAR FOUNDED: 2011

FOUNDER:
Bryan Brushmiller

ANNUAL PRODUCTION:
1,200 barrels

**YEAR-ROUND &
SEASONAL BEERS:** Just the Tip, Pale Ryeder, Rude Boy, Aboriginal Gangster, Bulletproof Tiger, Dirty Blonde, Hopless Beach, Bunker-C, SuperFun Stout, Barreled Brown Ale, Hugs & Nugs, Smokey the Beer, Wanker, Helter Spelter, Cabin Fever, Gingerbread Man, Wing Nut, Cherry Poppins, Cougar Juice

LOCAL FLAVOR: The Burley Inn, a popular eighteenth-century way station in Stevenson's Crossroads, eventually lent its name to the town, which became Berlin.

The eastern shore of Maryland isn't particularly expansive, but driving across it can feel like a long haul. Once you've crossed the Bay Bridge and made it as far as Berlin, you're ready to spend some time in the surf. If Bryan Bushmiller has his way, Berlin might end up attracting a growing number of visitors, some of whom might not be interested in beaches at all. His Burley Oak Brewing Company on Old Ocean City Boulevard has turned Berlin into a beer destination.

Bushmiller started the brewery in a 120-year-old building with equipment he found on Craigslist. He opened the same week Hurricane Irene struck the East Coast. Fittingly, the structure was a cooperage in the early 1900s. Today a small collection of barrels in the back contains beer, while those in the tasting room and bar have been converted into tables. Music is a given at Burley Oak. Tuesday is BYO vinyl night, and on Fridays a live band typically sets up in the corner. It's a fun, friendly, laid-back atmosphere, with Ping Pong, foosball, and a dartboard. Those spending the day (or an overnight) in Berlin, can take one of the beach cruisers out front for a spin. Tasters of beer are $2, pints cost $5 or $6, and growlers run from $12 to $22, with limited release, higher alcohol styles at the higher end of the scale. Meanwhile, their non-alcoholic root beer is a reasonable $3.

His brewery might still be relatively young, but Brushmiller doesn't seem interested in playing it safe with his beers. Yes, he has a classic German-style kolsch (although you will have to ask the bartender for "Just the Tip" with a straight face) and a citrusy IPA called Aboriginal Gangster (6.5% ABV), but he also makes a sessionable barleywine and a zippy, light-bodied wheat beer called Hopless Beach (4% ABV) that eschews beer's traditional bittering ingredient altogether. In general though, Burley Oak beers push the envelope. Take Night Ryeder (10% ABV), for instance, a chocolate rye milk stout that hides its boozy punch

CONTACT

10016 Old Ocean City
Boulevard
Berlin, MD 21811
443-513-4647
www.burleyoak.com
@burleyoak

TASTING ROOM HOURS:

Mon-Wed, 11am-11pm;
Thu-Sat, 11am-2am;
Sun, 11am-9pm
(Tours on Sat & Sun at 3pm)

LODGING:

The Atlantic Hotel
2 North Main Street
Berlin, MD 21811
410-641-3589
www.atlantichotel.com

behind a mocha aroma, a creamy mouthfeel, and the taste of bitter malt and tobacco. Taking a different approach to the fall seasonal, Not Your Average Gourd (6.5% ABV) derives its flavor from squash, vanilla, and toasted pumpkin seeds. Barreled (6.9% ABV), a nutty, buttery brown ale, and MOB Barley (7% ABV), an earthy, piney, and pungent black IPA are memorable beers, too.

If you're looking for the closest spot with Burley Oak on tap, follow North Main Street to The Globe (410-641-0784; www.globetheater. com) in the center of town. A former movie theater, this restaurant is a standout in the area with an extensive dinner menu and Sunday brunch. Should you find SummaRye (6% ABV) on tap, try this spicy saison brewed with local rye and Belgian rock candy with a big cup of cream of crab soup. Or for something lighter, match Cherry Poppins (4.5% ABV), a sessionable Belgian-style fruit beer, with The Globe's pear and spinach salad. Hooper's Crab House (410-213-1771; www.hooperscrabhouse.com) is just outside of Ocean City. Many of their items would go well with Cougar Juice (5% ABV), a saison that gets additional flavor from lemon verbena leaves, or Port d Orange (5% ABV), a Belgian wit.

One way to combine beer tasting with another activity is to book a kayaking trip with SuperFun Eco Tours (410-656-9453; www. superfunecotours.com). You'll meet at Burley Oak, board a bus to Assateague Island National Seashore for a guided paddle, and then return to the brewery for a tour and tasting. You can also check out Assateague (410-641-1441; www.nps.gov/asis/index.htm) on your own time, snapping photos of its famous wild horses, surfing, swimming, or even beach camping. Check out OC Parasail (410-723-1464; www. ocparasailing.com). Sure, there are cheaper ways to avoid the crowds on the boardwalk, but probably none quite so fun. 🍺

EVOLUTION CRAFT
BREWING COMPANY

YEAR FOUNDED: 2009

FOUNDERS:
Tom and John Knorr

ANNUAL PRODUCTION:
7,500-8,000 barrels

**YEAR-ROUND &
SEASONAL BEERS:** Exile ESB,
Lot 3 IPA, Lucky 7 Porter, Primal Pale Ale,
Rise Up Stout, Jacques Au Lantern, Secret
Spot Winter Ale, Sprung, Summer Session,
XO Stout

LOCAL FLAVOR: Evolution originally
started making beer due north of its
current home, in an old grocery store just
across the state line in Delmar, Delaware.

A career in food led Tom and John Knorr to beer. After college the two brothers worked for a Maryland restaurant chain called Phillip's Seafood. In 1996, they bought The Red Roost, a crabhouse and fried chicken joint in Whitehaven. They didn't know it yet, but it would be the start of their own restaurant group, Southern Boys Concepts. By the time they founded the Evolution Craft Brewing Company with brewmaster Geoff DeBisschop more than a decade later, they owned three restaurants in Maryland and another in Antigua, Guatemala. DeBisschop brought years of experience (plus a few prestigious beer awards) with him. Starting off in an old grocery store in Delaware with used brewpub equipment from Philadelphia, the team, which had added chef John Scheckells, realized they needed more space and moved to their current home, a former ice plant in downtown Salisbury.

Encompassing the brewery proper, a laid-back tasting room, and the Public House restaurant, Evolution is the kind of place where you could easily lose a couple of hours. On nice days, you might decide to spend some of that time on their patio or beer garden, an outdoor seating area elevated above the parking lot in front. Free tours (first-come, first-served) leave from the tasting room. The tasting room also serves cheese, charcuterie, and a daily special for visitors who finish a tour feeling a little peckish. Beer flights come four to an order and growlers run $9-$14, plus another $5 for the container itself.

In the beginning, DeBisschop brewed a pale ale, an ESB, and a porter, three versatile styles designed to fill food niches. The next addition was Lot No. 3 IPA (6.8% ABV). Today the Evolution lineup includes six year-round beers, four seasonals, limited runs of barrel-aged big beers, and an Incubator series of forty-barrel test batches released only once each. Incubator

#1 (5.6% ABV), the first beer in this project, was a peppery, dry, and refreshing Belgian pale ale with a flavor that brought to mind peaches or other ripe stone fruit. Their fall seasonal also puts a Belgian twist on a familiar style. Jacques Au Lantern (6.3% ABV), an amber ale that includes pie spices and roasted pumpkin, is fermented with a Belgian yeast strain. Somewhat uniquely, Evolution's year-round stout is cold-steeped with organic coffee. Dark, rich, and full of depth, Rise Up Stout (6.7% ABV) earned its name from its partner, Rise Up Coffee Roasters in nearby Easton. XO Stout (6.7% ABV) meanwhile, relies on the same base ingredients, but replaces the coffee with tart cherries and dark chocolate cocoa nibs.

When hunger strikes but you don't want to venture too far from a draft line, the easiest solution is to head next door to the Public House (443-260-2337; www.evolutioncraftbrewing.com/PublicHouse.aspx). Food and beer come together in a seemingly effortless manner here as dishes such as the duck confit shepherd's pie paired with Lucky 7 Porter (5.8% ABV) immediately demonstrate. The house-made pickled sampler and a Maryland-style crab dip with Parmesan flatbread can be even more enjoyable with a pint of Primal Pale Ale (5% ABV) or Incubator #1, a dry, spicy Belgian pale ale that might remind your taste buds of peaches and nectarines. Also in downtown Salisbury, the Market Street Inn (410-742-4145; www.msi.mojossalisbury.com) is a good bet for upscale cuisine in a casual atmosphere. The draft list here typically includes something from Evolution. A seasonal beer like the delicate Sprung (4.9% ABV) with its suggestion of honey and hibiscus would work well with a plate of fresh fruit and brie.

While at the Eastern Shore, stop at Greenbranch Organic Farm's store on a Friday or Saturday (443-736-7779; www.greenbranchfarm.com). Baseball fans might be more interested in the local team. Every summer, the Delmarva Shorebirds (410-219-3112; www.theshorebirds.com) host minor league opponents at Perdue Stadium just east of town. Another option is a fishing, crabbing, or sightseeing tour with Procrastinator Charters (443-783-0227; www.procastinatorcharters.com). 🍺

CONTACT

201 East Vine Street
Salisbury, MD 21804
443-260-2337
www.evolutioncraftbrewing.com
@evolutionbeer

TASTING ROOM HOURS:

Mon-Fri, 3-8pm;
Sat-Sun, 11:30am-8pm
(Tours Fri-Sun)

PUBLIC HOUSE HOURS:

Sun-Wed, 11:30am-Midnight;
Thu-Sat, 11:30am-12:30am

LODGING:

Whitehaven Hotel
2685 Whitehaven Road
Whitehaven, MD 21856
410-873-3099
www.whitehaven.tripod.com

FLYING DOG BREWERY

YEAR FOUNDED: 1990

FOUNDERS:
George Stranahan and Richard McIntyre

ANNUAL PRODUCTION:
90,000-100,000 barrels

YEAR-ROUND & SEASONAL BEERS: Raging Bitch, Snake Dog, UnderDog, Pearl Necklace, Wildeman, Doggie Style, In-Heat Wheat, Old Scratch, Double Dog, Gonzo, K-9 Cruiser, Kujo, Horn Dog, Lucky SOB, Woody Creek, Dogtoberfest, Secret Stash, The Fear

LOCAL FLAVOR: Many of Flying Dog's aged beers spend time in barrels from nearby Maryland wineries, such as Elk Run Vineyards in Mt. Airy.

Throughout the Northeast, the story of one beer business after another often begins the same way: a homebrewer dreams of going pro, scrapes together some money and equipment, and against all odds, brings a new, distinctive beer to market. The creation myth for Flying Dog in Maryland, however, starts a bit differently. First of all there's the central character, George Stranahan, the heir to the Champion spark plug fortune and a man who has at times been a cattle rancher, an author, a photographer, a philanthropist, and a restauranteur. But in fact, as much as Stranahan liked beer, it took a failed restaurant in Aspen (along with a strange bit of inspiration on a boozy mountaineering trip to Pakistan in 1983) to plant the seed for Flying Dog. With his longtime friend and business partner Richard McIntyre, Stranahan opened a brewpub named for a painting he'd seen in Rawalpindi. It thrived until the landlord raised the rent. Instead of packing up shop completely though, the partners switched to production brewing and later, via Gonzo journalist Hunter S. Thompson, met Ralph Steadman, a prolific artist who had illustrated *Fear and Loathing in Las Vegas*. The brewery moved operations from Colorado to Maryland in 2008, but Steadman's characteristic label art has appeared on every bottle of Flying Dog since 1996.

Tours, which start in the entry hallway decorated with a Steadman-esque mural, cost $5 and include samples of five beers and a souvenir glass. Reservations are required and can be made online. If you're not in a rush after the tour, pick your last sample from one of the nineteen taps at the long bar, grab a spot on the patio, and admire the hop garden on the other

side of the parking lot. Besides their weekly schedule, Flying Dog hosts the occasional event or concert, from Green Eggs and Kegs around St. Patrick's Day to Gonzo Fest in July (held every year on or near Hunter S. Thompson's birthday). Plus, on the second Tuesday of each month, they open up in the evening for a Brewhouse Rarities release where the lucky few have a chance to try beers like a Pineapple Saison, a Green Tea Imperial Stout, or a Gose brewed with Old Bay seasoning. An on-site gift shop stocks Flying Dog socks, underwear, and bottle opener dog collars along with individual bottles of seasonal and vintage beers. Growler fills range from $10 to $20.

It only makes sense that a brewery with such an irreverent company culture would push the limits with their products. Five of their ten year-round beers, including their flagship Raging Bitch (8.3% ABV), are hoppy pale ales or IPAs. In Heat Wheat Hefeweizen (4.7% ABV) is one of the exceptions to this rule, as is their amber lager and their oyster stout. Brewed with Rappahannock River oysters, Pearl Necklace (5.5% ABV) is an inky black, full-bodied beer brewed with midnight wheat and roasted barley. More sweet than bitter, it finishes with a subtle touch of minerality owing to the shellfish that end up in the beer. This one probably isn't for vegetarians. Outside of this core range, Flying Dog also releases a number of seasonal beers, many of which have connections to the area. Secret Stash Harvest Ale (5.5% ABV) is unique for its exclusive use of regional ingredients, from local wheat and rye to Maryland-grown hops. The intense, ebony-colored Kujo Imperial Coffee Stout (8.9% ABV) relies on a roast from Black Dog Coffee of West Virginia.

No more than two minutes from the brewery by car, a.k.a. Friscos (301-698-0018; www.akafriscos.com) on Wedgewood Boulevard is the closest place to go for food. Sandwiches here are large, filling, and reasonably priced. Case in point: the S. F. Fatboy with ham, salami, bologna, provolone, cheddar, lettuce, tomato, onion, and vinegar for $8. They also sell salads, ice cream, and (most importantly) beer, and devote an entire cooler to Flying Dog. If you've got the appetite, pair the Mud Pie Sundae with Gonzo Imperial Porter (9.2% ABV). To choose from a wider range of restaurants, head to downtown Frederick. At Firestone's Culinary Tavern on North Market Street, a Thai bouillabaisse made with lobster, littleneck clams, mussels, kimchi, bok choy, clams, yuzu fruit, chili peppers, and coconut milk would go well with a glass or two of Wildeman Farmhouse IPA (7.5% ABV), a dry, hoppy ale with a spicy nose. And although they don't carry Flying Dog, Brewer's Alley (301-631-0089; www.brewers-alley.com) just up the street from Firestone's is worth a stop if you have the time. They became Frederick's first brewpub when they opened their doors in 1996.

If you're the type who likes to road trip with a bicycle or two on the roof rack of your car, then scoot over to the Chesapeake & Ohio Canal National Historical Park (301-834-7100; www.nps.gov/choh/index.htm) before or after your stop at Flying Dog. The nearest visitor center is in Brunswick, to the west. The entire towpath stretches 184.5 miles from Washington, DC, to Cumberland; in other words, riders can choose their own distances. But if a shorter walk and some Civil War history are more of your speed,

head to Monocacy National Battlefield (301-662-3515; www.nps.gov/mono/index.htm) just outside Frederick. Meanwhile, the National Museum of Civil War Medicine (301-695-1864; www.civilwarmed.org) in downtown Frederick includes five galleries of exhibits, more than 1,200 medical artifacts, and a gift shop. Frederick also hosts the Maryland Shakespeare Festival each summer. And finally, for those who might want to try to squeeze in a seasonal farm visit while they're in the area, contact Sycamore Spring Farm (301-788-6980; www.sycamorespringfarm.org), a ten-minute drive from Flying Dog.

CONTACT

4607 Wedgewood Boulevard
Frederick, MD 21703
301-694-7899
www.flyingdogbrewery.com
@flyingdog

TASTING ROOM HOURS:

Thu-Fri, 4-8pm; Sat, Noon-4pm
(tours Thu & Fri at 4 & 6:30pm;
Sat at Noon & 2:30pm)

LODGING:

Hill House Bed & Breakfast
12 West Third Street
Frederick, MD 21705
301-682-4111
www.hillhousefrederick.com

MILKHOUSE BREWERY AT STILLPOINT FARM

YEAR FOUNDED: 2013

FOUNDERS:
Tom Barse and Carolann McConaughy

ANNUAL PRODUCTION:
200-250 barrels

YEAR-ROUND & SEASONAL BEERS: Haymaker XPA, Poor Butt Porter, Red-Eye Porter, Farmhouse IPA, Maryland Saison, Stillpoint Sour

LOCAL FLAVOR: Between the 1840s and the 1870s, German farmers planted the first hop fields in western Maryland. Tom Barse planted his field in 2008.

Silos alone make for great landmarks in farm country. So if the hand-painted sign and hop bines don't get your attention, look up on the hill for an old green Chevy pickup. When you see it, you've reached Mt. Airy's farmhouse brewery. While they'd been growing, picking, and sorting hops on the property for years, it wasn't until late 2012 that teachers Tom Barse and Carolann McConaughy could consider adding beer to the list of products available at Stillpoint Farm. Before that, state law only permitted brewpubs or production breweries. When the couple opened Milkhouse in the summer of 2013, they became the proprietors of Maryland's first farm brewery. After selling fresh Cascade and Chinook hops to larger local breweries like Flying Dog and Heavy Seas, Barse could finally start using them in larger batches of his own beer recipes.

With a hopyard, an apiary, and a twenty-seven-acre sheep farm to manage, Barse is a busy man and currently only brews once a week. Fortunately, the tasting room is open much more frequently. Knotty pine-paneled walls, plenty of natural light, and an attractive bar built from oak and chestnut make it a pleasant place to spend part of an afternoon—an oasis of beer a stone's throw from the Frederick Wine Trail. (In fact, there's a good chance you'll find Milkhouse ales aging in chardonnay barrels.) Several times a year, Tom and Carolann host events on the farm and invite area breweries like Monocacy, Flying Dog, and Barley and Hops to pour their beers, too. Besides growlers of Milkhouse beer ($18-$20), visitors to the brewery can also bring home raw honey, lotion, candles, yarn, local cheese, and seasonal veggies grown or produced in the area.

By focusing on freshness and locally grown ingredients, Milkhouse's full range of beers is necessarily—and understandably—limited. Brewed with black patent malt, Poor Butt Porter

(6% ABV) is a dark, rich, muscular ale that borders on a stout. On a chilly day it's a glass of comfort with an aftertaste akin to burnt toast. Barse's coffee-infused version, Red-Eye (5% ABV), is also reassuring under gray winter skies. At the other end of the color spectrum, Haymaker XPA has a sweet, floral nose and a pale straw color. Light-bodied with a crackery flavor, it's a beer for summer. Aiming for a crowd pleaser, Milkhouse also produces a Farmhouse IPA (6.5% ABV). Looking ahead, Barse plans to release a saison made with seasonal ingredients grown on the farm, as well as a barrel-aged sour partially inoculated with wild yeast cultured at Stillpoint.

A day or two of brewery touring is likely to work up an appetite. In Mt. Airy, hungry travelers should seek out Carterque (301-829-2222; www.carterque.com). They don't have Milkhouse on tap (yet), but can be depended on for a decent selection from other regional craft breweries. Or try the Mt. Airy Inn (301-829-1400; www.mountairyinn. com) on South Main Street. With a dozen beers on tap and more than twice as many in cans or bottles, you won't lack for pairing options. Flights of five run from $18 to $25.

You can find other green spaces close to Milkhouse, but Patuxent River State Park (301-924-2127; www.dnr.state.md.us/publiclands/central/patuxentriver.asp), at 5,000 acres, is the biggest place nearby to fish, hike, or horseback ride. To the east, Carroll County is a great place for road biking with ten different loop tours. For rentals, try Race Pace Bicycles in Westminster (410-876-3001; www.racepacebicycles.com). One route takes cyclists past the Carroll County Farm Museum (410-386-3880; www.ccgovernment.carr.org/ccg/farmmus). Open on weekends from May through October, the museum includes a nineteenth-century farmhouse, a Living History Center, livestock, gardens, and a nature trail. To see even more of western Maryland, sign up for a three-hour hot air balloon ride with Tailwinds Over Frederick (240-415-8094; www.tailwindsoverfrederick.com). 🍺

CONTACT
8253 Dollyhyde Road
Mount Airy, MD 21771
301-829-6950
www.milkhousebrewery.com
@MilkhouseBrew

TASTING ROOM HOURS:
Fri-Sun, Noon-9pm

LODGING:
Atlee House
120 Water Street
New Windsor, MD 21776
410-871-9119
www.atleehousebb.net

Element Brewing Co.
MILLERS FALLS

GLOUCESTER
Cape Ann Brewing Co.

Mystic Brewery
CHELSEA

BOSTON
Harpoon Brewery

Tree House Brewing Co.
BRIMFIELD

MASSACHUSETTS

CAPE ANN BREWING COMPANY

YEAR FOUNDED: 2004

FOUNDERS:
Jeremy Goldberg, Michael Goldberg, and Michael Beaton

ANNUAL PRODUCTION:
3,000-4,000 barrels

YEAR-ROUND & SEASONAL BEERS: Fisherman's Brew, Fisherman's Navigator, Fisherman's Ale, Fisherman's IPA, Fisherman's Pumpkin Stout, Fisherman's Imperial Pumpkin Stout, Fisherman's Rockporter, Fisherman's 70 Shilling Scottish Ale, Fisherman's Tea Party, Fisherman's Dead Eye DIPA, Fisherman's Winter Ale, Fisherman's Honey Pilsner, Fisherman's Sunrise Saison, Fisherman's Dunkleweiss

LOCAL FLAVOR: The image of the mariner that appears on Cape Ann's packaging is a nod to Gloucester's Fisherman Memorial or *The Man at the Wheel*, a bronze tribute to the thousands of fisherman who have lost their lives at sea.

Jeremy Goldberg took a circuitous route to his current position as owner of the Cape Ann Brewing Company. A New Jersey native and a hobbyist homebrewer, Goldberg was working on Wall Street when the Twin Towers fell in 2001. Shortly after the tragedy, he decided he no longer wanted to work in finance. But before updating his resume, he and a group of friends set out on a road trip to visit thirty-eight craft breweries in forty days. They documented their epic journey, which included on-camera interviews with numerous pioneering craft brewers, and ended up releasing the lighthearted if somewhat aimless result as a feature-length film called *American Beer*. Soon thereafter, Paul Kermizian, the director, and Jon Miller, the cinematographer, ended up opening Barcade, a hybrid beer bar and video arcade that now has four locations. Goldberg, with urging of his brother-in-law and some help from his father, relocated to Massachusetts and traded his silk tie for rubber brewing boots. Starting out in an old factory on Commercial Street, Cape Ann moved within town in 2009 and now occupies a larger site with more seating and a dozen tap lines instead of four.

Even if you didn't come to Cape Ann with an appetite, the brewpub is spacious enough for those who simply want to hang out with a beer or two. Inside the high-ceilinged room, air hockey, a foosball table, and darts provide entertainment while outside on the deck you can relax and watch vessels from the town's small fishing fleet enter and leave the harbor. Blonde wood, picnic table seating, and a wall of windows overlooking the water lend a casual, sunglasses-and-sandals vibe. Gloucester is very much a place with a seasonal population though, so

while it's not uncommon to wait for a table during the summer, you might find Cape Ann nearly empty at lunchtime in the winter. Free daily tours tend to be brief unless you bring lots of questions, so keep the brewpub's reasonably compact size in mind if you decide to check out the abbreviated experience. New growlers start at $15.50 and run all the way up to almost $25 for the rarest beers. As one might expect, the brewpub also sells branded apparel and glassware.

Cape Ann does distribute its core range of contract-brewed beers fairly widely, but in Gloucester, the lineup turns over frequently and often includes something that will never make it into bottles. Every once in a while you might turn up and discover a beer like Rumba (8.2% ABV), a reddish ale characterized by a low level of carbonation, a big-bodied chewiness, and almond and toffee flavors. Tea Party (9% ABV) is another unusual offering—a bitter, earthy, and somewhat murky barleywine made with three types of tea. More approachable beers include a Honey Pils (4.4% ABV) and Sunrise Saison (7% ABV), which pours with a lovely meringue-like head that slowly dissolves into a soft peachy-colored body. More tart than sweet with aromas of honey, strawberry blossoms, and a whiff of spice, this American take on a Belgian style adds whole strawberries and fresh rhubarb during the brewing process. In contrast, Imperial Pumpkin Stout (11% ABV) is an assertive beer with a pure black body and aromas of sweet potato, brown sugar, and pumpkin pie spices like cinnamon stick, allspice, nutmeg, and cloves. Thick and full-flavored, its earthy bitterness emerges late while a spirituous finish with hint of mocha lingers after your glass is empty.

As a brewpub, Cape Ann has a diverse menu of beer-friendly appetizers, sandwiches, and entrees, some of which are even prepared with the house beers. The generous fried

haddock sandwich, to mention just one example, is battered with Fisherman's Brew, Cape Ann's amber lager, while the P.E.I. mussels are sautéed in Fisherman's Kolsch. Whether you opt for a full meal or a few starters to share, ask for a cup of the thick, creamy New England clam chowder. Enjoy it with a pint of Fisherman's Clam Porter (6.5% ABV) or the rich, roasty Oyster Stout (4.4% ABV) made with crushed oyster shells. Across the inner harbor on Rocky Neck, a stretch of land that has attracted artists since the 1840s, the Rudder Restaurant (978-283-7967; www.rudderrestaurant.com) continues to serve hungry customers as it has since 1957. Naturally, seafood is the specialty, with entrees ranging from a locally caught two-pound lobster to pan-seared monkfish topped with a lemon butter sauce. Four of the six draft lines are usually devoted to Massachusetts breweries. If Fisherman's Dunkleweiss happens to be in the mix during your visit, give some thought to the dessert menu, especially the banana cream-filled burrito tossed in cinnamon sugar.

Perhaps you traveled to Gloucester for the sole purpose of visiting Cape Ann Brewing and maybe you want to get to a second brewery in Portsmouth or Boston before the end of the day, too. Before you rush off, spend some time walking the winding streets of America's oldest seaport. Or to get a taste of the mariner's life, arrange to go for a sail aboard a fifty-five-foot schooner or accompany a lobsterman out into the harbor through Maritime Gloucester (978-281-0470; www.gloucestermaritimecenter.org).

Seven Seas Whale Watch (888-283-1776; www.7seas-whalewatch.com) is also in town and runs regular boat trips from late April through October. During your three to four hour journey aboard the *Privateer IV*, you might see humpback, finback, sperm, minke, and blue whales as well as a pod of Atlantic white-sided dolphins. Alternatively, to learn more about the early days of this fishing village that dates back nearly four centuries, visit the Sargent House Museum or the Cape Ann Museum (978-283-0455; www.capeannmuseum.org) on Pleasant Street near the train station. A cultural center with an extensive collection of maritime art, artifacts from the shipping and granite industries, and two sculpture gardens, it's a worthwhile detour from an afternoon of beer tasting. 🍾

CONTACT

11 Rogers Street
Gloucester, MA 01930
866-BEER-MEN
www.capeannbrewing.com
@capeannbrewing

TASTING ROOM HOURS:

Sun-Sat, 11am-Midnight
(Tours Mon-Fri, 11am-5pm on request; Sat & Sun by appt.)

LODGING:

Blue Shutters Beachside Inn
One Nautilus Road
Gloucester MA 01930
978-283-1198
www.blueshuttersbeachside.com

ELEMENT
BREWING COMPANY

YEAR FOUNDED: 2009

FOUNDERS:
Daniel Kramer and Ben Anhalt

ANNUAL PRODUCTION:
700 barrels

**YEAR-ROUND &
SEASONAL BEERS:** Extra Special
Oak, Red Giant, Dark Element, Interval:
Summer Pilsner Fusion, Interval:
Altoberfest, Interval: Winter Ion,
Interval: Vernal, L.E.S.O. (Lavender Extra
Special Oak), Plasma

LOCAL FLAVOR: Originally known as
Grout's Corner, the town later changed its
name to Millers Falls after the manufacturer
that employed 500 people in 1912.

Before settling on the space their brewery now occupies, Dan Kramer and Ben Anhalt looked at thirty potential sites scattered across western Massachusetts. But when they came across the old five-and-dime storefront in Millers Falls, a former manufacturing town not far from New Hampshire, they knew their search was over. Here they saw opportunity where others had seen neglected buildings and a Main Street struggling to maintain its relevance. And so, confident that their small business could bring some money back to the area, and hoping to help turn around a community in decline, they decided to locate in Millers Falls. It seems like they made the right decision. With a positive reception from locals and a steady demand for the unusual beers Kramer and Anhalt brew, Element has grown considerably, doubling capacity and expanding into the adjacent storefront.

Despite a somewhat dated exterior, Element looks and feels modern inside, from the bright orange bar top and the quirky beaker-shaped pint glasses down to the wall-mounted representation of their logo, the structural formula for Xanthohumol, an antioxidant chemical found in hops. Think of it as geek chic. To Kramer and Anhalt, beer is a fusion of art and science, the marriage of creativity and precision. Stop by on a weekday and one of them will happily explain their brewing philosophy in more detail; visit on a Saturday and the steady stream of customers might make it harder to chat. Tours are casual and impromptu (just ask) and typically include a free sample of four beers. Merchandise (including gift baskets around the holidays) and corked-finished bottles wrapped in tissue paper are always available during retail hours, as are growler fills ($11-$24).

A tasting flight at Element might begin with one of their four seasonals, like Summer Pilsner Fusion (9% ABV), a deep golden or even brass-colored beer with a snappy bitterness and a smooth mouthfeel owing to the addition of English oats. On the opposite side of the calendar, Winter Ion (9% ABV), with a taste that brings to mind milk chocolate and oranges, is their popular cold weather release. From there you might sample Extra Special Oak (7.75% ABV), a malty, buttery, and aromatic ale, or Dark Element (9.25% ABV), an intriguing hybrid that walks the line between a bold American-style IPA and a German-style Schwarzbier, balancing the sweetness of espresso cookies and candied fruit with just enough piney, minty spice. Once a year, Element also releases an anniversary beer semi-cryptically called 6:56 (after the time of day they sold their first growler).

The closest place to find Dark Element and Extra Special Oak is across Bridge Street at Miller's Pub (413-659-3391; 25 East Main Street), a no-frills watering hole with a limited menu. For more options, try nearby Greenfield, where Magpie (413-475-3570; www.magpiepizza. com) and Hope and Olive (413-774-3150; www.oliveandhope.com) make an effort to source menu items from local farms and often carry Element beer. Greenfield is also home to The People's Pint (413-773-0333; www.thepeopespint.com), a brewpub with a commitment to seasonal, sustainable food.

Beer tourists with a pair of hiking boots and a bathing suit should seek out Wendell State Forest (413-659-3797; www.mass.gov/dcr), a large swath of parkland that includes a section of the New England National Scenic Trail and Ruggles Pond, a day-use area for boating, swimming, and fishing. Or, spend a few hours learning about early New England life at Historic Deerfield (413-774-5581; www.historic-deerfield.org), a group of eleven house museums featuring folk art, antiques, textiles, clothing, and engraved powder horns. In the autumn, this part of Massachusetts also attracts those who hope to view peak fall foliage in the Berkshires. The Mohawk Trail, one of the country's first scenic automobile routes, begins in Orange and passes by Millers Falls on its way toward Mt. Greylock, the highest point in the state. 🍾

CONTACT
30 Bridge Street
Millers Falls, MA 01349
413-835-6340
www.elementbeer.com
@elementbeer

TASTING ROOM HOURS:
Mon-Tue & Thu-Sat, Noon-6pm

LODGING:
The Brandt House
29 Highland Drive
Greenfield, MA 01301
413-774-3329
www.brandthouse.com

HARPOON BREWING

YEAR FOUNDED: 1986

FOUNDERS:
Rich Doyle and Dan Kenary

ANNUAL PRODUCTION:
190,000-200,000 barrels

YEAR-ROUND & SEASONAL BEERS: Harpoon IPA, Harpoon White IPA, Harpoon Black IPA, Rich & Dan's Rye IPA, Leviathan Imperial IPA, Leviathan Quad, Leviathan Red Squared, Leviathan Baltic Porter, Leviathan Great Scott Ale, Leviathan Czernobog, Harpoon Grateful Harvest Ale, Harpoon Chocolate Stout, Harpoon Dark, Harpoon Celtic Ale, Harpoon Summer, Harpoon Octoberfest, Harpoon Winter Warmer, UFO Hefeweizen, UFO Raspberry Hefeweizen, UFO White, UFO Pale Ale, UFO Pumpkin, Harpoon Cider, Harpoon Pumpkin Cider

LOCAL FLAVOR: Although they are reviving, South Boston's docks aren't as busy as they were in 1926, when Fish Pier distributed 250 million pounds of seafood.

Only a handful of craft brewers around the country surpass Harpoon in terms of output. But, like the many tiny one- or two-barrel businesses that have recently popped up across the United States, Harpoon also has humble origins. In the summer of 1986, on the heels of another now-famous Boston brewery started by another Harvard alum, three former classmates—Rich Doyle, Dan Kenary, and George Ligetti—decided they wanted to make beers like those they had enjoyed in Europe. The only catch was that none of them knew how to brew. So they wrote up a business plan, applied for (and received) Brewing Permit #001 from the state, and hired Russell Heissner, a graduate of the brewing program at the University of California, Davis. One year later, the Massachusetts Bay Brewing Company had its first product: the mild, somewhat fruity Harpoon Ale.

A short distance from the busiest stops on Boston's tourist trail, the long brick building on the waterfront is hard to miss, thanks to the collection of tanks and grain silos lined up outside. With the new Visitors Center and Beer Hall open, the interior of the brewery will probably leave an impression, too. Enter from the parking lot through glass double doors and climb the staircase (or take the elevator) past a wall plastered in beer bottle caps to reach an enormous room humming with activity and filled with natural light. If you plan on taking a guided tour ($5, includes a tasting and a souvenir glass), be sure to sign up as soon as you arrive; tickets are sold on a first–come, first–served basis. If you miss the chance for a behind-the-scenes tour, grab a seat at the bar or find a spot at one of the many polished wooden tables and enjoy the view of Boston's skyline. With fourteen draft beers to choose from and warm handmade soft pretzels, the Harpoon Beer Hall is not a bad place for a craft beer enthusiast to spend an afternoon.

After making their mark with Harpoon Ale (5% ABV), Doyle and Kenary introduced Harpoon Winter Warmer (5.9% ABV), a copper-colored ale spiced with cinnamon and nutmeg and one of the country's first seasonal beers. They then went with a golden lager as their other year-round beer, adding a stout, a festbier, and a few others to their seasonal range. It was the bitter yet balanced IPA (5.9% ABV) that really catapulted Harpoon forward, however. The IPA has come a long way since 1993, and visitors can now regularly expect to find a black IPA (7% ABV), white IPA (6.2% ABV), rye IPA (6.9% ABV), and a pungent, powerful imperial IPA (10% ABV) pouring in the Beer Hall. Ask a bartender for the IPA flight to compare the flavors of four different varieties against one another. Because you have the option of limited release batches fresh from the tap, also ask about the pilot series and the 100 Barrel Range, beers that have included Vermont spruce tips, Duxbury Bay oysters, and fresh ginger.

Once a bit of a wasteland in terms of dining and drinking, South Boston has undergone a transformation in the last decade. At Blue Dragon (617-338-8585; www.ming.com/blue-dragon.htm), Boston's first Asian gastropub, bring a few friends and go for the buttermilk tempura whole chicken with sweet chili sauce, which should work nicely with UPO White (4.8% ABV). Also, fast approaching its one hundredth birthday, No Name Restaurant on Fish Pier (617-338-7539; www.nonamerestaurant.com) is a good bet.

Non-beer activities abound in this neighborhood. Follow a segment of the scenic Boston Harborwalk to the Institute of Contemporary Art (617-478-3100; www.icaboston.org) or Castle Island and Fort Independence (617-727-5290; www.mass.gov/dcr/parks/metroboston/castle.htm). For more history, head to the Boston Tea Party Ships & Museum (617-338-1773; www.bostonteapartyship.com) on the Congress Street Bridge, or see Boston's Harbor Islands (617-223-8666; www.bostonharborislands.org) by hopping on a ferry from Long Wharf at the end of State Street. 🍾

CONTACT

306 Northern Avenue
Boston, MA 02210
617-456-2322
www.harpoonbrewery.com
@harpoon_brewery

TASTING ROOM HOURS:

Visitors Center
Mon-Wed, 11am-7pm; Thu-Fri,
11am-11pm (Tasting starts
promptly at 2pm and 4pm daily);
Sat, 11am-11pm; Sun 11am-7pm
(Tours on the half hour
from 11:30am-6pm)
Beer Hall
Mon-Wed, 2pm-7pm;
Thu-Fri, Noon-11pm;
Sat, 11am-11pm; Sun, Noon-7pm

LODGING:

Seaport Boston Hotel
1 Seaport Lane
Boston, MA 02210
617-385-4000
www.seaportboston.com

MYSTIC BREWERY

YEAR FOUNDED: 2009

FOUNDER:
Bryan Greenhagen

ANNUAL PRODUCTION:
300-400 barrels

**YEAR-ROUND &
SEASONAL BEERS:** Mystic Saison,
Mystic Descendant, Saison Renaud, Saison
Asterix, An Dreoilin, Old Powderhouse,
Vespula Mysticus, Day of Doom, Vinland
One, Three Cranes, Mary of the Gael,
Auerbach's Rauchbier, Entropy

LOCAL FLAVOR: The tasting room's
bartop is made from floor beams recovered
from an old mill in Lowell; the structure
itself is fieldstone from Massachusetts.

I n Belgium, the type of nondescript building where Bryan Greenhagen creates his beers would be referred to as a *geuzestekerij*. But in Chelsea, Massachusetts, the founder and head fermenterer of Mystic Brewery can call his "blending house" whatever he wants; there's never been one here before. So he settled on Fermentorium, which sounds more fun, anyway. Whichever name you give it, Mystic is not a brewery in the traditional sense of the word. Every Mystic beer actually begins its life in another brewhouse. Instead of taking his ideas from start to finish in a single location as most breweries do, Greehagen and his small team of "mystics" actually handle the brewing—mashing, or making the wort that will become fermentable sugars; sparging, or rinsing the grains; and then adding hops to a boil lasting an hour or more—off site. After finishing these steps, the proto-beer is trucked back to the Fermentorium on Admiral Hill where yeast that will eventually produce alcohol is added.

Greenhagen, who worked as a fermentation scientist at biotechnology companies and homebrewed for fourteen years before starting the Mystic Brewery, can often be found in the tasting room, leading tours and pouring samples from one of the ten taps at the bar. Showing groups around the space, he might qualify his passion for pre-industrial style beers, offer a quick explanation of how he collects and propagates local yeast strains, or reveal the identities of the quartet of brewing luminaries depicted in large banners that resemble stained glass windows. (Hint: one of them is Father Theodore, a monk at the Scourmont Abbey who isolated the yeasts still used in the world famous Chimay Trappist beers.) Drop by on a Friday or Saturday to fill a 32- or 64-ounce growler ($15-$19) or join a tour for $6, a cost that includes samples, a souvenir goblet, and a small donation to local charities like the Mystic River Watershed Association. T-shirts and patches bearing the company's logo, a Celtic-looking mystic knot, are also for sale.

Start with a taste of their Table Beer (4.5% ABV), a deliciously delicate saison with a warm yellow color that shimmers when held up to the light. Next you might move on to Saison Reynaud (6.5% ABV). Its success lies in its simplicity: Saaz hops lend it a floral nose with accents of green apple, Pilsner malt provides a light body and a clean taste with the essence of lemon and warm honey, while their house yeast strain gives it a zesty sharpness, a pillowy head of snow white foam, and a dry finish. And don't miss the chance to try a taproom-only release, many of which are designed by Alastair Hewitt, an award-winning homebrewer turned research and development specialist. A step up in strength from the saisons with 6 and 7 percent alcohol by volume, his first contribution to the Mystic lineup was the Old Powderhouse Wheat Wine (11% ABV). Similar in some ways to a barleywine with a full body, lots of malt complexity, and a wine-like character, this American twist on an English style relies on red winter wheat grown and malted in Massachusetts for much of its flavor. Cloudy, earthy, and dry, Old Powderhouse is also suitable for aging. And the most unusual of the lot is probably Entropy (14.2% ABV), a barrel-aged quad fermented in four stages with their house Belgian yeast, a French white wine yeast, a sherry yeast, and an English barleywine yeast. Rather than try to shoehorn this potent beer into a style category, Greenhagen likes to refer to it as "Boston Cognac."

Enjoyable on their own, most of Mystic's saisons practically ask to be served with a meal. Or at least a filling snack of some kind. Greenhagen is especially fond of steamers (clams) and mussels with his Mystic Saison. At Saus, a pint-sized joint near Faneuil Hall that specializes in pommes frites and Liege waffles, you might find Auerbach's Rauchbier (5.3% ABV) on tap. Go for the regular-sized order of fries served with a free dipping sauce like applewood smoked bacon and parmesan, and have fun trying to choose the dip that best complements your beer. Meanwhile, at the south end of the Freedom Trail and steps from the Common, Stoddards Fine Food & Ale (617-426-0048; www.stoddardsfoodandale.com) on Temple Place is one of several newer gastropubs in Boston that reliably have Mystic on tap or in bottles. Their P.E.I. mussels in a red coconut curry with dark rum would work with Descendant (7% ABV), a dark saison brewed with molasses. Back across the Charles River in Cambridge, Mead Hall (617-714-4372; www.themeadhall.com) is noteworthy for its number of taps: one hundred in all, situated in the middle of a cavernous space near MIT's campus. They describe their menu as farm fresh Belgian American, an ideal canvas for almost any one of Mystic's nuanced beers.

On Tap

Bourbon Barrel-aged
Old Powderhouse 11% wheat wine

Vespula Mysticus 4.5% Saffron Saison
(collaboration w/ Bluejacket DC)

Three Cranes 7% Cranberry Saison

An Dreoilin 7% Winter Solstice Saison

Vinland One 7.25% Native yeast wild Ale

Day of Doom 12% Quadruple Ale

~ Brewery Only ~

Roswell 8.6% Double IPA

CONTACT

174 Williams Street
Chelsea, MA 02150
617-800-9023
www.mystic-brewery.com
@MysticBrewery

TASTING ROOM HOURS:
Fri, 3pm-7pm;
Sat, Noon-4pm
(Tours Sat at 1pm & 2pm)

LODGING:
The Constitution Inn
150 Third Avenue
Boston, MA 02129
617-241-8400
www.constitutioninn.org

Just across the Mystic River is Charlestown, a neighborhood of the modern city that actually predates Boston and briefly served as the original capital of the Massachusetts Bay Colony. The northern terminus of the well-known Boston Freedom Trail can be found here, along with the Bunker Hill Monument and the USS *Constitution*, the world's oldest commissioned naval vessel that's still afloat. Both sites have museums today that are worth visiting. Charlestown is also noteworthy to beer travelers for being the former site of Three Cranes Tavern, one of the first brewpubs in Massachusetts, and the colonies in general. Built in 1635, the tavern sadly fell victim to fire (during the Battle of Bunker Hill no less) and is marked by a plaque in City Square today. Stop by on your way to the Charlestown Bridge and the continuation of the Freedom Trail in the North End. 🍾

TREE HOUSE
BREWING COMPANY

YEAR FOUNDED: 2012

FOUNDERS:
Dean Rohan, Nathan Lanier, Jonathan Weisbach, and Damien Goudreau

ANNUAL PRODUCTION:
600-700 barrels

**YEAR-ROUND &
SEASONAL BEERS:** Curiosity One, Julius, King Julius, Dirty Water, That's What She Said, Sap, Snowtober, Old Man, Green, Eureka, Dirty Berry, Tornado, Space & Time

LOCAL FLAVOR: Damien's father, Roc, an accomplished professional illustrator, designed and sketched the artwork that would become the Tree House logo.

Growing up in the country or even suburbia, kids often dream about one day having their own backyard tree house. For friends Damien, Nate, Johnny, and Dean, the dream was to build a brewery in western Massachusetts. Unlike a childhood fortress high in the boughs of a native hardwood though, Tree House Brewing Company is a project without a definite end. These four friends are trying to make the best beer they can. Saturday is usually brew day, when Damien and Nate handle the mashing, sparging, and wort boiling, while Dean serves as the master of ceremonies, and Johnny makes sure the tap lines in the tasting room don't run dry. All four still have full-time jobs, but in their spare time have managed to turn a shared hobby into a busy local business.

Depending on when you turn up, parking can be a challenge, and you might have to wait a while to get a growler ($10-$16, plus a one-time container fee) or 750ml bottle ($5-$8, plus a one-time container fee), but in Brimfield, the waiting is half the fun. On any given weekend you'll find four or five beers on tap in their rustic tasting room, and on winter days they'll fire up the wood-burning stove to keep everyone toasty warm.

If you happen to catch Lanier during a free moment, he might tell you that a certain farmhouse brewery in Vermont's Northeast Kingdom serves as a source of inspiration, but the best way to understand his beers is, of course, to try them. Fans of IPA will want to spend some time with Julius (6.8% ABV), a fragrant, tart beer with an apricot orange hue and a creamy meringue-like head. Bright not biting, it bursts with flavors of ripe tropical fruit. Double and even triple versions of Julius have been known to make the occasional appearance on the Tree House tap list chalk board. That's What She Said (5.6% ABV), a creamy, chocolately, comforting milk stout, is another

CONTACT

63 St. Claire Road
Brimfield, MA 01010
413-949-1891
www.treehousebrew.com
@TreeHouseBrewCo

TASTING ROOM HOURS:

Fri, 6-9pm; Sat, 11am-6pm

LODGING:

The J.C. Spring House
51 West Old Sturbridge Road
Brimfield, MA 01010
413-245-1062
www.jcspringhouse.com

memorable offering that lends itself to food pairings and bad jokes. And while this beer is good enough to share, its relatively restrained level of alcohol might make you want to keep it to yourself. Speaking of sessionable, the quenching blonde ale the Tree House crew has dubbed Eureka (3.9% ABV) also lends itself to multiple servings, and might just convince your white wine–drinking friends to broaden their horizons. Brewed using pale barley malt and a hop with qualities akin to the Sauvignon grape varietal, it's light, dry, and very drinkable.

Outside of Brimfield, Tree House can be hard to track down. Back in Sturbridge, the Cedar Street Grille (508-347-5800; www.cedarstreetgrille. com) concentrates on small plates made with fresh ingredients. If it's available, try the malty special bitter called Old Man (5.4% ABV) with Caribbean scallops and toasted macadamia nuts in an apricot glaze. Or fill up a growler or a hand-labeled 750ml bottle at the brewery (maybe something big and rich like the 6.6% ABV Snowtober) and head to B.T.'s Smokehouse (508-347-3188; www.btsmokehouse.com), a BYOB barbecue joint on Main Street. If you're heading east before 3 p.m., consider a stop in Worcester at Armsby Abbey (508-795-1012; www.armsbyabbey.com) for brunch.

Outdoor-minded travelers will find Wells State Park (508-347-9257; www.mass.gov/dcr) 1,400 acres of woods and water just five miles from Old Sturbridge Village (800-SEE-1830; www.osv.org). Far from an ordinary museum, this complex of more than forty buildings includes a tin shop, a printing office, a shoe shop, a cooper, and a cider mill. Just under twenty-five miles west of Brimfield, the Naismith Memorial Basketball Hall of Fame (413-781-6500; www.hoophall.com) is a magnet for anyone hung up on hoops.

LOVE ME LONG TIME - bohemian pilsener - 4.9
OMA'S TRIBUTE - black lager - 4.9%
DIPPITY DO american brown ale.
AMBER'S AMBER - amber rye ale - 5.2
HOPSTRUCK - red ipa - 6.4% ABV
MAPLE-KISSED WHEAT PORTER - 4.9% A
CAMPFIRE - smoked robust porter - 6.
NOSIE'S OATMEAL STOUT - 5.1% A
DONKEY-HOTÉ DOUBLE IPA - 8.2
DOUBLE DIPPITY slightly smokey double bro
SPICY BOHEMIAN jalapi
CHOCOLATE MINT STOUT - 5.6

NORTH
WOONSTOCK
Woodstock Inn

Moat Mountain
NORTH CONWAY

White Birch Brewing
HOOKSETT

Throwback
Brewery
NORTH HAMPTON

HAMPTON
Smuttynose Brewing Co.

NEW HAMPSHIRE

MOAT MOUNTAIN SMOKEHOUSE & BREWING COMPANY

YEAR FOUNDED: 2000

FOUNDERS:
Stephen Johnson and Vicky Valentino

ANNUAL PRODUCTION:
2,000 barrels

YEAR-ROUND & SEASONAL BEERS: Hoffman Weiss, Violet B's Blueberry, Czech Pilsner, Iron Mike Pale Ale, Bone Shaker Brown, Square Tail Stout, Helles Lager, Cathedral Ledge Lager, Matilda's Red Ale, Scotty's IPA, Oktoberfest Lager, Smoke House Porter

LOCAL FLAVOR: Due to space limitations in the brewpub's cramped basement, Moat creatively uses an old Ben & Jerry's tractor-trailer as their cold storage.

A full day on the trail or eight hours on the slopes tends to work up an appetite. It often leaves you thirsty, too. Which might explain why business at the Moat Mountain Smokehouse and Brewing Company took off so soon after it opened on the White Mountain Highway. Beer and barbecue can be a persuasive combination. Co-owner Stephen Johnson, a graduate of the Johnson & Wales College of Culinary Arts, already had experience running a restaurant when he and his wife acquired the Scottish Lion Inn and began making plans for its renovation. Before moving to New Hampshire, he had launched an Asian fusion restaurant in the foodie town of Portland, Maine, watching as enthusiasm for locally brewed beer grew and grew. When he saw the chance to open his own brewpub within easy striking distance of Mount Washington, one of the biggest tourist attractions in the state, he didn't hesitate. The next phase for Moat Mountain involves converting a historic barn and former dance hall in Bartlett into their new brewery and canning facility. Even with double brew days they outgrew their cramped, seven-barrel basement brewhouse years ago and have been packaging by hand and struggling to keep up with demand ever since.

With so many shops, restaurants, and hotels along Route 16, Moat doesn't necessarily leap out from its spot near the Memorial Hospital, but if you somehow miss the big house with yellow siding, look for the purple ski chair out front. Inside, the atmosphere is fun, friendly, and focused on service. The smell

of house-smoked ribs, pork, and brisket will probably be the first things to greet you, followed by the sound of something classic, like Johnny Cash's 1956 hit "I Walk the Line." Executive chef Scott Ross prepares beer dinners on occasion, usually announced via social media or via advertisements in the brewpub. During peak season in the summer and winter, lunch is the time to go if you don't want to wait. In the evening and on weekends, seats—even at the bar—are not easy to come by. A seven-beer sampler will cost $7 and beer to go is available in 24-ounce cans, 22-ounce bomber bottles, and refillable growlers. You can also pick up T-shirts, koozies, and "Fear No Beer" bumper stickers on your way out. Plans for the new brewery include a growler fill station and a retail space.

In the beginning, Moat brewed three beers: Lager, Hoffman Weiss (5.7% ABV) a hazy, medium-bodied German-style wheat smelling of banana and clove with nip of white peppery spiciness, and Violet B's Blueberry (4.5% ABV), a pale ale with a mild hop presence and subtle fruitiness that blends with sweetness of the malt. And while two of these beers remain in regular rotation, the brewery has expanded its range considerably over the years. All along though, the goal has been to produce drinkable beers that are true to style and appealing to beer geeks and grandmothers alike. Given their proximity to White Mountain National Forest, they've also made an effort to be as sustainable as possible, boiling their wort with energy collected from solar panels on the roof and recaptured from their pizza ovens. While Weiss and Blueberry might be ideal for the heat of summer, Bone Shaker Brown (5.5% ABV), a well-hopped and medium-bodied ale with a flavor that approximates a loaf of crusty rustic European bread, wants to be consumed in cooler conditions, as does Square Tail Stout (5.8% ABV). Its deep, dark, and malty body draws you in again and again, only to finish with a trace of coffee and snap of bitterness.

They do serve a veggie hummus wrap at Moat, but I don't think most people turn up in North Conway with a hankering for a garlicky chickpea paste. The half rack of ribs, dry-rubbed, smoked, and smothered in tangy, tomato-based barbecue sauce is more like it. Plus the latter tastes that much better with Bone Shaker Brown, or better yet, Smoke House Porter (5% ABV), their winter seasonal. Smoked salmon brined in cane sugar and dark rum and served with a side of mango pineapple salsa isn't a bad option, either. For more of an upscale dining experience, drive north to Glen where Culinary Institute of America graduates Teresa and Scott Stearns run a restaurant, deli, and cider mill collectively known as the Cider Company (603-383-9061; www.ciderconh. com). Once a week they offer a burger and beer special that has included such inspired creations as the Leaky Goat, a patty topped with sautéed ramps, Vermont goat cheese, and smoked tomato mayonnaise. It begs to be paired with Moat Stout (5.8% ABV). If you only want a snack though, munch on an order of the goat cheese and local mushroom wontons and enjoy the way Hoffman Weiss (5.7% ABV) harmonizes with them.

In North Conway, most of the action revolves around Mount Washington, the high point of the White Mountains and the tallest peak in the Northeast. Serious hikers like to test themselves on an eight-hour round-trip trek to the summit, but it's also possible to drive to the top or ride the historic Mount Washington Cog Railway (603-278-5404; www.thecog.com). Opened in 1869 as the world's first mountain-climbing railroad, steam- and biodiesel-powered trains run rain or shine from late April through the end of December. At the top, you can visit the museum in the Mount Washington Observatory (603-356-2137; www.mountwashington.org), where weather researchers have been collecting and interpreting data on the planet's climate and weather since 1870. This non-profit organization also operates a free museum in North Conway called the Weather Discovery Center. West of the peak, the Mount Washington Resort (603-278-1000; www.brettonwoods.com) has an embarrassment of activities, whether or not you spend the night at one of their three hotel properties. At their adventure center you can learn to rock climb inside or outside, play eighteen holes of disc golf, take a canopy tour, or go horseback riding.

CONTACT

3378 White Mountain
Highway Route 16
North Conway, NH 03860
603-356-6381
www.moatmountain.com
@moatmountain

TASTING ROOM HOURS:
Daily, 11:30am until last call

LODGING:
Wildflowers Inn
3486 White Mountain Highway
North Conway, NH 03860
866-945-3357
www.wildflowersinn.com

SMUTTYNOSE
BREWING COMPANY

YEAR FOUNDED: 1994

FOUNDERS:
Peter and Janet Egelston

ANNUAL PRODUCTION:
45,000–50,000 barrels

YEAR-ROUND & SEASONAL BEERS: Shoals Pale Ale, Old Brown Dog Ale, Finestkind IPA, Star Island Single, Robust Porter, Summer Weizen, Pumpkin Ale, Winter Ale, Big A IPA, Noonan Black IPA, Vunderbar Pilsner, Strawberry Short Weiss, ParadoX

LOCAL FLAVOR: The brewery still owns the old red and white camper trailer that appears on the packaging for their Finestkind IPA. Its location remains a secret.

Located on New Hampshire's seacoast, Smuttynose takes its name from an island in the Isles of Shoals group, a small Atlantic archipelago between the Granite State and Maine. Over the years, the scenery, serenity, and remoteness of these little landmasses have attracted artists, vacationers, and buccaneers—most famously, Edward Teach, the English pirate better known as Blackbeard. After college, Peter Egelston worked as a teacher in New York until his sister Janet persuaded him to relocate to Massachusetts to help her start the Northampton Brewery, now the oldest brewpub in the Northeast. In 1991, the pair opened the Portsmouth Brewery, the first brewpub in New Hampshire. Smuttynose, their production operation, came next when they unexpectedly ended up winning the bankruptcy auction for the brewery formerly occupied by the Frank Jones Brewing Company. Three expansions later, Peter, who had since bought his sister out of both New Hampshire businesses and sold his share of their Northampton company to her, finally decided to upgrade and custom-build a new brewery from the ground up.

Though farther from Portsmouth, the reborn Smuttynose is able to offer more regular tours, a full flight of samples served at a dedicated tasting bar, a 95-seat LEED-certified restaurant with a kitchen that uses beer in its recipes, a growler station, and a retail shop. Sitting on fourteen wooded acres, the new brewery is surrounded by an apple orchard, an apiary, a patio area, and a nineteenth-century barn. Plus, instead of tearing down the Victorian-era farmhouse, Egelston shifted it over, altered its orientation, and turned it into the Farmhouse Kitchen with twenty draft lines and a wide selection of foods grown or raised locally and/or sustainably. An adjacent kitchen garden also supplies ingredients for the seasonal menu.

A relatively hoppy example of the style when it was first released, Shoals Pale Ale (5.6% ABV) seems less aggressively bitter now than it must have in the mid-1990s. Today, hop lovers are more likely to seek out Smuttynose's unfiltered, lip-smacking Finestkind IPA (6.9% ABV) or the newer still Noonan Black IPA (5.9% ABV) with its piney, herbal aroma. Over the years, Smuttynose has worked hard to prevent their portfolio from stagnating, however, debuting a Big Beer Series in 1998 and releasing small or "short" batches of unusual beers like a Strawberry Short Weiss (3.7% ABV), a deliciously tart wheat ale with strawberry puree added to the boil. ParadoX (5.3% ABV) is another example of the brewery's willingness to shake things up. Conceived of as a sessionable IPA, ParadoX is brewed with an as-yet-unnamed experimental hop variety and a portion of locally grown and malted barley that give it a lemony flavor and a subtle, grainy sweetness.

With a sophisticated menu and a James Beard–finalist chef, Black Trumpet (603-431-0887; www.blacktrumpetbistro.com) is one of the hottest dining destinations in the Northeast. Black Trumpet typically uses its four tap lines to feature regional breweries. The other obvious place to go for ale and a meal is New Hampshire's first brewpub, the Portsmouth Brewery (603-431-1115; www.portsmouthbrewery.com). Nearly everything is sourced locally and prepared in house.

Farther down Towle Road, the James House (www.jameshousemuseum.org) is open to the public between May and October. Built in 1723, this National Historic Site is regarded as the earliest surviving example of a center chimney colonial home in the state of New Hampshire. To the north in Portsmouth, the ten-acre Strawberry Banke Museum (603-433-1100; www.strawberybanke.org) tells the story of coastal life in New England from the Colonial Period until World War II. If beaches and old houses don't appeal, book a cruise with the Isle of Shoals Steamship Company (603-431-5500; www.islesofshoals.com). Not only will you get to see the nation's oldest active naval yard from the water, you'll have the chance to look at an abandoned prison and five forts guarding the harbor.

CONTACT

Towle Farm Road
Hampton, NH 03842
603-436-4026
www.smuttynose.com
@smuttynosebeer

BREWERY RESTAURANT HOURS:

Daily, 11:30am-11pm
(Tours Sun-Thu, 1-5pm;
Fri-Sat, Noon-6pm)

LODGING:

Ale House Inn
121 Bow Street
Portsmouth, NH 03801
603-431-7760
www.alehouseinn.com

THROWBACK BREWERY

YEAR FOUNDED: 2011

FOUNDERS:
Annette Lee and Nicole Carrier

ANNUAL PRODUCTION:
400-500 barrels

YEAR-ROUND & SEASONAL BEERS: Hog Happy Hefeweizen, Love Me Long Time Bohemian Pilsner, Oma's Tribute Black Lager, Dippity Do American Brown Ale, Hopstruck Red IPA, Maple Kissed Wheat Porter, Campfire Smoked Porter, Rhubarb Wit, Spicy Bohemian, Fat Alberta Imperial Stout

LOCAL FLAVOR: Nicole and Annette didn't realize the twelve-acre Hobbs Farm they bought as a new home for their brewery included a donkey. His name is Jericho.

Some beer companies spring from the dreams of hopeful brewers, individuals with plans to one day be their own boss and develop their own recipes. Others result from efforts of talented homebrewers, people who yearn to turn a serious hobby into a full-fledged profession. After a twenty-year career as an environmental engineer, Annette Lee decided she needed to do something different. Committing to a career change can be daunting and time-consuming, but she had a goal in mind, choosing to put more than a decade of homebrewing experience to the test. Coursework at the Seibel Institute, America's oldest brewing school, and an internship up the road at Smuttynose followed, and then she and partner Nicole Carrier—who handles most of the tech and marketing—started the Throwback Brewery, crafting fresh, idiosyncratic beers three barrels at a time. Sometimes they brew test batches to determine whether their ideas will translate on a scale larger than a stovetop setup, but just as often, they simply go for it, using an ingredient one of them might have spotted in a cookbook or at a farmers market.

For a community brewery that makes every effort to source its ingredients from a 200-mile radius, Throwback isn't exactly in the most scenic location, squeezed into an industrial park off Lafayette Road just south of Portsmouth. Fortunately for Lee and Carrier, they were able to acquire the historic twelve-acre Hobbs farm, an aging yet handsome property in North Hampton, when it went up for auction. Within a year, they expect to be brewing beer and greeting visitors in the old barn. Until they move to their new address across the road, Throwback offers ad hoc, spontaneous tours during their

"Growler Hours" on Thursday, Friday, and Saturday. It's a relatively short affair befitting a small facility with only a handful of staff members. Don't be disappointed if you can't poke around the brewery though; pay a dollar for a tasting glass and try four ounces of anything (or everything) available from the eight tap lines at their little tasting bar. Seating is at a premium on Saturday afternoons, though, so be prepared to stand, and give in to the urge to ask the person next to you what they liked best. New growlers are $13, T-shirts reading "No Farms, No Beer" cost a few dollars more.

Seasonal and food-inspired might be the best way to describe Throwback's beers. From Fat Alberta (9.5% ABV), a chocolate peanut butter imperial stout, to a pumpkin chai porter, and their Rhubarb Wit (5% ABV), a Belgian-style wheat beer that also incorporates oats and chamomile, the duo aims to please taste buds with every new release. And whether they're brewing with fennel flowers, apples, watermelons, or coffee, they always look to local producers first. Even Hopstruck Red IPA (6.4% ABV), a popular perennial that they've sold since opening their doors in 2011, is made with organic barley grown in Maine and malted in western Massachusetts, and organic hops grown in upstate New York. Besides the seven beers Throwback tries to keep available

year-round, they also brew the occasional one off and, for about twelve weeks during the coldest, darkest part of the year, focus on porters and stouts with their Unafraid of the Dark series. Past releases have included a chocolate mint stout and No More Mr. Fungi (5.9% ABV), an earthy, bitter porter brewed with ten pounds of chaga mushrooms.

The philosophy is simple, the motto catchy, and most importantly, the food at Lexi's Joint (603-319-4055; www.lexiesjoint.com) in Portsmouth is good. Plus they almost always have Throwback on tap. It's hard to argue with Peace, Love, and Burgers. Select beef, chicken, or black bean and then pile on the toppings—up to six if you're feeling adventurous. First-timers might want to start with one of the originals, though, like the Stairway to Heaven: a medium rare patty topped with braised short ribs, caramelized onions, barbecue sauce, and cheddar. Wash it down with a pint of brown ale like Dippity Do (5.7% ABV). Closer to Market Square, Moxy (603-319-8178; www.moxyrestaurant. com) serves modern American tapas, or small plates from small farms. The prix fixe five-course option is a fun and affordable way to explore the menu, but you can do your own choosing from whimsical categories like Fish, Shellfish, and Beach Bums. A light German-style wheat beer like Hog Happy Hefeweizen (4.9% ABV) might be nice with the sauteed Rhode Island fluke, Maine lobster, brown butter cauliflower, carrot puree, and crispy celery root chips. A third possibility for small bites and beer is Portsmouth Book & Bar (603-427-9197; www.bookandbar.com) in the old Customs House.

Recreation-wise, New Hampshire's entire eighteen-mile seacoast is essentially one long stretch of public land, beginning with Hampton Beach State Park (603-926-3784; www.nhstateparks.org/explore/state-parks/hampton-beach-state-park.aspx) near the Massachusetts state line. Pack a picnic lunch and head to the park for views of the Atlantic, or depending on the water temperature and your tolerance for cold, take a quick dip in the ocean. Just outside of Portsmouth on Wentworth Road, Portsmouth Kayak Adventures (603-559-1000; www.portsmouthkayak.com) leads guided tours for paddlers of all interests and ability levels. So whether you're looking for a leisurely sunset cruise, a more strenuous circumnavigation of New Castle Island, a trip that includes a yoga session on the beach, or even a private lesson, this company has you covered. But if splashing around on Sagamore Creek doesn't sound like as much fun as, say, eating locally made ice cream, you'll want to check out the state's Dairy Trail instead. West of Throwback in Kingston, Memories Ice Cream (603-642-3737; www.memoriesicecream.com) is one of the closest participants. Flavors include Kahlua chip and bananas foster, a scoop of which would be wonderful in a pint of Fat Alberta's Imperial Stout. 🍶

CONTACT

121 Lafayette Road, Unit 3
North Hampton, NH 03862
603-379-2317
www.throwbackbrewery.com
@thrwbck

TASTING ROOM HOURS:

Thu-Fri, 4-6pm; Sat, 1-4pm

LODGING:

The 1810 Pickering House
195 Portsmouth Avenue
Greenland, NH 03840
603-430-0111
www.1810pickeringhouse.com

WHITE BIRCH
BREWING

YEAR FOUNDED: 2009

FOUNDERS:
Bill and Ellen Herlicka

ANNUAL PRODUCTION:
1,200 barrels

**YEAR-ROUND &
SEASONAL BEERS:** Belgian Style
Pale Ale, Hop Session Ale, Hooksett Ale,
Tripel, First Sparrow, Our Humble Porter,
Berliner Weisse, Crown of Gold, Hop to Wit,
Farmhouse Red, Oude Timey, Nyx, Tavern
Ale, Rusalka, Ol' Cattywhompus

LOCAL FLAVOR: Roughly 100 years
before the arrival of White Birch, the town
of Hooksett had another successful food
business: J. S. Burbank's Tomato Ketchup.

For dedicated beer travelers, New Hampshire's Route 28 north of Manchester is worth a drive. Just off Interstate 93, not far from the Merrimack River, White Birch Brewing in Hooksett produces some of the state's finest beers. Started by Bill Herlicka in 2009, the brewery has grown from fifteen-gallon batches to fifteen-barrel batches. The rapid expansion required a move, which is how White Birch ended up in its current space, the former site of a used-car dealership. In the back, Bill has installed a brewhouse filled with fermentation tanks and whiskey barrels for aging strong beer.

Thanks to big picture windows, the front tasting room is light-filled and, on many weekends, a lively environment. Surrounding the central bar, a handful of cushy armchairs await visitors who plan to take their time trying the half dozen beers typically offered as samples. Bottles of new releases, flagship beers, and one-off specials resulting from White Birch's Apprentice Program occupy much of the remaining wall space while the small kettles Bill started his company with have a reserved corner of their own. An empty growler is $7 but $3 more will get it filled with one of the three flagship beers. Or take home a half-gallon of a seasonal beer like Oude Timey (8% ABV), a Flemish-style brown ale with a reddish hue and a kiss of sourness for $15. The shop also sells individual bottles as well as T-shirts and bags of spent grain dog treats for fashion mavens and pet owners. Tours are a buck but entitle you to 10 percent off anything in the shop.

Begin your visit with a small pour of the Belgian Style Pale Ale (6.3% ABV), a very drinkable beer with a floral scent reminiscent of apple blossom or pear. Follow that up with the aromatic and more assertively bitter Hop Session (5.2% ABV), and Hooksett Ale (7.5% ABV), a Belgian-style IPA with a piney, peppery, and decidedly American hop character. But don't stop there. Because in spite of producing this trio of beers year-round, Herlicka and Head Brewer Chris Shea aren't afraid to experiment the rest of the time. The best example of this might be their Anniversary Ale, released annually and ranging from 7.6% to 9.7% ABV (so far). The beer in the ninety-six bottles of First Anniversary included white birch sap, while the Belgian-style quadrupel bottled and released in 2012 was aged in oak barrels.

You won't find anything to eat at the brewery, so head south to Manchester. On either side of Elm Street between Bridge and Lake, a number of inviting restaurants present a challenging decision for the hungry traveler. At Republic (603-666-3723; www.republiccafe.com) the red lentil cake appetizer with a lemon caper remoulade could play well with the tart, dry Berliner Weisse (5.5% ABV). If a full meal sounds like too much and you'd rather satisfy your sweet tooth, drop by Queen City Cupcakes (603-624-4999; www.qccupcakes.com) and order a maple bacon Rocky Road cupcake. You could get a cup of coffee, but Tavern Ale (8% ABV), White Birch's smoked imperial brown ale, might just be the perfect match. At River Road Tavern (603-206-5837; www.riverroadtavern.com) on the other side of the Merrimack, the beef stroganoff begs for a glass of First Sparrow (3.8% ABV), a hoppy smoked wheat ale with Polish origins.

Manchester is a pleasant city to linger in for an afternoon or an evening. During the winter months the Manchester Monarchs (603-626-7825; www.manchestermonarchs.com) own the ice at the Verizon Wireless Arena, and when the minor league baseball season begins, the New Hampshire Fisher Cats (603-641-2005; www.milb.com/index.jsp?sid=t463) call the city's riverside stadium home. To learn something about Manchester's history, visit the Millyard Museum (603-622-7531; www.manchesterhistoric.org) and head upstairs to the SEE Science Center (603-669-0400; www.see-sciencecenter.org) if only to marvel at the LEGO Millyard Project, a record-setting installation built to represent the Amoskeag Millyard, once the world's largest textile company. For a little outdoor recreation, drive north from White Birch on Route 28 to Deerfield Road and Bear Brook State Park (603-485-9874; www.nhstateparks.org), where forty miles of multi-use trails crisscross over 10,000 acres of forested public land. 🍺

CONTACT

1339 Hooksett Road
Hooksett, NH 03106
603-206-5260
www.whitebirchbrewing.com
@Bill_WBB

TASTING ROOM HOURS:
Thu-Fri, Noon-7pm;
Sat, Noon-5pm (Tours on Sat)

LODGING:
Ash Street Inn
118 Ash Street
Manchester, NH 03104
603-668-9908
www.ashstreetinn.com

WOODSTOCK INN
STATION & BREWERY

YEAR FOUNDED: 1995

FOUNDERS:
Scott and Peggy Rice

ANNUAL PRODUCTION:
5,000-6,000 barrels

YEAR-ROUND & SEASONAL BEERS: Pig's Ear Brown Ale, Red Rack Ale, White Mountain Weasel Wheat, White Mountain Raspberry Weasel Wheat, Pemi Pale Ale, Through Hiker Double Rye Pale Ale, Old Man Oatmeal Stout, Loon Golden Ale, Kanc Country Maple Porter, Scottish Ale, Autumn Ale Brew, Wassail Ale, Cogsman Ale, Good Old Time Root Beer

LOCAL FLAVOR: Moved from Lincoln in 1984, the train station that's now part of the Woodstock Inn once stood at the end of the line of the Boston, Concord, and Montreal Railroad's White Mountain Branch.

How do you improve on a quirky, family-run hotel in scenic northern New Hampshire? By adding a brewery, of course. Established as the premiere spot for dining and lodging in the quaint town of Woodstock, the Woodstock Inn Station and Brewery has slowly expanded over the years, adding more rooms, another dining area, a brewpub, and most recently, a second much larger brewhouse, a fourth bar, and private function hall. There may still be a few people who turn up at the front desk without realizing that beer has become a big part of their business, but it's highly unlikely that anyone leaves before trying a pint or two. The hotel complex is easy to find in this tiny town, especially in the summer, when beer drinkers congregate near the main entrance at the fittingly named Dam Bar (guess where the wood came from). It's also impossible to forget with backwoodsy kitsch like taxidermy animals giving the interior a personality seldom seen at other accommodations. Over time, Scott Rice and his wife, Peggy, have carefully managed the growth of both sides of the business, maintaining the rustic character of the property alongside the accessibility of their English- and American-style beers.

Spread across five historic buildings with thirty-three rooms to stay in, bars everywhere you turn, live entertainment, and two different places to eat with their own unique menus, the Woodstock Inn Station and Brewery can feel like a beer vacationer's dream come true. This is no accident. Daily tours take place at noon. For $5 you'll get a souvenir Shaker pint, a guided explanation of the brewing process from grain to glass, and the requisite tasting. Roll the dice and sign up in person, or plan ahead and book a spot online before you arrive. To learn

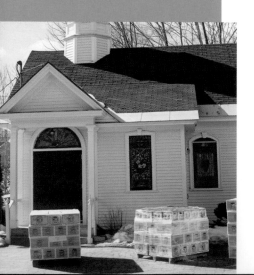

even more about beer, check Woodstock's calendar for the dates of their immersive brewer's weekends, held four times in the spring and four times the fall. These two-day experiences include a five-course beer dinner, a hat, a T-shirt, and the satisfaction of knowing that your labor will be enjoyed in liquid form by a number of future guests. All of the beers brewed at the Woodstock Inn Station are available to go, either in growlers or bottles. If you do spend the night here, be sure to wake up early enough for the complimentary breakfast. The portions are exceedingly generous, but besides that, you'll want to have some food in your stomach before tackling another beer tasting.

Overall, the brewery aims to produce beers that are fun, approachable, and easy to drink. That said, Woodstock uses something in the neighborhood of eight tons of hops every year, favoring varieties such as Zythos, Fuggle, Golding, Cascade, Columbus, and Willamette. Of the five mainstay beers and the ten rotating selections, about 20 percent of the total volume is consumed on site. That also includes the odd test batch brewed on the old Peter Austin brewpub system. The first beers to appear under the Woodstock name were Red, Brown, and Golden. Pale Ale (5.7% ABV) and Weasel Wheat (4.13 % ABV), brewed with New Hampshire maple syrup, came next. Their newest offering is Fellowship IPA (6.4% ABV), a beer that gives back by donating $0.50 from the sale of every pint to Rotary International, an organization working to eradicate polio. Smooth, creamy, and chocolatey, their oatmeal stout has milk chocolate on the nose, and earthy, almost leathery bitterness supplied by earthy British hops.

Over the years, the Woodstock Station has received lots of attention for its beers, but as locals know, its menu is nothing to scoff at either. A number of items actually include Woodstock beers into their recipes and many of their sandwiches are served on spent grain bread. From the chili made with Red Rack Ale (5.5% ABV) to the Pig's Ear Brown Ale pulled pork sandwich topped with cheddar and onion rings, the food here is just the stuff to fill up on after a long hike or a day out on the slopes. Indulge in an order of poutine with sweet potato fries, mini marshmallows, and a Kanc Country Maple Porter demi-glace, or go with a healthier salad (dressed

with an oatmeal stout balsamic vinaigrette, of course). Maybe you want something a little spicier though. To get your Mexican fix, you don't have to run all the way to the border, you only need to go as far as Burrito Me (603-238-3410; www.burritome.com) in Plymouth. The formula is simple with low prices and local breweries like Moat Mountain, White Birch, and Woodstock regularly earning a spot in the tap rotation. They also host three- and four-course Brewer's Dinners. Build your own Mission-style burrito with meat or veggies, choose a medium, mild, or habanero salsa, and wash it down with Pemi Pale Ale.

Often referred to by its nickname, the Granite State, New Hampshire is truly a mountainous domain, a fact that attracts a certain type of person to its northern reaches. Active, outdoorsy individuals tend to be the majority, but contemplative types like poets and writers find the state's north country appealing, too. Robert Frost, for instance, lived on a farm in Franconia that is now a museum and cultural center open from Memorial Day until Columbus Day (603-823-5510; www.frostplace.org). Between the Frost Place and North Woodstock, Franconia Notch State Park and Cannon Mountain (603-823-8800; www.cannonmt.com) in particular, attract visitors year round. During the warmer months, people come to mountain bike, walk to the Flume Gorge, and ride the Aerial Tramway to the summit of the 4,080-foot peak, while the winter brings skiers and snowboarders. Closer to the Woodstock Inn, Loon Mountain Resort (603-745-8111; www.loonmtn.com) also gets busy as the snow begins to accumulate. And then, for the thrill-seeker, there are the zipline tours offered by Alpine Adventures (603-745-9911; www.alpinezipline.com) in Lincoln. It's not every day you can fly through the treetops at forty to fifty miles per hour. 🍺

CONTACT

135 Main Street
North Woodstock, NH 03262
603-745-3951
www.woodstockinnnh.com
@WoodstockBrew

TASTING ROOM HOURS:
Daily, 11:30am-10pm
(Tours at noon)

High Point Brewing Co.
BUTLER

Carton Brewing Co.
ATLANTIC HIGHLANDS

OCEAN
Kane Brewing Co.

SOMERDALE
Flying Fish Brewing Co.

Cape May
Brewing Co.
RIO GRANDE

NEW JERSEY

CAPE MAY
BREWING COMPANY

YEAR FOUNDED: 2011

FOUNDERS:
Ryan Krill, Bob Krill, and Chris Henke

ANNUAL PRODUCTION:
1,000 barrels

YEAR-ROUND & SEASONAL BEERS: Hefeweizen, Cranberry Wheat, Honey Porter, Centennial IPA, Saison, Blonde Ale, Cape May IPA, Stout, Altbier, Roggenbock, Pale Ale, Apple Bomb, Winter Wheat, Devil's Reach

LOCAL FLAVOR: Just behind the brewery, Hangar One at the Cape May Airport served as a pilot training center for dive-bombers during the Second World War.

Chris Henke and Ryan Krill became friends while attending Villanova University and after graduation, began their respective careers in engineering and banking. Ryan's father, Bob, had professional experience as a carpenter. All three of them enjoyed craft beer. Cue the cartoon lightbulb. Inspired by the ultra-local philosophy of New Glarus Brewing in Wisconsin and noting the fact that while Cape May County had a number of wineries, no one had yet started a brewery, the trio set about remedying that situation. They started very small, and then, as they watched their following grow, decided to take the next step. Sticking to a tight budget, they bought brewing equipment from a defunct brewpub in Annapolis, Maryland, called Castle Bay and acquired a walk-in cooler that had been used by a Quiznos franchise in Philadelphia. Henke put his satellite-building skills to use designing a keg washer, and they cut out another expense by making their wood tap handles—which resemble the state's outline—themselves. Mark McPherson has since joined the team as an additional full-time brewer.

Now that Cape May has added a sizeable and attractive tasting room that serves full pints, a detour to their brewery on a visit to south Jersey shouldn't be treated as a mere option for beer drinkers, it should be seen as essential. To keep the experience exciting for visitors, they make an effort to have eleven draft beers at all times; try a pint of anything on tap for $5, or for the same $5, buy four wooden tokens to cash in for four-ounce tasters. A pint in a souvenir Cape May Brewing glass is $11. Once you've got your beer, find a spot at one of the picnic tables opposite the long concrete bar and consult the giant beer flavor wheel on the back wall as you look, smell, and taste. During the summer months, you might arrive at the brewery to find food trucks slinging barbecue, fish tacos, or handmade empanadas outside. Grab a bite and play around with different beer pairings. When you're ready to leave, check out their well-stocked shop to go home with a hat, hoodie, onesie, or koozie. You can also buy beach totes sewn from Weyermann malt bags or bars of beer soap made with Cape May Stout and Honey Porter.

To some, Cape May might seem like a long drive for beer. The good news is that they have a style or flavor combination for just about everyone. From their piney, orange-hued, Centennial IPA (7% ABV), abundantly hopped with—surprise—a variety called Centennial, to the smooth, light-bodied Kolsh-style Blonde Ale (5.3% ABV) and the dark and roasty Honey Porter (5.2% ABV) brewed with local buckwheat honey, Cape May doesn't seem interested in self-imposed limitations. They also make the fragrant and pleasantly tangy Cranberry Wheat (5.6% ABV) that from a distance could almost masquerade as a glass of pink grapefruit juice. Regardless of color, it's a quenching beer with a hit of fruit that doesn't hurt one bit. Their malty Altbier (5.9% ABV), a tasty ale with the color of

cut garnet and a herbal accent from Noble German hops, is another standout. So far though, the most unusual product to come out of the Cape May brew kettle is Apple Bomb (8.2% ABV), a strong beer steeped on fresh apples to impart a tart flavor.

Assuming you didn't buy something from a food truck, you'll want to head south toward Cape May Point for the widest variety of dining choices. Half a block from the beach, the Mad Batter (609-884-5970; www.madbatter.com) in the Carroll Villa Hotel is regularly picked as the best brunch in town. The thick-sliced orange and almond French toast will satisfy those with a sweet tooth, but the Chesapeake Bay Benedict with lump crabmeat and caper Hollandaise stands out from the crowd. To cut through the creamy sauce, ask for a pint of Cape May IPA (6.1% ABV), which is usually on tap. Citrusy Cascade hops will play nice with the lemon notes, while this beer's malty side will complement the caramelized flavors you taste in the home fries. One block over on Beach Avenue,

Cabanas (609-884-4800; www.cabanasonthebeach.com) has a rotating selection of local craft beers that often includes something from Cape May. If it's Pale Ale, the Cabanas beer-battered fish tacos filled with avocado, shredded cabbage, and pineapple mango salsa are a compatible match. Overlooking the harbor, Lucky Bones Backwater Grille (609-884-2663; www.luckybonesgrille.com) has also been supportive of their local brewery. Both the herbed chicken salad sandwich and the shrimp salad sandwich work with Cape May's characteristically dry Saison (6.2% ABV).

Next to the brewery at the Cape May Airport, the Naval Air Station Wildwood Aviation Museum (609-886-8787; www.usnasw.org) is open daily from April through November, and on weekdays during the rest of the year. Visit to see numerous fighter jets, Huey and Cobra helicopters, military photographs and memorabilia, and interactive exhibits on the science of flight. Marshes, dunes, and wildlife might hold more appeal than

CONTACT

1288 Hornet Road
Rio Grande, NJ 08242
609-849-9933
www.capemaybrewery.com
@CapeMayBrewCo

TASTING ROOM HOURS:

Wed-Thu, 4-8pm;
Fri-Sun, Noon-8pm
(Tours Sat every hour;
Sun-Fri, 2:30pm & 5:30pm)

LODGING

The Star Inn
29 Perry Street
Cape May, NJ 08204
800-297-3779
www.thestarinn.net

aircraft for some though, and those people will want to squeeze in a morning or afternoon stop at Cape May Point State Park (609-884-2159; www.state.nj.us/dep/parksandforests/index.html) with its 157-foot-high lighthouse looking out over Delaware Bay and the Atlantic. Go for a short hike on one of the three trails, climb to the top of Cape May Light, or watch a hawk banding demonstration on Saturdays and Sundays in the fall. (Note: beer tourists who plan to visit Dogfish Head, 16 Mile, and any of Maryland's Eastern Shore breweries can cut out a lot of driving by taking the Cape May-Lewes ferry.) A third option is a dolphin or whale-watching cruise aboard the *Spirit of Cape May* or the *Cape May Whale Watcher* (609-884-5445; www.capemaywhalewatcher.com).

CARTON
BREWING COMPANY

YEAR FOUNDED: 2011

FOUNDERS:
Chris and Augie Carton

**YEAR-ROUND &
SEASONAL BEERS:** Boat Beer,
Brunch Dinner Grub, 077XX, Carton of
Milk, Red Rye Returning, Launch Golden
Ale, Monkey Chased the Weasel, Carton
Canyon, Pumpkin Cream Ale, Harvest
2012, Epitome, Decoy, Intermezzo

LOCAL FLAVOR: Before
incorporating in 1887, the town of Atlantic
Highlands was a Methodist summer
colony; tents were kept in the building
that is now the brewery.

If you ask Augie Carton why he decided to start a brewery with his cousin Chris, he has a short yet compelling answer: there are flavors that don't exist but should. Sitting around a beach bonfire, the two decided they would make a beer akin to the big, hoppy, West Coast IPAs they liked to knock back, but sessionable. Enlisting the help of Jesse Ferguson, their favorite homebrewer, they proceeded to work on the recipe for Boat Beer. Roughly two years later they had their flagship, and in the summer of 2011, they opened Carton Brewing, a company that, in spite of its name, definitely does its thinking outside of the box.

Fittingly, the second floor tasting room feels like a den or a family room. Exposed brick walls, big old couches, a coffee table littered with magazines, and a TV set all create the impression that this is a space for loitering, preferably with a taster glass of beer in hand. With Ferguson as the only full-time employee, Chris and Augie try to treat their brewery like a hobby and can usually be found behind the bar pouring samples. Like any two guys who share a passion for something, they're more than happy to tell you all about whatever experimental batch they currently have in the "Tippy," a twenty-gallon pilot system that they use to try out new ideas. Impromptu tours on Thursday and Friday nights or weekend afternoons allow a glimpse of Carton's junior fermenter and the rest of the fifteen-barrel brewhouse.

At the bar, consider starting with Boat (4.2% ABV), a delicious blend of Old World malt and New World hops that adds up to a delicious IPA without head-spinning levels of alcohol. Next, move on to Brunch Dinner Grub (6% ABV), a medium-bodied brown that is an especially tasty example of beer as liquid bread. Relying on a reasonably new French hop variety called Aramis for its lemon and tarragon flavors, this is a great choice for the dinner table (hence the name). Make sure you try something adventurous like Monkey Chased the Weasel (3.9% ABV), a sour wheat ale that resembles the tart Berliner Weiss style, except the Carton boys add mulberries from a tree in the brewery's backyard. For outdoorsy types there's G.O.R.P. Trail Ale (8.4% ABV), a nutty, chocolately beer fermented on black raisins to evoke the taste of the popular hiking snack. Finally, the remarkably successful Decoy (12% ABV), is a dark, strong winter ale that piles on cumin, coriander, honey, lavender flowers, Belgian candi sugar, and Sichuan peppercorns to mimic the complexity of Chinese five-spice duck.

A handful of nearby restaurants offer Carton on tap. A few blocks away on First Avenue, Copper Canyon (732-291-8444; www.thecoppercanyon.com) bills itself as a restaurant and tequila bar, yet has served Carton Canyon (6.4% ABV), a lager brewed with blue agave nectar. If you're in beach attire after a few hours at Sandy Hook, head to the Chubby Pickle (732-872-7000; www.thechubbypicklenj.com), a sports bar and grill that has held Carton tap takeovers in the past. Otherwise, make the short drive south to Dish in the town of Red Bank (732-345-7070; www.dishredbank.com), a casual BYOB restaurant with a menu that emphasizes seasonal ingredients. Bring a growler with Carton of Milk (4% ABV) and try it with an order of stout-braised beef short ribs.

A range of activities make it easy to turn a short visit to the New Jersey coast into a full-day affair. You might decide to spend an afternoon on the beach at the Sandy Hook unit of the Gateway National Recreation Area (718-354-4606; www.nps.gov/gate/index.htm). Weather permitting, you might want to spend half a day fishing aboard the *Sea Tiger* (732-872-9231; www.seatiger2.com) or the *Atlantic Star* (732-291-5508; www.atlanticstarfishing.com). Hartshorne Woods Park, about four miles from the brewery, includes more than fourteen miles of multi-use trails. 🍶

CONTACT
6 East Washington Avenue
Atlantic Highlands, NJ 07716
732-654-BEER
www.cartonbrewing.com
@cartonbrewing

TASTING ROOM HOURS:
Thu-Fri, 5-7:30pm;
Sat-Sun, Noon-5pm
(Tours on request)

LODGING:
Blue Bay Inn
51 First Avenue
Atlantic Highlands, NJ 07716
732-708-9600
www.bluebayinn.com

FLYING FISH
BREWING COMPANY

YEAR FOUNDED: 1995

FOUNDER:
Gene Muller

ANNUAL PRODUCTION:
18,000-20,000 barrels

**YEAR-ROUND &
SEASONAL BEERS:** Abbey Dubbel, ESB Ale, Extra Pale Ale, Hopfish, Exit 4, Exit 16, Red Fish, Oktoberfest, Farmhouse Summer Ale, Grand Cru Winter Reserve, Imperial Espresso Porter, BlackFish, Big Fish Barleywine

LOCAL FLAVOR: In the 1970s, the Kennedy Boulevard building was the home of Superior Record Pressing, a manufacturing plant owned by Motown Records.

Flying Fish started out as a website, the world's first online brewery. Gene Muller, who refers to himself these days as the safety director or president and head janitor, advertised it as "a true life Internet soap opera... about suds." Of course the idea was to generate attention and attract investors, but the fact remains: this brewery began as virtual reality. Flash-forward a couple of decades, and it's now the largest production brewery in the state with the ability to get even bigger. After operating out of a space in Cherry Hill for years, Muller, envisioning greater capacity and a modern facility that could eventually become a showcase for sustainability, moved Flying Fish to Somerdale in 2012. Instead of investing in new construction, however, he went with a building that had been a record factory and warehouse for none other than Barry Gordy, founder of Motown records. Not that anyone would guess—the roof is blanketed with solar panels and the front entrance has been entirely redesigned to include a wall of glass beer bottles.

Surrounded by five acres of property that includes undeveloped wetland and resident turkeys, skunks, woodchucks, and beavers, Flying Fish is poised to be one of the most compelling breweries to visit in the Northeast. Muller (who is a gardener as well as a brewer) wants to add a rain garden with native plants to attract butterflies, bees, and hummingbirds, and plans to one day offer demos showing visitors how to construct a rain barrel or build their own bog. In the meantime, his 4,000-square-foot tasting room features wood reclaimed from an old water tower and is meant to serve as a community space as much as it is a bar. The ten taps at the bar almost always include a brewery-only release, and occasionally a cask-conditioned beer, too. Guided tours shed light on the art and science of brewing, while video screens in the tasting room show camera views of the action for beer tourists on a tight schedule. An outdoor seating area is also planned for the future.

From day one, Muller has designed his beers to go with food. Each Flying Fish beer is multi-dimensional and, even in hoppier styles, the malt character holds its own. XPA (5.2% ABV) a luminous, golden yellow ale with a snow-white head and a nose that evokes cut grass or hay, was one of two beers originally available from the brewery. Its crackery flavor with a touch of sweetness and a snappy bit of bitterness in the finish make XPA an excellent crossover drink for those who insist that they don't like craft beer. XPA might have longevity, but OktoberFish (6% ABV) is a frequent contender for the most popular Flying Fish. European malt, hops, and yeast pay tribute to the classic German festbiers, and its alluring reddish color makes it hard to resist. The first batch, released in 2002, sold out in two weeks. And then there's BlackFish (5.2% ABV), a draft-only hybrid beer that joined the lineup after Muller learned that a bartender in Charlottesville, Virginia, was blending XPA with Flying Fish Porter to the delight of his patrons. For a first class food beer though, Abbey Dubbel (7.2% ABV) takes the cake. Dark amber in color with aromas of dates and walnut liqueur, it's been used for a washed-rind cheese by a creamery in New Jersey. Remarkably complex, Abbey Dubbel is simultaneously sweet like panettone, nutty and spicy like a clove cigarette.

Somerdale itself doesn't have much to offer in the way of interesting food and drink, but fortunately Philadelphia isn't far. Closer than that, the Pour House (856-869-4600; www.pjspourhouse.com) in Westmont does craft beer with upscale pub fare and a running special on Flying Fish drafts. When their hoppy amber ale Red Fish (7% ABV) is in the mix, opt for the spicy cheddar fondue, with chorizo, milky queso fresco, tomato, and fresh cilantro, or the Mexican Caesar Salad made with grilled chicken, black beans, tomatoes, onions, pumpkin seeds, and a lime Caesar

dressing. Across the state line in Pennsylvania's largest city, the Industry (215-271-9500; www.theindustrybar.com) is a warm, wood-clad space with a menu that says: Welcome home. You'll definitely spot tap handles from well-regarded West Coast breweries here, but locals like Yards and Flying Fish are almost always in the mix, too. Farmhouse Summer Ale (4.9% ABV), a grassy, dry drinker, would be great with their Bahn Mi, a Vietnamese sandwich layered with chicken terrine, liver pâté, shredded carrot and cucumber, sprigs of cilantro, pickled jalapeño, and a spicy mayonnaise. In Northern Liberties, the Standard Tap (215-238-0630; www.standardtap.com) has long been regarded as one of the best bars in the city, and from the beginning they've also prioritized local craft beer. Similarly, their menu relies on local produce and seasonal ingredients. Give it a try if you have time.

As with restaurants, the immediate points of interest around Flying Fish are few, and the action is closer to Philadelphia and the river. A short walk from Camden's waterfront, the humble, two-story Walt Whitman House (856-964-5383; www.nj.gov/dep/parksandforests/historic/whitman) still stands more than 130 years after the author of *Leaves of Grass* bought the Greek-revival style building for $1,750. Today it's a National Historic Landmark and a museum offering free, guided tours from Wednesday

CONTACT

900 Kennedy Boulevard
Somerdale, NJ 08083
856-504-3442
www.flyingfish.com
@jerseyfreshale

TASTING ROOM HOURS:

Tue-Fri, 2:30-7:30pm;
Sat, Noon-6pm

LODGING:

Haddonfield Inn
44 West End Avenue
Haddonfield, NJ 08033
856-428-2195
www.haddonfieldinn.com

to Sunday. Another possibility is spending a few hours at Adventure Aquarium (856-365-3300; www.adventureaquarium.com). There you can see sharks, stingrays, sea turtles, jellyfish, a giant Pacific octopus, and much more. You can, of course, also cross the Delaware River to watch the Phillies, Eagles, Flyers, or 76ers compete in downtown Philadelphia, but for a low-key—and less expensive—sporting venue, consider a night on the Jersey side of the river at Campbell's Field, home of the Camden Riversharks (856-963-2600; www.riversharks.com) and a Flying Fish Pub on the main concourse. Fireworks follow games on Friday and Saturday nights. 🍾

HIGH POINT
BREWING COMPANY

YEAR FOUNDED: 1994

FOUNDERS:
Greg Zaccardi

ANNUAL PRODUCTION:
3,000-4,000 barrels

**YEAR-ROUND &
SEASONAL BEERS:** Ramstein
Blonde, Ramstein Classic, Ramstein
Double Platinum Blonde, Ramstein Amber
Lager, Ramstein Revelation Golden Lager,
Ramstein Imperial Pilsner, Ramstein Winter
Wheat, Ramstein Maibock, Ramstein
Oktoberfest, Ramstein Summer Bock

LOCAL FLAVOR: For close to a
century, Butler was known as a center
of rubber manufacturing. In 1974, the
Amerace Corporation (American Hard
Rubber Company) was the last rubber
company to close its plant in town.

When Greg Zaccardi made the decision to start a brewery after spending time in Germany, he was well aware of the fact that the American craft beer scene had fallen hard for pale ales. And he wasn't interested in being a Sierra Nevada imitator. Figuring he might stand out better in the market by trying something else, he went into business as a brewer of German styles, the beers he had come to love during his years in Bavaria. When he got back to the United States, he discovered that the area around New Jersey's High Point State Park reminded him of the German countryside, specifically the pastoral hills and the foothills of the Swiss-German Alps. He named his brewery accordingly, and even chose to use the stone obelisk in the park in the High Point logo. As for what to call the beers themselves, Zaccardi went with Ramstein, after the town that had been his home for a while. For the first few years, he hand-sold every single case that left his warehouse. But even if it took time to win converts, his passion and dedication paid off. Zaccardi's beers are truly world class; served from the tap without their own glassware, you'd be forgiven for guessing they were imports.

The High Point Brewing Company occupies part of a huge complex that once manufactured all sorts of rubber products, including bowling balls, which employees tested by dropping them from a tall tower. Business dried up in the mid-twentieth century, and a devastating fire closed the factory completely for about fifteen years after that. Today, Zaccardi's footprint includes his brewhouse, a tasting room, a small amount of office space, and an area for storage and warehousing. The tap room, which tends to be busiest on Mondays, Fridays, and Saturdays, has the feel of a beloved tavern, with a wood-burning stove, some beat-up old stools at the bar, and a bourbon barrel or two to rest a Weissbier vase on. Beer awards, a plastic hop bine, cones and all, as well as a few displays explaining the brewing process, hang on the walls. Beer samples at the bar don't cost anything, but a full pour is $3. High Point runs guided tours once a month, and also holds an open house four times a year to launch brewery exclusive beers. When it comes time to leave, pick up some Ramstein merchandise or save your money for a growler, which can cost as much as $40 new.

Zaccardi's started out by brewing draft-only blonde wheat beer and quickly realized he would need to bottle and to diversify. He's up to eleven varieties now, including a popular Oktoberfest, his first non-wheat beer. Pouring a friendly warm orange or medium amber color, Ramstein Amber Lager (5% ABV) is a bready, medium-bodied beer with a toasty character, a trace of caramel sweetness, and a crisp finish. Ramstein Classic (5.5% ABV) is a darker beer, full-bodied and malty with a smell reminiscent of fresh-baked spice cake. Double Platinum Blonde (7% ABV) meanwhile, is transparent gold and impresses immediately, producing a huge pillow of foam and appetizing aromas of banana and clove. Several times a year, High Point brews limited-edition beers. During the winter of 2012-2013 it was a strong eisbock Zaccardi dubbed Ice Storm (14.5% ABV). To get the beer to freeze, he chained kegs outside the brewery for Mother Nature's help. This seasonal proved extremely popular, selling out in just three hours.

Other than the somewhat unremarkable Trackside Bar and Grill, Butler isn't a town where you'll necessarily find Zaccardi's lagers on tap. Up the road in West Milford though, Tuscany Brewhouse (973-545-2700; www.tuscanybrewhouse.com) is a dependable place to find Ramstein seasonals like Winter Wheat (9.5% ABV) alongside handles from Ithaca and Saranac. The rich complexity of this dopplebock is well-suited for many of the grilled items on the menu, such as the blackened Delmonico's steak topped with mushrooms and pan-fried onions. Continuing west, you'll reach Sparta and its Mohawk House restaurant (973-729-6464; www.mohawkhouse.com) serving seasonal American fare in an elegant main dining room with a vaulted ceiling and a huge fieldstone fireplace. Ramstein Blonde (5.4-5.5% ABV), which is exceptional on its own, intertwines perfectly with the berry parfait tart on the dessert menu, matching the sweetness of the cream filling and the buttery texture of the pastry shell. East of High Point, the Taphouse Grille (973-832-4141; www.taphousenj.com) in Wayne serves a bratwurst with applewood smoked bacon, roasted potatoes, and lager-infused sauerkraut that wants to be washed down with Revelation (3.9% ABV), Ramstein's crisp, effervescent golden lager.

Follow Route 23 northwest, and you'll eventually end up at High Point State Park (973-875-4800; www.state.nj.us/dep/parksandforests/index.html), more than 14,000 acres of forests, fields, ponds, and lakes. The monument that is the centerpiece of the park, a 220-foot-tall granite obelisk, appears on Zaccardi's beer labels. Spend a few hours or an entire afternoon here boating, swimming, hiking, or cross-country skiing. Somewhat closer to Butler, Mountain Creek (973-827-2000; www.mountaincreek.com) is a four-season destination with downhill skiing and snowboarding, more than forty miles of mountain biking trails, a unique alpine mountain coaster, and a waterpark with thirty different rides and slides. Either of these options will appeal to those who

like to work up a sweat on vacation. A third attraction in the area requires considerably less physical fitness—just the ability to maintain a leisurely stroll. Due north of the brewery, Skylands Manor and the New Jersey State Botanical Garden (973-962-9534; www.njbg.org) occupy more than a thousand acres altogether and represent the state's finest example of landscape architecture. Join a free tour of the gardens every Sunday from May through October or learn about the Tudor Revival Mansion designed by John Russell Pope, who was also the architect for the National Gallery of Art.

CONTACT

22 Park Place

Butler, NJ 07405

973-838-7400

www.ramsteinbeer.com

TASTING ROOM HOURS:

Mon-Fri, 9am-6:30pm;

Sat, 1-4pm (Tours on the second

Sat, Mar to Dec)

LODGING:

Alpine Haus Bed & Breakfast Inn

217 State Route 94

Vernon, NJ 07462-3305

973-209-7080

www.alpinehausbb.com

KANE
BREWING COMPANY

YEAR FOUNDED: 2011

FOUNDER:
Michael Kane

ANNUAL PRODUCTION:
2,500-3,000 barrels

**YEAR-ROUND &
SEASONAL BEERS:** Head High,
Afterglow, Drift Line, Single Fin, Overhead,
Cloud Cover, Port Omna, Malus, Morning
Bell, Solitude

LOCAL FLAVOR: Yorktowne Caskets
Incorporated formerly occupied the
nondescript building that now houses
the brewery.

Hard as it is to believe, the Jersey Shore does in fact have a mild-mannered, unassuming side—one that bears little resemblance to the version you've seen on television. And Ocean Township is a good place to find it—starting with a young brewery just off Sunset Avenue. The building itself doesn't look like much from the outside, but most weekends, this is where you'll find Michael Kane, behind the bar in his taproom, pouring samples of his latest seasonal release, filling growlers, and making conversation with the throng of beer pilgrims who have turned up to try his American and Belgian-influenced ales.

Behind a glass door on the other side of a pint-sized lobby, Kane, VP Glenn Lewis, and head brewer Matthew Czigler have turned a homebrewing dream into a serious business with serious ambition. Tired of the corporate grind, Kane traded in his suit and tie for a brewer's apron, leasing a 7,000-square foot industrial space in late 2010 and moving a brewhouse in at the end of the following February. As a finishing touch, he created a tiny garden outside— one just large enough to grow eight Cascade, Chinook, Columbus, and Nugget hop plants. Demonstrating a conviction common among many entrepreneurial craft brewers, Kane literally chose to put down roots in low-key Ocean. In the relaxed tasting room, Modest Mouse, the Black Keys, Radiohead, and the Pixies play from corner speakers and framed photographs of the nearby dunes hang at regular intervals around the small, white-washed space. From the adjacent brewhouse, shiny stainless-steel fermenters and a bright beer tank gleam through a large picture window. Stemmed tulip glasses, Shaker pint glasses, hats, T-shirts, and growlers are all available for sale, the latter for $5 empty or $12-$20 for sixty-four ounces of your favorite beer style.

Starting off with a golden ale for the summer debut of Kane Brewing Company, he's since added a tangy, ruddy-colored rye ale called Afterglow (5.5% ABV) and Head High (6.5% ABV), a resinous IPA with a prominent piney aroma and a shade akin

CONTACT

1750 Bloomsbury Avenue
Ocean, NJ 07712
732-922-8600
www.kanebrewing.com
@kanebrewing

TASTING ROOM HOURS:

Fri, 5-8pm; Sat, Noon-5pm
(Tours Sat, 1, 2, 3, & 4pm)

LODGING:

Asbury Ocean Beach Inn
404 Asbury Avenue
Asbury Park, NJ 07712
732-539-8440
www.asburyoceanbeachinn.com

to saffron. On the darker end of the spectrum, Drift Line (5.8% ABV), a medium-bodied, chestnut-hued oatmeal brown ale is joined by Port Omna (6% ABV), a gorgeous stout perfect for winter days when the Atlantic's cold wind reaches farther inland. Meanwhile, within boxes stacked along the walls, Malus (9.5% ABV), a strong Belgian ale brewed with local apple cider, grains of paradise, cinnamon, and orange zest, might be finishing the maturation process known as bottle conditioning. You might also find them pouring their newest Mysterioso small-batch beer, an experimental brew that could be anything from a farmhouse saison with honey to a Belgian-style IPA.

Of course as time goes on, it becomes easier to find Kane's beers along the Jersey Shore. At Nicchio (732-280-1132; www.nicchiorestaurant.com), a short drive away in Belmar, try the sweet sausage and broccoli rabe orecchiette alongside the hoppy Head High. Slightly closer to the brewery at Brickwall Tavern and Dining Room (732-744-1264; www.brickwalltavern.com) in Asbury Park, start off with a savory appetizer such as stuffed whole artichoke washed down with the somewhat spicy Afterglow.

While you're in Asbury Park, find out who's playing at the Stone Pony (732-502-0600; www.stoneponyonline.com), a legendary music club where Steve Van Zandt first made a name for himself before joining his friend Bruce Springsteen's E Street Band. If you turn up early, take a stroll on the recently renovated boardwalk. For an even better view of the ocean, venture south to the little town of Sea Girt. Built in 1896 as the last live-in lighthouse on the Atlantic Coast, Sea Girt Lighthouse (732-974-0514; www.seagirtlighthouse.com) can be toured on Sunday afternoons from mid-April until mid-November. Book lovers might want to make a quick stop at Arbutus Cottage on Asbury Park's Fourth Avenue, a modest two-story house that was the home of Stephen Crane in 1883 (732-775-5682; www.thestephencranehouse.org).

BUFFALO
The Pan-American
Grill & Brewery

Hopshire Farm & Brewery

FREEVILLE

BURDETT
Two Goats Brewing Co.

LAKEWOOD
Southern Tier Brewing Co.

Brewery Ommegang
COOPERSTOWN

ATHENS
Crossroads
Brewing Co.

Greenport Harbor
Brewing Co.
GREENPORT

Captain
Lawrence
ELMSFORD

BROOKLYN
Brooklyn Brewery

NEW YORK

BREWERY OMMEGANG

YEAR FOUNDED: 1997

FOUNDERS:
Don Feinberg and Wendy Littlefield

ANNUAL PRODUCTION:
35,000-40,000 barrels

YEAR-ROUND & SEASONAL BEERS: BPA, Witte, Rare Vos, Hennepin, Abbey Ale, Three Philosophers, Scythe & Sickle, Gnomegang, Adoration, Fleur de Houblon, Duvel

LOCAL FLAVOR: Built on a former hop farm, Ommegang is roughly fifty miles east of tiny Bouckville where James D. Coolidge planted root stock he brought from Massachusetts to start New York's first commercial hop yard in 1808.

B rewery Ommegang began as a love story. Actually, it was more of a love triangle between beer, Belgium, and baseball that all started at Yale University when Don Feinberg met Wendy Littlefield. Smitten, the two eloped to Brussels, where they soon discovered the country's beer. Following a few years in the advertising industry, they moved back to the United States where Don established an import business to introduce Americans to the abbey ales, witbiers, and lambics he had grown so fond of. Wendy joined the company, now called Vanberg & DeWulf, in 1990, and they increased their educational outreach, even publishing the first U.S. edition of Michael Jackson's *Great Beers of Belgium*. On a birthday trip to the Baseball Hall of Fame, Feinberg and Littlefield fell in love with Cooperstown and ended up choosing a former hop farm south of town as the site for the farmstead brewery they wanted to start. With investments from Duvel Moortgat and other family-owned Belgian breweries they'd worked with in the past, they opened their brewery, taking the name from a Flemmish expression meaning "to walk about." Ommegang's beer range has grown over time but continues to draw from Belgian brewing traditions like open fermentation.

Built to resemble a Belgian farmhouse, Brewery Ommegang is easily one of the most striking examples of brewery architecture in the Northeast. A long, curving white barn stands out against the wooded hill behind it and almost appears as if it's been picked up and moved from the European countryside. Drive through the arched gateway in the center of the building to reach the parking lot, tasting room, and café. Informative tours leave from the brewery shop and last about thirty

minutes. For $3 you can add on a tasting of six different beers and go home with a souvenir glass. A more leisurely visit might include a full serving of Belgian Pale Ale or Witte out on their patio, perhaps accompanied by an order of frites. Or, save your money for the snacks and swag in the shop. Ommegang also hosts regular events including summer concerts, an annual Belgium Comes to Cooperstown festival, and a birthday party called Waffles and Puppets.

When Ommegang introduced Abbey Ale (8.5% ABV) in 1997, the availability of Belgian or Belgian-style beers in the United States remained limited. Bottle conditioned for additional complexity, this beer produces a fruity bouquet when uncorked, and offers a range of flavors from sweet fig and prune to spicy coriander and cumin, and bitter, earthy licorice. It remains an excellent interpretation of the Belgian dubbel. They followed their first release with the medium-bodied Hennepin (7.7% ABV), the first saison brewed in the United States. Juggling orange zest, peppery spice, bright ginger, and an herbal bitterness, Hennepin is easy to like and refreshing to drink. A newer addition to Ommegang's lineup, Scythe & Sickle (5.8% ABV) is the color of marmalade and pours with a sandy-colored head. Brewed for the harvest with four different grains, it gives off aromas of cracked wheat, white pepper, and rye, evoking the inviting scent of a loaf of rustic bread. This beer has a generous level of carbonation and a creamy mouthfeel, with slightly bitter, earthy flavors that turn up midway and blend into a dry, crackery finish. Keep an eye out for some of the brewery's limited releases such as the funky Adoration (8.9% ABV) brewed with raspberries and pear, too.

Italian food with Belgian beer? Don't listen to skeptics, it can be done, and done well. In Cooperstown, Bocca Osteria (607-282-4031; www.boccaosteria.com)

carries Ommegang on draft and in bottles, often with as many as six styles to choose from. They also offer helpful pairing suggestions, recommending the fragrant, lemony, and approachable Witte (5.2% ABV) with the Bocca Salad, a mixture of greens, red onion, candied pecans, oranges, and Gorgonzola dressed with balsamic vinaigrette. For a hearty entrée, they encourage diners to try Abbey Ale with Fettuccine Ai Funghi, ribbon-like pasta in a cream-based sauce topped with mushrooms and shaved parmesan. Near the corner of Chestnut and Main, Alex and Ika's (607-547-4070; www.alexandika.com) typically has Duvel and BPA on draft, the latter of which is delicious with any of the six gooey sandwiches grouped together on the menu as "The Grilled Cheese Bazaar." Or, drive a short way up the western side of Otsego Lake, the body of water James Fennimore Cooper referred to as Glimmerglass in his *Leatherstocking Tales* to reach The Blue Mingo (607-547-7496; www.bluemingogrill.com). The produce is fresh, herbs come from their own garden, and the beer is Cooperstown's own. Match Hennepin with the Bangkok Bird, Asian grilled chicken with a Thai peanut sauce.

If you already know the name Cooperstown, chances are it's because of the Baseball Hall of Fame (888-425-5633; www.baseballhall.org). Since 1939 this popular museum has collected and displayed artifacts and memorabilia telling the story of a game that has grown into a professional sport watched around the world. If you've ever cheered for a walk-off home run or a nail-biting double play, you won't want to miss this three-story building on Main Street. At the other end of Otsego Lake, another hall will appeal to travelers more interested in New York's history than baseball's history. A country mansion with almost fifty rooms, Hyde Hall (607-547-5098; www.nysparks.com/historic-sites) was one of the largest homes in the still-young United States of America when finished. House tours of the historic site are offered on the hour from early May through the end of October. Extend your visit by spending time in neighboring Glimmerglass State Park. Just west of town, Fly Creek Cider Mill and Orchard is, like Ommegang, a member of the Cooperstown Beverage Trail and a fun place to stop to try hard cider, apple wine, fudge, and cheese. Or continue on to Munnsville, where Foothill Hops (315-495-2451; www.foothillhops.com) sells all things related to the climbing bine. 🍺

CONTACT

656 County Highway 33
Cooperstown, NY 13326-4737
607-544-1800
www.ommegang.com
@BreweryOmmegang

TASTING ROOM HOURS:

Daily, Noon-5pm; 11am-6pm from
Memorial Day to Labor Day
(Tours on the hour)

LODGING:

The Inn at Cooperstown
16 Chestnut Street
Cooperstown, NY 13326
607-547-5756
www.innatcooperstown.com

BROOKLYN BREWERY

YEAR FOUNDED: 1987

FOUNDERS:
Steve Hindy and Tom Potter

ANNUAL PRODUCTION:
180,000-200,000 barrels

YEAR-ROUND &
SEASONAL BEERS: Brooklyn Lager, Brooklyn Brown Ale, Brooklyn East India Pale Ale, Brooklyn Pilsner, Brooklyn Pennant Ale, Brooklyn Blast!, Brooklyner Weisse, Brooklyn Black Chocolate Stout, Brooklyn Winter Ale, Brooklyn Monster Ale, Brooklyn Dry Irish Stout, Brooklyn Summer Ale, Brooklyn Oktoberfest, Brooklyn Post Road Pumpkin Ale, Local 1, Local 2, Sorachi Ace

LOCAL FLAVOR: In 1898, the same year it was incorporated into New York City, Brooklyn had forty-eight breweries; twelve of these big buildings still stand today.

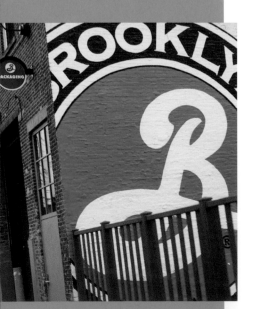

Walking around New York City, you might see the Brooklyn Brewery logo and guess that it's been around forever. The elegant white "B" on a field of green designed by Milton Glaser, the same artist who created the iconic "I Love New York" logo somehow has a timeless feel to it. In fact, this brewery founded by a couple of neighbors in Park Slope is approaching its thirtieth birthday. Along the way it outlasted a number of peers and competitors, helped revitalize a neighborhood, and challenged popular notions of a historic beverage by aging beer on wine sediments, brewing a cocktail-inspired beer, and collaborating with chefs and other breweries. When journalist Steve Hindy moved back to the United States after working in the Middle East as a foreign correspondent, his homebrewing ambitions were to save money, not to start a brewery. But a small yet growing market for domestic beer, a book about Brooklyn's brewing history, and most importantly, the partnership of Tom Potter, a banker friend who lived in the same building, led Hindy to take the first steps toward starting a beer business that now numbers among the most successful in the country. Challenges ranging from pure inexperience to mob intimidation beset them along with way, but in March 1988, they sold the first bottles of the dry-hopped lager that started it all.

In the beginning, there was no Brooklyn brewery per se, every drop of the company's original lager was made upstate in Utica at F.X. Matt Brewing and warehoused on Meserole Street in the former Huber-Hittleman brewery. Then, after moving to an old matzo factory in Williamsburg, founders Hindy and Potter, along with current brewmaster Garrett Oliver, began brewing their own beers in 1996. The space has expanded considerably since, and now encompasses much of the block along with part of a warehouse on the other side of the street.

Inside the public entrance, a fascinating collection of antique beer bottles is tastefully exhibited, backlit in their case to glow a soft blue, green, or brown. It's a tiny museum of New York's beer history when companies like Nassau (1898-1916) and Beadleston & Woerz Empire (1877-1920), respectively, pumped out 150,000 and 225,000 barrels per year. Beyond the display, oak columns break up the space in the brewery's tasting area, a cavernous room populated by long picnic tables and barrels. Even in a neighborhood full of bars, this is a popular place on weekends. At the rear, visitors exchange a wooden token ($5 apiece or five for $20) for a full pour from one of eight taps or a special cask offering. They also sell jerky, potato chips, and peanut brittle, but if you're really hungry, call in an order from Carmine's original pizza—you'll find menus near the gift shop.

Even as they've grown to become an international player (they opened a second brewery in Sweden in 2013), Brooklyn has always kept an eye on the artisanal side of craft beer. Occasional casks make their way to gastropubs around the five boroughs such as the Spotted Pig and the Breslin while bottles of experimental "Ghost" beers end up appearing at beer dinners and special events. Brooklyn Brown Ale (5.6% ABV) followed on the heels of their debut lager, and offers a rich, fruity, and roasty flavor with a caramel smoothness that's excellent with a variety of meats and cheeses. Black Chocolate Stout (10% ABV) is a dessert beer that might be at its best with a scoop of gourmet vanilla ice cream floating on top. And the lemony, effervescent Sorachi Ace (7.6% ABV), an unfiltered saison refermented with Champagne yeast and named after a Japanese hop variety, is delightful with jerked chicken or lobster on the half shell.

Rarefied Brooklyn releases are worth tracking down, too. Chat with Oliver at an event and he might tell you that getting the desired character out of barrels is one of the joys of brewing to him. That should be reason enough to track down Black Ops (10.5% ABV), an imperial stout aged in Woodford Reserve bourbon barrels that does in fact exist.

Spend any amount of time in Brooklyn and you'll quickly realize: the beers made in and named for the borough are no longer hard to find. They haven't been for years. The tough part is deciding where to settle in for some beer-worthy dining. You are, after all, in a city with an embarrassment of dining options. About the closest you can get is Mable's Smokehouse and Banquet Hall (718-218-6655; www.mablessmokehouse.com) on the other side of North 11th. Go for the regular platter—one meat and two sides—or bring an appetite and tackle the deluxe platter with three sides and three meats. They've got longnecks of Lone Star, but you're in New York, so wash it down with Brooklyn Lager instead. A few blocks away on Wythe Avenue, Fat Goose (718-963-2200; www.fatgoosewilliamsburg.com) changes their New American menu seasonally. Before a weekend tour of the brewery, brunch on a fried egg sandwich with escarole, aged gouda, and chili and sip on the sessionable, draft-only Radius (4.8% ABV), a dry, hoppy beer with a whisper of orange zest. No visit to New York is complete without a stop at a pizza joint, so if you can't decide where to eat in Williamsburg, make your way north to Paulie Gee's (347-987-3747; www.pauliegee.com) in the neighborhood of Greenpoint. The six craft beers on tap tend to be local, so pair the smooth, crisp Brooklyn Pilsner (5.1% ABV) with a simple yet original pie like the Red, White, and Greenberg: mozzarella, guanciale, baby arugula, and pickled red onions.

It should come as no surprise that, in a foodie city like New York, its hippest borough has plenty of other delicious culinary activities to fill your itinerary. On the other side of McCarren Park, a short walk from the brewery, the New York Distilling Company (718-412-0874; www.nydistilling.com), offers free tastings and tours on Saturdays and Sundays between 3 and 5 p.m. with live music at 4 p.m. Started by one of the co-founders of the Brooklyn Brewery, this distillery produces Perry's Tot Navy Strength Gin, Dorothy Parker American Gin (with elderberries, citrus, cinnamon, and hibiscus along with the juniper), and a rye whiskey. While you're visiting Brooklyn, don't miss the chance to stroll through Prospect Park or spend a few hours literally smelling the roses at the Brooklyn Botanical Garden (718-623-7200; www.bbg.org). From Temperate, Tropical, and Desert Pavilions to a bonsai museum and more than a dozen gardens, this living attraction opened in 1910. When the evening rolls around, check to see what's on at the Brooklyn Academy of Music (718-636-4100; www.bam.org), a concert hall, performance space, and movie theater that holds the title of America's oldest continually operating performing arts center. Known for world-class, avant-garde programming, this cultural center commissioned the Brooklyn Brewery to make a limited edition bottle release called BAMBoozle Ale for its 150th anniversary.

CONTACT

79 North 11th Street
Brooklyn, NY 11249
718-486-7422
www.brooklynbrewery.com
@BrooklynBrewery

TASTING ROOM HOURS:

Mon-Thu, 5pm tours; Fri, 6-11pm;
Sat, Noon-8pm; Sun, Noon-6pm
(Tours Sat on the hour 1-5pm;
Sun on the hour 1-4pm)

LODGING:

Wythe Hotel
80 Wythe Avenue
Brooklyn, NY 11249
718-460-8000
www.wythehotel.com

CAPTAIN LAWRENCE
BREWING COMPANY

YEAR FOUNDED: 2006

FOUNDER:
Scott Vaccaro

ANNUAL PRODUCTION:
20,000 barrels

YEAR-ROUND & SEASONAL BEERS: Freshchester Pale Ale, Liquid Gold, Captain's Kolsch, Captain's Reserve, Brown Bird Brown Ale, Smoked Porter, Pumpkin Ale, Espresso Stout, Winter Ale, Saison, Sun Block

LOCAL FLAVOR: When he decided to open a beer business in New York, Scott named his brewery after the road he grew up on in South Salem.

Some high school students dream of sports careers and others see themselves one day pursuing medicine, but for Scott Vaccaro, brewing beer has been the job he knew he wanted almost as soon as he finished his first batch of homebrew with a friend's father at age seventeen. Inspired by Belgian breweries such as De Dolle and Brasserie d'Achouffe as well as home-grown successes like New Belgium and New Glarus, he convinced his skeptical parents that transferring from an accounting program at Villanova University to a fermentation science program at the University of California, Davis was a good idea. All along, starting his own brewery had been in the back of his mind, and so, following short internships in England and Connecticut and six years at the Sierra Nevada Brewing Company, he moved back east and struck out on his own soon thereafter. It wasn't easy. He drew the original Captain Lawrence logo himself, hired his cousin to handle sales, and delivered kegs out of his Volkswagen Jetta. But he persisted and made steady progress, winning seven big beer medals in the first seven years.

Since moving to Elmsford from Pleasantville, Captain Lawrence has expanded its tasting room as well as the brewhouse. With potted plants, polished wood floors, cream-colored walls, and soft overhead lighting, the space has the feel of an upscale bar, the kind of place where you might bring a book to read while you savor a pint of beer. If that's your style, Wednesdays, Thursdays, and Saturday afternoons tend to be quieter times to visit. On the walls, framed medals and magazine articles tell the story of the brewery's steady growth and hard-earned popularity, while steel kegs and handsome wood barrels scattered around the room serve as stools and tables. Enjoy a full pour with a small order of assorted nuts ($3) or beef jerky ($6), or for a reasonable two bucks, sample everything available at one of the tap towers at either end of the long oak bar. A small outdoor beer garden with a bocce ball court and the presence of Village Dog slinging grass-fed beef and heritage pork dogs topped with kimchi and plum ketchup or braised onions and provolone also encourages visitors to linger on temperate afternoons. Hats, glassware, sweatshirts, and other typical brewery merchandise is available for sale at the bar, as are growlers for about $10-$13.

Freshchester Pale Ale (5.5% ABV) is the brewery's flagship beer, a style that Vaccaro first brewed upon relocating to California to study brewing. A deep orange color with aromas of pine and citrus, his pale ale doesn't shy away from hop bitterness, using three West Coast varieties recognizable for their moderate pungency. From the beginning though, he's also brewed a

series of sophisticated beers that hardly seem related to the sometimes run-of-the-mill stouts, porters, and amber ales that once dominated the craft beer landscape. A wine glass filled with Cuvee de Castleton (9% ABV) for instance, might have you wondering exactly what you're drinking. Oaky tannins, overripe fruit, and a bit of funk replace hop aroma in this wild ale that pours with a Champagne-like froth. Muscat grapes, wild yeast, and wine barrels work together to produce the tart flavors and dry finish in this singular beer. By including the complex Smoked Porter (6.4% ABV) in his regular lineup, Vaccaro chose another style that's less common than the classic pilsner or the ubiquitous IPA. It's a beer that evokes the past, and rewards those who sip slowly. One more reason to visit Elmsford is the chance to try the test batch beers that show up in the tasting room from time to time. It's just about the only place to find experiments like a sweet milk stout inspired by dulce del leche, or a fiery chile beer brewed with habaneros called El Scorcho.

As one of the first new breweries to pop up in the Hudson Valley, Captain Lawrence has had time to make inroads into the local restaurant scene. In nearby Tarrytown, Sweet Grass Grill (914-631-0000; www.sweetgrassgrill.com) serves a varied menu that depends on close to a dozen local farms for much of their ingredients. Captain's Reserve (9% ABV), a big, hoppy imperial IPA would complement the citrus and shaved fennel salad with orange, grapefruit, and candied walnuts from their lunch menu. Of course, you might need to order the cheese plate for dessert to reset your palate. To the south in Dobbs Ferry, The Cookery (914-305-2336; www.thecookeryrestaurant.com) is another supporter of Vacarro's beer and has collaborated with Captain Lawrence on special events like an Oktoberfest celebration at the brewery. Order the crisp heritage pork osso bucco with apple mustard and creamy white polenta and, if possible, pair it with a bottle of Golden Delicious (12% ABV), a strong, golden-hued ale dosed with extra hops at the end of fermentation and aged in apple brandy barrels. And then, for a truly fine dining experience, there's Blue Hill at Stone Barns (914-366-9600; www.bluehillfarm. com), one of the premiere restaurants in the Hudson Valley. Eschewing a traditional

CONTACT
444 Saw Mill River Road
Elmsford, NY 10523
914-741-2337
www.captainlawrencebrewing.com
@cptlawrencebeer

TASTING ROOM HOURS:
Wed-Fri, 4-8pm;
Sat-Sun, Noon-6pm
(Tours Sat & Sun, 2 & 4pm)

LODGING:
Crabtree's Kittle House Inn
11 Kittle Road
Chappaqua, NY 10514
914-666-8044
www.kittlehouse.com

menu altogether, Blue Hill offers a five-, eight-, or twelve-course tasting that revolves around the day's harvest. During the spring, that might mean green garlic, fiddlehead ferns, and lamb. Both Liquid Gold (6% ABV) and Captain's Kolsch (5% ABV) make regular appearances on their beer list.

Much of Westchester County is dotted with golf courses, but once you venture upriver into Putnam and Dutchess counties, the fairways give way to forests, with parks becoming more common. Teatown Lake Reservation (914-762-2912; www.teatown.org) is one such spot that's easy to reach from the brewery. There, fifteen miles of trails will appeal to hikers, gardeners will enjoy seeing Wildflower Island, and birdwatchers will take pleasure in observing the resident owls, hawks, and kestrels. History buffs, meanwhile, will want to visit one of the historic homes in the Lower Hudson Valley, like Washington Irving's Sunnyside or Kykuit, the Rockefeller Estate in Sleepy Hollow (914-631-8200; www.hudsonvalley.org/historic-sites/kykuit). This grandiose stone mansion was home to four generations of the influential family, beginning with John D. Rockefeller, the founder of Standard Oil and once the richest man in the country. Tours include the house, its surrounding gardens, and the Coach Barn. In addition to a highly regarded restaurant, Blue Hill operates an eighty-acre farm and nonprofit institution called the Stone Barns Center for Food and Agriculture (914-366-6200; www.stonebarnscenter.org). Drop by to take a guided or self-guided tour, shop at their weekly farm market, or attend an event such as an afternoon of foraging or their annual sheep shearing festival. 🍾

CROSSROADS
BREWING COMPANY

YEAR FOUNDED: 2010

FOUNDERS:
Ken Landin and Janine Bennett

ANNUAL PRODUCTION:
850 barrels

**YEAR-ROUND &
SEASONAL BEERS:** Lighthouse
American Wheat, Athens Mill Honey Rye
Amber, Angry Pete's Pale Ale, Outrage IPA,
Homewrecker Double IPA, Fat Boy Porter,
Brooks Brown Ale, Black Rock Stout, Brady's
Bay Cream Ale, First Pitch Pilsner, Brick Row
Red Ale, Abbey Road Belgian Dubbel

LOCAL FLAVOR: Abandoned when
they found it on their real estate hunt, the
building at 21 Second Street opened as
the Brooks Opera House in 1893.

For Kenny Landin and Janine Bennett, the path that led to Crossroads Brewing wasn't an easy one to follow. Launching their plan in Queens, New York, but knowing they wanted to open a brewery in the Hudson Valley, they spent months looking at close to a hundred sites. When they finally found a location they liked in Columbia County, it fell through at the last minute, taking their pre-approved loans with it. Almost at the point of abandoning the dream they'd shared for years, Landin and Bennett happened to see a "For Sale" sign in the window of an old opera house in the sleepy town of Athens. Luck had decided to show up in the nick of time. Enamored with the riverside community and the historic three-story brick building (the sale of which ended up taking close to a year), they rolled up their sleeves and went to work renovating it, installing brewing equipment Landin had acquired from the Defiant Brewing Company in Peal River. Starting with a tiny tasting room and growler sales, Crossroads has since grown into a full-fledged brewpub with a rotating menu that complements their draft beers.

Built on the corner of Second and Franklin streets in 1893, the Brooks Opera House was in bad shape when Landin and Bennett showed up to assess their new property. The roof, for example, was doing very little to prevent water from pouring down to the first floor. Gradually and lovingly, they patched, painted, and pieced the landmark back together, preserving as much of its original detail as they could. Behind the forty-six-foot bar for instance, you might notice that some of the tap handles look like banister rails. In a nod to the history of the building and the town, they've also hung black and white

photos of Athens and the opera house along the hallway to the kitchen and the bathrooms. Fittingly, this space that would have been a community hub at the turn of the century is bringing people together again. Eventually they also plan to turn the second floor—which still shows signs of earlier uses as a playhouse, basketball gym, and small garment factory—into a 350-seat concert venue. Until they do, belly up to the bar and ask for a tasting flight ($12). If the brewmaster, Hutch Kugeman, is around on a Saturday afternoon, inquire about a short tour. Then, before you leave, fill up a Crossroads growler with one of their beers ($15).

As Landin likes to tell it, Crossroads Brewing introduced themselves to a Coors town with an IPA. Medium amber with an assertive hop aroma of citrus and pine, Outrage IPA (7% ABV) is anything but a light lager. Persistently bitter from start to finish, this popular beer's flavors of juicy grapefruit and pine resin stand out against an ever-so-sweet background. Golden-hued with a smooth mouthfeel, Brady's Bay Cream Ale (5.2% ABV) followed on the heels of Outrage, joined soon thereafter by Black Rock Stout (6.8% ABV), a medium-bodied roasty ale with notes of espresso and bittersweet chocolate. When Kugeman took over the brewing reins, he added a handful of other plucky beers to the lineup, including a double IPA, a honey rye amber ale, and a single

hop pale ale called Angry Pete's (5.3% ABV). This beer changes from batch to batch, depending on the hop variety he chooses, but generally ends up the color of sun tea, transparent with small head that quickly fades. Fresh smelling, leafy, and pungent, it offers a measured level of bitterness throughout, a medium level of carbonation, and wave after wave of hop flavor followed by a lingering finish.

With ten beers on tap at any given time, it's easy enough to dedicate yourself entirely to sipping ales at Crossroads. Except that you'd be missing half the fun of a visit. A seasonal menu sourced from Hudson Valley farms includes an Empire Salad with mixed greens, walnuts, goat cheese, and New York apples in a cider vinaigrette, a savory Catskill Mushroom Casserole with white beans and crispy beer-battered shallots, and smoked wings in a sauce made from their own Black Rock Stout (6.8% ABV). Cocoa, espresso, and a hint of charred wood in this beer pick up on the smoky taste of the meat and the umami flavor of the sauce. And although they don't have a kitchen, one of the more interesting places in Hudson to go for a pint of Crossroads is Spotty Dog Books and Ale (518-671-6006; www. thespottydog.com). Occupying an old firehouse on Warren Street, this small business has eight beers on tap and a collection of about 10,000 books for sale. Drop in to browse their new titles, hear some live music on Friday and Saturday nights, or just to sit at the bar with a full pint of Athens Mill Amber (5.5% ABV) and a new novel. To get a locally raised grass-fed burger with your pint of Outrage, continue driving east to the Main Street Public House in Philmont (518-672-7346; www.philmont.org/local0609_mainstreetpublichouse.html).

About the best thing to do in Athens on a hot day is to find Paddlehead Boards (518-755-4052; www.paddleheadboards.com) on the river. Between May and October this little business rents kayaks and stand-up paddleboards out of a storefront on North Water Street. In the past, they've also co-sponsored an event with Crossroads called the Reel Paddling Film Festival. Instead of doing your own paddling, you can also join the Hudson-Athens Lighthouse Preservation Society (518-828-5294; www.hudsonathenslighthouse.org) on one of their semi-regular tours out to the two-story Hudson Athens Lighthouse. Finished in 1874 and attached to an eight-room keeper's residence, this building was occupied for seventy-five years until the Coast Guard automated the light. As for a land-based activity, think about visiting the Olana State Historic Site (518-828-0135; www.olana.org) across the river in Hudson. This walkable town also has the largest number of hotels in the area. To reach Hudson during the summer, make the short drive over the Rip Van Winkle Bridge, or hop the evening ferry, which runs Fridays and Saturdays 5-10 p.m. Home to Hudson River School artist Frederick E. Church, the Olana house museum is surrounded by acres of landscaped grounds and contains many original furnishings as well as well-known works by the painter. 🍾

CONTACT

21 Second Street
Athens, NY 12015
518-945-BEER
www.crossroadsbrewingco.com

TASTING ROOM HOURS:

Mon, Wed, & Thu, 4-9pm;
Fri, 4pm-Midnight;
Sat, 1pm-Midnight; Sun, 1-9pm

LODGING:

The Country Squire Bed &
Breakfast
251 Allen Street
Hudson, NY 12534
518-822-9229
www.countrysquireny.com

GREENPORT HARBOR
BREWING COMPANY

YEAR FOUNDED: 2009

FOUNDERS:
Rich Vandenburgh and John Liegey

ANNUAL PRODUCTION:
4,000-5,000 barrels

YEAR-ROUND & SEASONAL BEERS: Harbor Ale, Black Duck Porter, Canard Noir, Summer Ale, Leaf Pile Ale, Anti-Freeze, Hopnami, Havre Rouge, Triton, Spring Turning Rye Saison, Weesh'd Scotch Ale

LOCAL FLAVOR: The squat brick building next door to the brewery on Carpenter Street is Greenport's former jailhouse, built in 1917.

One hundred miles east of Manhattan's buzzing beer scene and a stone's throw from Gardiner's Bay, the smell of malted barley wafts out of a former firehouse on a quiet residential street. Just look for the whale sign. Deciding to chase a college dream they couldn't shake in the years since graduating, friends John Liegey and Rich Vandenburgh bought the historic building in 2008 and set about converting it into a brewery. Months of cold, hard work later (much of the construction took place during the winter), the duo could proudly claim to be the first brewers on Long Island's North Fork. Joined soon thereafter by professional brewer D. J. Swanson, the threesome quickly put the tiny town of Greenport Harbor on the craft beer map—a feat all the more impressive given its location in the thick of a well-known wine region.

On any given weekend, classic rock can be heard spilling from open windows, and a steady stream of thirsty visitors climbs a side staircase to the second floor. Here, a sun-bathed tasting room cum art gallery welcomes neighbors and out-of-towners with bowls of pretzels and six taps of fresh, locally brewed beer. Stand at the long, polished bar and chat with other beer enthusiasts or sit and admire paintings by local artists on one of the kegs that have been creatively repurposed as cushy stools. Several times a year, the brewery also hosts receptions for area artists. Eight dollars will buy you a Greenport pint glass along with a taste of the available ales, while growler fills run anywhere from $16 to $25, depending on the style. In 2013, Liegey and Vandenburgh opened a second larger brewhouse with a beer garden and a bottling line on Route 25 and Peconic Lane in Peconic.

Debuting with Harbor Ale (5.3% ABV), an American pale ale brewed with 50 percent wheat malt, and Black Duck Porter

CONTACT

234 Carpenter Street
Greenport, NY 11944
631-477-6681
www.harborbrewing.com
@greenportbrew

TASTING ROOM HOURS:

Sun-Thu, Noon-6pm;
Fri-Sat, Noon-7pm

LODGING:

Ruby's Cove Bed & Breakfast
151 Bay Avenue
Greenport, NY 11944
631-477-1837
www.rubyscovebnb.com

(4.7% ABV), a thick, roasty dose of barley, Greenport Harbor has gone on to release more than a dozen other beers, from a formidable barleywine to a delightfully tart citrus IPA brewed with whole oranges, lemons, limes, grapefruits, and tangelos. And in April 2011, Liegey and Vandenburg enlisted family and friends to plant roughly 300 hop bines, beer's all-important bittering agent. As the plants matured, they created recipes that would allow them to use fresh hops in future beers. Their collective interest in *humulus lupulus* also led them to experiment with "Project Hoppiness," an ongoing series of distinctive IPAs that range from herbal and earthy to bold and bright.

Greenport Harbor's town center doesn't lack for restaurants. Head to the upscale North Fork Oyster Company (631-477-6840; www.northforkoystercompany.com), just around the corner from the brewery on Bay Avenue. Farther down Front Street, Noah's (631-477-6720; www.chefnoahschwartz.com) works with local farmers and devotes a tap to their neighborhood brewer. Another option is Love Lane Kitchen (631-298-8989; www.lovelanekitchen.com) in nearby Mattituck, which also sources its ingredients locally and hosts beer dinners.

Once you've finished your beer tasting, stroll to the nearby marina or window shop on Main Street. History buffs will want to stop by the East End Seaport Museum or the Railroad Museum of Long Island, and sailors should time their visit with the annual Maritime Festival in September. Those looking for bit of human-powered adventure can pick up a retro cruiser from Port Side Rentals (631-477-6585; www.portsiderentals.com) and pedal around town, or rent a kayak from Eagle's Neck Paddling Company in nearby Southold (631-765-3502; www.eaglesneck.com). At the end of Route 25, Orient Beach State Park (631-323-2440; www.dec.ny.gov/outdoor/72049.html) offers the chance to fish, swim, picnic, or hike in a maritime forest.

HOPSHIRE
FARM & BREWERY

YEAR FOUNDED: 2013

FOUNDERS:
Diane Gerhart and Randy Lacey

ANNUAL PRODUCTION:
300 barrels

**YEAR-ROUND &
SEASONAL BEERS:** Blossom,
Beehave, Brambles, Daddy-O, NearVarna,
Shire Ale, Zingabier, Sneaky Weasel,
Shenanigans, Dragon's Milk

LOCAL FLAVOR: In 1880, upstate
New York had reached its peak as the
nation's leading hop growing region,
producing roughly 20 million pounds
in a single year.

Randy Lacey doesn't just want to make beer. He wants to make New York beer, using local ingredients. At one point, he thought about opening a homebrew shop, and then opted to grow hops instead, starting with seventy-five rhizomes. More than another homebrewer with lofty dreams, he saw a future in the state's brewing history and wanted to raise the bar, making beer touring a classier experience. Located in the heart of a region that once produced record-setting hop yields, he thought he might be able to create a beer destination that paid tribute to this agricultural heritage. Taking inspiration from a dismantled hop kiln at Brewery Ommegang as well as a few other examples of these barns that still stand in central New York in defiance of time, Lacey, an engineer at Cornell University, and his wife, Diane Gerhart, resolved to start a farmhouse brewery. Once they found a plot of land big enough, they enlisted their family to help put the pieces together for Hopshire Farm and Brewery. With the brewhouse finished, their plans include a four-acre hopyard and fields for berries to use in their beers.

From concept to completion, attention to detail and an effort to use sustainable materials were both important to Lacey and Gerhart. The building itself is a precise recreation of a New York hop kiln, and much of the wood in the tasting room was either salvaged locally or cut from property they own. Vintage globe lamps hanging from the ceiling come from nearby Cortland, the handsome L-shaped mahogany bar was rescued from a restaurant in Ithaca, and their son designed and made the leaf-shaped tap handles. As for the beer, Lacey works hard to keep six to eight selections on tap at all times.

A full tasting flight is $3 and growler fills cost between $10 and $12, depending on the style. Beer tourists sticking to a tighter budget can also go home with a half growler for $6 to $8. Barbecues are not unheard of in the summer—grab a seat at one of the picnic tables outside—and visitors will also find local honey and maple syrup as well as Hopshire T-shirts and pint glasses for sale.

Ask one of the bartenders for advice choosing a beer and they'll tell you that Hopshire divides their range into three categories: mellow, middling, and mighty. Behind the bar, the name of each beer on tap appears on a maple board hanging from a brass chain. Zingabier (5.5% ABV), a Belgian pale ale brewed with ginger and coriander pours with a dense head of foam, and smells strongly of its spicy additions. Amber in color, its bright ginger flavor makes it a great choice on a hot summer day. So far, NearVarna (7.5% ABV) has proven to be one of their most popular beers—five hop additions make this IPA a deliciously bitter brew. Sticking to their local philosophy, both Hopshire's cherry wheat ale and their blonde ale Beehave (4.2% ABV) are made entirely with ingredients from New York. The latter includes barley from Canastota, honey from Moravia, and hops grown in Lansing. Every year Lacey also brews Maple Nut Brown Ale (10% ABV) using maple syrup instead of water. Strong and boozy with a syrupy sweetness in the aftertaste, it pours a dark ruby brown and has a rich, sherry-like nose. Hops take the backseat in this big beer made for central New York's cold winters.

There's no guarantee that Ithaca's Bandwagon Brew Pub (607-319-0699; www.bandwagonbeer.com) will have Hopshire on draft the day of your visit, but it's a safe bet for good beer and food nonetheless. Sourcing their beef, pork, cheese, and

eggs locally, Bandwagon dedicates many of its tap lines to their own beers while supporting other New York State breweries with the remainder. When hunger strikes, order a big ribeye steak with grilled asparagus, roasted garlic mashed potatoes, and crumbles of Gorgonzola cheese. It's all the more satisfying with a pint of lightly hopped, malt-forward Shire Ale (6.3% ABV). Between Ithaca and Freeville on Dryden Road, the Ithaca Plantation Bar & Grill (607-273-4950; www.theithacaplant.com) also prepares uncomplicated, beer-friendly food. But if you're looking for something different, Taste of Thai Express (607-272-8424; www.tasteofthaiexpress.com) in Ithaca has a BYOB policy, which means you can fill up a growler with your favorite Hopshire beer and try it with spicy Southeast Asian cuisine. Made with fresh ginger, Zingabier is well suited for one of the restaurant's spicy curries, like the Indian-influenced massaman.

Located in the eastern part of the Finger Lakes region, Freeville is surrounded by natural beauty, from farms and orchards to undisturbed state forests and the waters of Cayuga Lake, less than a dozen miles west. Not far from the brewery, the Jerry Dell Farm Store (607-351-8747; www.jerrydellfarm.com) sells maple syrup and raw honey, organic produce, and free-range eggs from the farm next door, as well as their own raw milk cheddar cheese and other artisan cheeses from around the Finger Lakes. Certified organic and a member of the Finger Lakes Cheese Trail, the farm is a great place to stop if you need something to go with the growler of beer you just bought at Hopshire.

Closer to Ithaca, the largest city in the region, Buttermilk Falls State Park (607-273-5761; www.nysparks.com) and Robert H. Treman State Park (607-273-3440; www.nysparks.com) each contain swimming areas, campgrounds, and hiking trails leading past scenic waterfalls. Both can be relaxing places to unwind after a long road trip by car or bus. After dinner in or around this college town, find entertainment at the Ithaca College Main State Theatre (www.ithaca.edu/hs/depts/theatre/mainstage) or Cornell University's Schwartz Center for Performing Arts (607-254-2787; www.pma.cornell.edu/schwartz-center). Count on everything from plays to dance festivals and student film screenings, but remember shows taper off between June and August over the school's summer break.

CONTACT
1771 Dryden Rd (State Route 13)
Freeville, NY
607-229-6700
www.hopshire.com
@HopshireBrews

TASTING ROOM HOURS:
Wed-Fri, 4-8pm;
Sat, 11am-6pm; Sun, 1-6pm

LODGING:
Rogues' Harbor Inn
2079 East Shore Drive
Lansing NY 14882
607-533-3535
www.roguesharbor.com

THE PAN-AMERICAN GRILL & BREWERY

YEAR FOUNDED: 2012

FOUNDERS:
Earl and Joshua Ketry

ANNUAL PRODUCTION:
400-500 barrels

YEAR-ROUND & SEASONAL BEERS: City of Light Lager, Rough Rider, Roosevelt Red, The Terminator, Nickel Town Brown, Th' Wee Beastie, Dusseldorf Altbier, Hooligan Dry Irish Stout, Honey Brown Lager, German Kolsch

LOCAL FLAVOR: After William McKinley's assassination at the Pan American Exposition in 1901, Theodore Roosevelt was sworn in as the twenty-sixth president of the United States at Ansley Wilcox Mansion, just over a mile from the Lafayette.

I t can be tempting to skip the long drive through the Finger Lakes to the Niagara region, but no good brewery tour should neglect western New York. And by the time you make it all the way to Buffalo, you'll definitely want a beer. Located on the ground floor of the Lafayette Hotel, the Pan-American Grill and Brewery is part of a group of businesses owned by Earl and Joshua Ketry and collectively referred to as the Brewery District of Buffalo. Overseeing brewing operations at both the Pan-American and the Pearl Street Grill and Brewery about five blocks away is Phil Internicola, a friendly, mustachioed man whose great grandfather had been brewmaster at the Tonawanda Brewing Company. His appreciation for Buffalo and its brewing history is part of what led him to trade a job at Flying Bison Brewing Company for a position at Pearl Street. Taking inspiration from the World's Fair held in the city in 1901, as well as the larger than life twenty-sixth president, the Pan-American is a history-lover's brewpub on the shores of Lake Erie.

Located on the corner of Clinton and Washington Streets across from Lafayette Square, the Lafayette Hotel was designed by Louise Bethune, the first woman to be professionally licensed as an architect in the United States. Designed in a French Renaissance style and constructed between 1902 and 1911, this impressive seven-story brick building features terra cotta trim and wrought-iron window balconies that give it a striking appearance. The interior lobby and adjacent brewpub are equally impressive with considerable detail and handpainted ceilings. Ask for a seat in the elegant Taproom, the colorful Murals Room, or the Teddy Roosevelt–inspired Trophy Room with a large fireplace and taxidermy game animals. On Sundays during the warmer months, while brunch is served at the

Grill, the brewery also offers forty-five-minute walking tours ($5) on the hour. Focusing on the architecture around Lafayette Square and including a behind the scenes look at the hotel, these events are a fun way to learn something about the history of Buffalo without venturing too far from the beer you traveled to try. Or, from the end of May until late September you can join a guided pub crawl to three bars in the Brewery District, including the Pan-American ($20).

Younger than Pearl Street by well over a decade, the Pan-American is still tinkering with its beer lineup in an effort to remain distinctive yet broadly appealing. City of Light Lager (4.5% ABV), a pale gold beer styled in the tradition of German Helles has a low level of bitterness that arguably makes it the most approachable of the four beers in regular rotation. The Terminator (4.5% ABV), on the other hand, a beer named for Rocco Termini, the local developer behind the Hotel Lafayette's restoration, is a classic hoppy American pale ale with citrusy and floral flavors and aromas attributable to the popular Cascade hop variety. Darker beers with more body and more of a malty profile include Rough Rider (4.4% ABV), an English-style porter with toasty, sweet, and slightly chocolatey flavors and earthy undertones supplied by Kent Golding hops and Hooligan Dry Irish Stout (4.5% ABV). In the past, the seasonal beers at the Pan-American have also leaned toward maltier ales like a German altbier, a honey brown lager, and a Scotch ale called Th' Wee Beastie.

The key to two of the successful items on the menu is, as might be expected at a brewpub, beer. In the French onion soup, Roosevelt's Red Ale informs the flavor of the beef broth, while the grilled ribeye sandwich on toasted ciabatta bread is topped with mushrooms marinated in Rough Rider. Either would be a filling meal at lunchtime. From the dinner menu, the slow-roasted Red Stag Half Chicken with Yukon mashed potatoes

could be paired with almost any one of the Pan-American's standard offerings, but the medium-strength Nickel Town Brown (4.5% ABV) is a particularly nice match, with its dark malts picking up on the char-grilled flavors in the poultry. Wander down the street to Pearl Street Grill and Brewery (716-856-2337; www.pearlstreetgrill.com) for more food and options as well as a completely different range of beers crafted by Internicola. The open-faced pot roast sandwich served on a golden fried potato pancake with a side of apples stewed in the brewpub's cherry wheat beer is every bit as good as it sounds.

While the Brewery District does include an ample number of places for food, drink, and entertainment, you might decide to see more of the city during your stay. Beyond the metro area, Niagara Falls State Park (716-278-1796; www.niagarafallsstatepark. com) has attracted a steady stream of tourists since 1885, when environmentalists persuaded the New York legislature to establish the country's first state park. Take the Cave of Winds Tour, buy tickets for a ride aboard the *Maid of the Mists*, or simply stand back and snap photos, just don't skip Niagara Falls on your first trip to the area. Back downtown, you can get out on Lake Erie by going sailing with the Seven Seas Sailing Center (716-880-5154; www.sevenseassailing.com) or register for a Buffalo Niagara River Tour (716-852-7483; www.bnriverkeeper.org/get-involved/rivertours) from May through October to see this waterway by bicycle or boat. Admirers of the work of architect Frank Lloyd Wright on the other hand, will want to visit his Martin House

Complex (716-856-3858; www.darwinmartinhouse.org) near the zoo. And then to round out your Buffalo experience, cheer on the Sabres during hockey season at the First Niagara Center, a venue that also hosts concerts, ice shows, and other sports teams. 🍺

CONTACT

391 Washington Street

Buffalo, NY 14203

716-856-0062

www.panamericangrill.com

TASTING ROOM HOURS:

Daily, 11am-9pm

LODGING:

The Lafayette Hotel

391 Washington Street

Buffalo, New York 14203

716-853-1505

www.thehotellafayette.com

SOUTHERN TIER
BREWING COMPANY

YEAR FOUNDED: 2002

FOUNDERS:
Phineas DeMink and Allen Yahn

ANNUAL PRODUCTION:
70,000-80,000 barrels

YEAR-ROUND & SEASONAL BEERS: IPA, Phin & Matt's, Porter, 422 Pale Wheat, Live Pale Ale, 2XStout, 2XIPA, 2Xmas, Old Man Winter, Eurotrash Pilz, Hop Sun, Harvest, 2XSteam, 2XRye, UnEarthly IPA, Iniquity, Backburner, Krampus, Pumpking, Compass

LOCAL FLAVOR: Southern Tier began its life in the Stoneman Business Park, named for one of the first few farming families that owned land in Lakewood in the nineteenth century. George Stoneman Jr. served as the fifteenth governor of California.

What a difference a decade makes. When Southern Tier took its first steps as a brewery, it was headquartered in a small industrial park in Lakewood, New York, and had four employees. Flash forward and the brewery is still in Lakewood, but now it's on the other side of Hunt Road in a much larger, recently expanded, newly built facility. It also employs more than forty people. Co-founder Phin DeMink initially went to school for furniture design and tinkered around with homebrews in his free time. His first batch was a cinnamon nut brown. After meeting his wife and current co-owner at a ski resort in Ellicotville (where he had landed his first brewing job), DeMink relocated to Chicago and ended up working at Goose Island Brewery, makers of the widely praised Bourbon County Stout. He later moved back to the Southern Tier, or the southwestern corner of New York State, to open the Back Burner Beer Company with Allen Yahn. A soft-spoken guy in person, DeMink has nonetheless built a brand around a number of beers that are anything but mild mannered. And while still very much a production brewery at its core, Southern Tier has evolved into a gathering place for fans of craft beer.

Tour the brewery on Saturday afternoons for $12, which includes a tasting and a Q&A session with a guide. Southern Tier's brewery pub, the Empty Pint, is a great place to hang out before or after, with fourteen beers on tap, one of which is usually reserved for guest beers and ciders. They also have a decent bottle selection with ales and lagers from Canada, Spain, Belgium, Germany, and the United Kingdom. The room itself is a striking space with stone floors, a high ceiling, and lots of wood, that give it the appearance of a ski chalet or an elegant

mountain lodge out west. Additional seating in the covered patio includes picnic tables as well as a number of weather-worn boulders scattered around the lawn. Free outdoor concerts are commonplace during the summer, and every so often Southern Tier runs a Brewer for a Day program that includes lunch. New growlers run from about $15.50 to as much as $25.50, with refills usually topping out at $18.

DeMink started off with three beers: a pilsner that has changed somewhat over the years, a mild ale that has since been retired, and an IPA (7.3% ABV). Copper-colored, medium-bodied, and triple-hopped, the surviving member of Southern Tier's original lineup uses four varieties of malt to balance the generous level of bitterness. The brewery's range has since expanded, with roughly two dozen beers in regular production. This includes common styles such as a porter, a pale ale, and a stout, but it also covers a number of imperial beers, ales that don't shy away from hops and alcohol, and often contain other ingredients. Mokah (11% ABV) for instance, is a unique creation best described as an imperial milk stout. It pours black and opaque with a thick, creamy, khaki-colored head. Full-bodied and luscious, this beer smells of milk chocolate and brown sugar and offers a malty sweetness, with lots of coffee flavor in the background. "Brewed with a pagan spirit," Pumpking (8.6% ABV) is a warm transparent orange color with the aroma of pumpkin bread. Vanilla, nutmeg, and a tickle of allspice stand out in the flavor and an almost candy-like sweetness distinguishes this seasonal release from some of the more highly hopped Southern Tier beers.

With beer as the priority, a lengthy menu of entrees and appetizers might seem superfluous. In that case, tide yourself over at the end of a Saturday afternoon tour with a hickory-smoked pulled pork sandwich topped with coleslaw at the Empty Pint,

Southern Tier's pub and gift shop. If that doesn't appeal, ask about the soup of the day, or bring your own snacks. For a much wider selection and outdoor seating with a view of Lake Chautauqua, go to the Harbor Grill (716-720-5959; www.harborgrillceloron. com) in the village of Celoron, the childhood home of Lucille Ball. Meat lovers will want to match the citrusy and moderately bitter Live Pale Ale (5.5% ABV), which has a dry finish, with a messy yet mouth-watering Pat LaFrieda steak burger with melted cheddar on a flaky croissant. Vegetarians (or Elvis fans) on the other hand, might like to try The King, a fried peanut butter and banana sandwich. On the side, you'll get sweet potato fries with a trace of vanilla and a cinnamon sugar glaze. To cut the sweetness, pair it with Porter. A few miles away in Jamestown, Forte (716-484-6063; www.fortetherestaurant. com) offers an eclectic menu from sushi to chipotle chicken sopes. They also serve Southern Tier. If you have room for dessert, split a bottle of creamy, bittersweet Choklat (10% ABV) and a thick slice of red velvet chocolate mousse cake.

The proximity of Southern Tier to Lake Chautauqua makes a boat trip easy to squeeze in for those who enjoy being out on the water. Take a ride aboard the *Chautauqua Belle* (716-269-2355; www.269belle.com) which offers daily round-trip cruises from Mayville and Chautauqua at the north end of the seventeen-mile long lake.

Back in Jamestown, the Roger Tory Peterson Institute of Natural History (716-665-2473; www.rtpi.org) will appeal to birdwatchers and armchair naturalists. With a museum, a nature center, an exhibition gallery, and an interpretive walking trail, the organization seeks to preserve and further the work of the naturalist, artist, and author. If you're looking for a place with fewer people around, drive east to Alleghany State Park (716-354-9121; www.nysparks.com), the largest state park in New York with miles of hiking trails, two small beaches, multiple campgrounds, and a ski touring area. And that's not the only place to go for winter activities. At the nearby Holiday Valley Resort (716-699-2345; www.holidayvalley. com) in the little town of Ellicotville—which also happens to have a brewery—downhill skiers can ride one of thirteen lifts up to fifty-eight trails and slopes for a day of wintry excitement.

CONTACT

2072 Stoneman Circle
Lakewood, NY 14750
716-763-5479
www.stbcbeer.com
@stbcbeer

TASTING ROOM HOURS:

Thu-Fri, 4-10pm; Sat, Noon-10pm
(Tours Sat, 12:15, 1, 1:45,
2:30, 3:15 & 4pm);
Sun, Noon-6pm

LODGING:

The Oaks Bed & Breakfast Hotel
1103 West Third Street
Jamestown, NY 14701
716-720-5267
www.theoaksbandbhotel.com

TWO GOATS
BREWING COMPANY

YEAR FOUNDED: 2010

FOUNDER:
Jon Rodgers

ANNUAL PRODUCTION:
250 barrels

**YEAR-ROUND &
SEASONAL BEERS:** IPA, Redbeard Red Ale, Cream Ale, Amber Logger, Dirty Shepherd Brown Ale, Hefeweizen, Wyck'd Nuggets IPA, Headbutt, Goat Master Ultra Pale Ale, Oatmeal Stout, Danger Goat, Whiskey Richard Stout

LOCAL FLAVOR: To create his brewery on the lake, Rodgers dismantled an old barn that had been sitting empty down the road and reassembled it where it stands today.

N ew York's Finger Lakes are supposed to be wine country. From the highly regarded terroir to the stunning views across any one of these bodies of water, the setting is perfect for a vineyard. It's just that the wineries now have some company: beer. Two Goats Brewing is one such newcomer, an intentionally small, under-the-radar establishment just up the road from Watkins Glen on Seneca Lake. Funky, fun, and far from ordinary, it's a spot worth visiting on the still-young Finger Lakes Beer Trail. Founder and brewer Jon Rodgers grew up about an hour south of his brewpub, and at different times worked in a winery tasting room and a cellar. After spending some time out west, his affection for the region and its aesthetic led him to try to do something with beer. Enlisting some friends, he disassembled, cleaned, and rebuilt a nineteenth-century barn on a postcard-like perch of land east of the lake, using pieces of another barn to construct the roof, bathroom, and entryway. Boxy and unpainted with a steep peaked roof, it's a photogenic little building with a deck that wraps around two sides. Rodgers refers to it as his dream come true.

Approaching the entrance from the gravel parking area, a sign posted next to the threshold gives visitors a sense of what to expect inside: "Hippies use backdoor, no exceptions." From this lighthearted warning to rainbow-colored billy goat tap handles and the dollar bills tacked to the underside of the roof—Rodgers calls them his retirement fund—this is one brewery that makes it abundantly clear that enjoyment is a big part of the reason for drinking craft beer. Unlike many other places that prefer to stick their own paraphernalia on the walls,

Two Goats is decorated with tin beer signs from Pabst, Sierra Nevada, Dogfish Head, and Blue Point, to name a few. A handful of high-top tables give you a place to lean or rest your glass. A pair of dartboards serves as the lone diversion; otherwise it's live music on weekends, birdwatching from the deck (Rodgers has seen bald eagles), or old-fashioned conversation. No tasting flights here, but you'll probably get a small pour and a quick explanation if you ask for a sample. Inquire about Danger Goat, however, and you're just as likely to be told about a chubby superhero.

So far, Rodgers guesses he's brewed about fourteen different beers at Two Goats, but he doesn't plan to stop there. He'll tell you that he tries to brew beers that are simple and beautiful like the barn, but he also likes to try new things every once in a while. Hence his barrel-aged stout. Among a family of hoppy IPAs and amber ales, the Whiskey Richard Stout, with its ivory head and inky black body, occupies the role of patriarch: strong, aged, and worthy of admiration. Starting off with his Oatmeal Stout, Rodgers lets it sit in whiskey barrels from neighboring Finger Lakes Distilling, which lend the final product layers of complexity that

distinguish it from many of the best beers in its category. This is one drink that's sure to win over malt lovers who appreciate a kiss of bourbon with their beer. Wyck'd Nuggets IPA (9% ABV) is another memorable ale, brewed in limited quantities. Continually hopped with fifty pounds of the Nugget variety grown locally, it pours deep amber and offers a green, herbal aroma and plenty of bitterness. And then there's the Headbutt, a twist on the classic Black and Tan that combines the sweet, biscuity Cream Ale (7.2% ABV) with Oatmeal Stout.

Two Goats is only about eight miles away from Watkins Glen and a number of restaurants, but if you're sitting out on the deck admiring the view with a pint of Goat Master at your side, you might not feel like making the trip. Fortunately, this little brewery has anticipated just such a scenario. Don't bother looking around for a menu though—the only choice to worry about is whether to get your roast beef sandwich with pickles and potato chips or without. You could ask for it without the homemade au jus and creamy

horseradish sauce, too, but that wouldn't make any sense. The rolls are baked at Glen Mountain Market in Watkins Glen, and all together, this filling, no-frills meal makes for a mean complement to almost anything on tap. If you can't decide, try the IPA. Show up on the early side and there's a good chance you'll find a warm pile of buttery popped kernels waiting in the old-fashioned popcorn maker in the corner.

East of the brewpub, the sprawling Finger Lakes National Forest (607-546-4470; www.fs.usda.gov/main/fingerlakes/home) contains more than thirty miles of multi-use trails suitable for hiking, mountain biking, or cross country skiing. It also includes a small seasonal campground. Watkins Glen State Park (607-535-4511; www.nysparks.com) is an even more impressive example of natural beauty, with nineteen different waterfalls sculpting the shale and limestone walls on either side of Glen Creek into photogenic shapes and forms. Follow the Gorge Trail into the hanging valley for the most dramatic views. Instead of hiking, you might continue south to the Hoffman family farm. Better known as Sunset View Creamery (607-594-2095; www.sunsetviewcreamery.com), this working dairy farm offers tours seven days a week from Memorial Day through Labor Day. Meet the animals, sample their cheddar and monterrey jack, shop for maple syrup, local honey, coffee from Keuka Lake Coffee Roasters, or apple, plum, and apricot butter. Closer to Two Goats, you'll find Finger Lakes Distilling (607-546-5510; www.fingerlakesdistilling.com), which produces small batches of whiskey, a gin made with eleven botanicals, brandy, grappa, and several fruit-based liqueurs. With a canoe chandelier hanging above the bar, a tasting room overlooking their 4,000-pound copper still, and handsome oak floors reclaimed from a Kentucky tobacco barn, this distillery has created an attractive welcoming space for visiting whiskey (and beer) connoisseurs. 🍾

CONTACT

5027 State Route 414
Burdett, NY 14818
607-546-2337
www.twogoatsbrewing.com

TASTING ROOM HOURS:

Mon, Tue & Thu, Noon-10pm;
Fri & Sat, Noon-Midnight;
Sun, Noon-8pm

LODGING:

Magnolia Place Bed & Breakfast
5240 New York 414
Hector, NY 14841
607-546-5338
www.magnoliawelcome.com

YEAR ROUND BEERS:
BIG HOP I.P.A. -12
MONKEY BOY HEFEWEIZE
FAT GARY NUT BROWN
BLACK STRAP STOUT -
EASONALS & ONE OFFS
SNOW MELT -13
COFFEE PORTER -1
OLD NEBBY STOCK A
STEEL CUT OATMEAL S

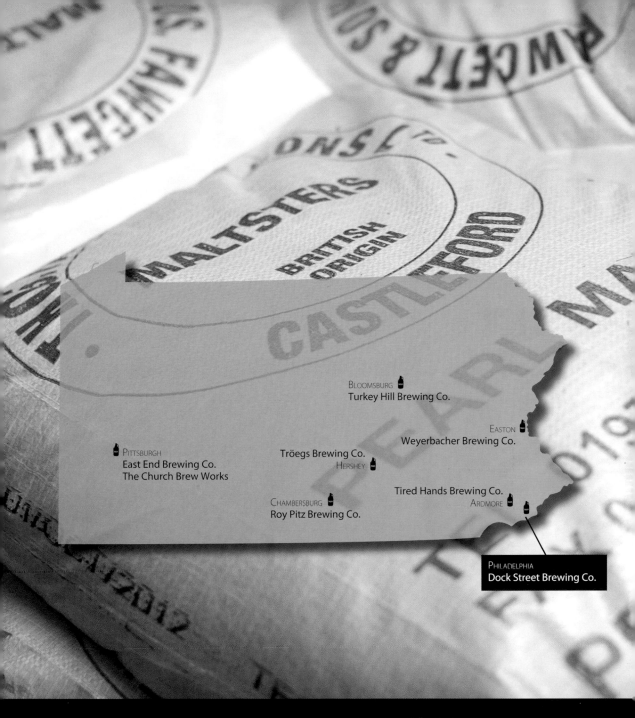

BLOOMSBURG
Turkey Hill Brewing Co.

EASTON
Weyerbacher Brewing Co.

PITTSBURGH
East End Brewing Co.
The Church Brew Works

Tröegs Brewing Co.
HERSHEY

Tired Hands Brewing Co.
ARDMORE

CHAMBERSBURG
Roy Pitz Brewing Co.

PHILADELPHIA
Dock Street Brewing Co.

PENNSYLVANIA

THE CHURCH BREW WORKS

YEAR FOUNDED: 1996

FOUNDER:
Sean Casey

ANNUAL PRODUCTION:
3,000 barrels

YEAR-ROUND & SEASONAL BEERS: Celestial Gold, Pipe Organ Pale Ale, Pious Monk Dunkel, Blast Furnace Stout, Mad Brewer Maibock, Saaz Monster, Millennium Tripple, D'Pomme Rye Saison, Thunder Hop IPA, Oak Aged Wheat Wine, Cherry Quadzilla, Heavenly Hefeweizen

LOCAL FLAVOR: In 1869, the Pittsburgh Brewing Company, also known as Iron City, was the largest brewer in Pennsylvania. Production took place in a massive brick facility at Liberty Avenue and 34th Street, a block from where the church is today.

Around the northeastern and Mid-Atlantic states, old churches have been repurposed as schools, museums, and apartments. In Pittsburgh, entrepreneur Sean Casey decided that an abandoned parish church in Lawrenceville on the edge of Little Italy might be a perfect venue for an upscale brewpub. His intentions caused some controversy at first, as neighbors envisioned (perhaps) drunk and debauched customers spilling out of a former house of worship in the wee hours of the morning. The community came around once he explained the concept and pledged to restore the landmark building to its former grandeur. As it approaches its twentieth anniversary, The Church Brew Works is more popular than ever, having helped to revitalize a neighborhood and introduce a major city to craft brewing. Now serving a secular purpose and no longer in danger of becoming a derelict part of Pittsburgh's urban landscape, St. John the Baptist is as beautiful as it must have been in 1903 at the end of construction. Plus, the kitchen turns out top quality appetizers and entrees, and a skilled team of brewers has brought Church a number of coveted beer awards over the years. A visit to Pittsburgh without a stop here would be a mistake.

When you step inside The Church Brew Works, eager to taste your first beer, pause at the end of the nave for a minute to soak it all in: stained glass glows on either side of the enormous room, huge columns guide your eyes to the altar and the apse where, against a cerulean blue backdrop, the brewhouse proudly stands. To the left, the long bar wiggles around more columns while to the right, church pews have been repurposed as booth seating. The restoration process also uncovered the original Douglas fir flooring, polished to shine like new today. On one side, a confessional has been cleverly transformed into a closet for brewery merchandise, while the confessional on the other side of the room now provides access to the kitchen. Next to it, a door leads to the old rectory courtyard, a patio that serves as a hop garden between April and June. Once you've seen it, the Church is not the kind of brewpub you're likely to forget. To familiarize yourself with their beer lineup, begin by ordering the tasting flight. From time to time they also hold events that enable attendees to get to know their food and beer. A prix fixe option on weekends and Brewer's Dinners every two or three months are two other easy ways to delve into the menu and experiment with beer pairings.

While The Church Brew Works is a place that's always tinkering with new beer recipes, four beers that range from light to dark will always remain on tap. Pious Monk Dunkel (4.3% ABV), a medium-bodied, malty lager that finishes clean and keeps within the boundaries of its style, has long been considered the brewery's flagship, but a second offering has gained ground. With the significant and sustained taste for India pale ales around the country, the brewery introduced Thunderhop IPA (6% ABV). Hops from Australia and the Pacific Northwest (although not the ubiquitous Cascade variety) give this beer its bite, even as a generous malt bill tips the scale back to the sweeter side. Relatively light-bodied and tangerine in color, Pipe Organ Pale Ale (4.3% ABV) is another that stays in rotation and complements many of the items on their menu. Candied orange and citrus leap out from the layers of flavor. Those who enjoy stouts will also want to taste the rotating version the brewery is pouring at the time. Past examples have included a mole stout, a pumpkin stout, and a supple coconut stout made even better by the tannic and vanilla flavors contributed by bourbon-barrel aging.

Often spotted together at pubs and restaurants nationwide, beer and pizza are a tried and true combination. But in a city where pierogie mascots race around the baseball field between innings at Pirates games, Church Brew Works needed something different. And so, alongside a traditional cheese pie, a portobello pesto pizza, and another topped with chicken and sun dried tomatoes, they also serve the Pittsburgh Pierogie Pizza. Try it with their dark lager, Pious Monk Dunkel (4.3% ABV), or go bold and ask for a pint of their rotating stout. Fans of the dunkel might also want to consider the Wild Boar BBQ Pizza topped with red onion, corn, and slow-roasted pulled wild boar in a barbecue sauce made with the malty beer. The kitchen at the Church goes beyond the predictable bar food options, however. Buffalo meatloaf in a roasted tomato demi glace is served with sautéed mushrooms and pesto potatoes while the braised chicken Madrid comes with polenta, smoked pineapple, and a celery, radish, and fennel salad on the side. Mad Brewer Maibock (7% ABV), a beer that's won bronze, gold, and two silver medals at the Great American Beer Fest, might balance some of the intense flavors in the latter. And don't skip dessert. A simple bowl of vanilla ice cream drizzled with a sweet cinnamon and lager syrup is simply too good to miss.

If you enjoy craft spirits as much as you like craft beer, you'll want to stick around in Pittsburgh long enough to visit the Strip District and Wigle Whiskey (412-224-2827; www.wiglewhiskey.com). Open six days a week for cocktails, drams, or sample flights of their organic white rye whiskey, white wheat whiskey, and ginever, Wigle also offers hour-long guided tours on Saturdays. On 39th Street and Penn Avenue, Arsenal Cider House and Wine Cellar (412-260-6968; www.arsenalciderhouse.com) is a third place to go for a sample of Pittsburgh's liquid culture. For a different perspective of the city, rent a boat from Kayak Pittsburgh (412-969-9090; www.kayakpittsburgh.org) and paddle under the bridges on the Allegheny River for an hour or two. Don't worry about reservations, just walk up, get in, and enjoy views of the skyline, Point State Park, and Heinz Field, home of the Steelers. When you're back on solid ground, make your way to one of the four Carnegie Museums of Pittsburg (412-622-3131; www.carnegiemuseums.org), whether it's the Science Center, the Museum of Art, the Museum of Natural History, or the Warhol. See European works of art from the sixteenth and seventeenth centuries, Andy Warhol film and video from the '60s and '70s, or dinosaur fossils millions of years old.

CONTACT

3525 Liberty Avenue
Pittsburgh, PA 15201
412-688-8200
www.churchbrew.com
@ChurchBrewWorks

TASTING ROOM HOURS:

Mon-Thu, 11:30am-11pm;
Fri-Sat, 11:30am-Midnight;
Sun, Noon-9pm

LODGING:

The Priory Hotel
614 Pressley Street
Pittsburgh, PA 15212
412-231-3338
www.thepriory.com

DOCK STREET
BREWING COMPANY

YEAR FOUNDED: 1985

FOUNDERS:
Rosemarie Certo (and earlier Jeffrey Ware)

ANNUAL PRODUCTION:
1,200 barrels

**YEAR-ROUND &
SEASONAL BEERS:** Rye IPA, Man Full of Trouble Porter, Royal Bohemian Pilsner, Bubbly Wit, Barley Wine, Little Prince Stout, Devil's Double IPA, Illuminator Dopplebock, Born Again Tripel

LOCAL FLAVOR: Before becoming the second home of Dock Street, the historic brick firehouse in Cedar Park served as the neighborhood's farmers market.

Scattered across the Northeast from Lake Champlain to the Chesapeake Bay, observant travelers will find a number of fine brewpubs, quiet yet committed to slaking the thirst of their respective communities. Many of them are worth visiting. But Philadelphia's Dock Street, reborn in the Cedar Park neighborhood after starting out near Logan Square downtown, has a unique distinction: the endorsement of the late Michael Jackson, still regarded as an authority on the great beers of the world. The brainchild of Rosemarie Certo and her husband, Jeffrey Ware, the business caught the first craft beer wave in 1985 and became the first brewpub in the City of Brotherly Love. Over the next decade it grew into a nationally recognized brand and the partners decided to sell. Certo, who spent her early childhood in Sicily in a family of winemakers and olive oil makers, decided to buy Dock Street back in 2004, making its new home an old Italianate-style firehouse built in 1928. Today the brewpub shares the building with a community acupuncture center and a bike shop. As a gourmet cook and a lover of food, she's also succeeded in turning the second incarnation into one of Philadelphia's best places for wood-fired pizza.

Stepping into Dock Street from busy Baltimore Avenue, you'll likely see the slate-topped Man Full of Trouble Bar first. That or the wood burning stove, just to the left of the entrance. Cement floors and thick, tiled walls keep it cooler and quieter inside, and soft light from the many exterior windows shines on tables occupied by professors, punks, and students from the University of Pennsylvania. Behind the bar, two big copper kettles gleam from behind their own window. It's not a huge seating area, but high ceilings keep it from ever feeling too crowded. Six rotating beers on draft greet visitors from a chalkboard, all of which are available in growlers for $14-$16 plus the price of the container if you arrive without one. To try any of the house beers for a dollar less than usual, turn up any weeknight during Happy Hour 4-6 p.m. Tuesday nights are movie nights with discounts on pizza and beer. Dock Street does give tours of the brewhouse for small groups, but these need to be scheduled in advance by phone or email.

Continuity over time can be important to a brewery and helps with brand recognition. So as much as experimentation is a part of Dock Street's identity, they have also kept a few favorites from the beginning. Along with an amber ale and a beer called St. Albans Ale of Health Strength, Royal Bohemian Pilsner (5% ABV) was one of their first beers, and it remains in the lineup today. This soft, golden lager is well suited to many of the items on the pub's menu and, along with Illuminator Dopplebock (7.5% ABV), comes highly recommended by Michael Jackson. If Dock Street has a flagship beer, it's Rye IPA (6.8% ABV), a coppery liquid with gold highlights and lots of spicy flavor due to

aggressive hopping and a percentage of rye malt. It's frequently brewed twice a week. Fermented with Champagne yeast, Bubbly Wit (7.1% ABV) is a cloudy, grassy witbier with prominent coriander notes, a whisper of pepper in the background, and a fairly clean, dry finish, providing an interesting twist on a familiar style. In the last few years, the brewery has also collaborated with the Four Seasons Hotel Philadelphia to release an annual series called Beer Four All Seasons. Past examples have included Crackle and Squeeze brewed with pink and black pepper as well as Meyer lemon, and O. P. Yum, a wheat beer with oats and pomegranate.

Diners at Dock Street can order char-grilled burgers and hand-cut fries, but brick oven pizza is really the way to go here. The Fig Jam pie with mozzarella, gorgonzola, crumbled applewood smoked bacon, and gooey fruit is a standout, and a wonderful partner to a flute of crisp Bohemian Pilsner (5% ABV) and its gentle honey sweetness. From the vegetarian side, the Florentine, topped with spinach, sliced tomatoes, mozzarella, crème fraiche, and crispy leeks wants for nothing except a pint of spicy Rye IPA. For dessert, the choice is easy. Pick either tiramisu or a cannoli and, assuming you're not in a hurry, order a Man Full of Trouble Porter (6% ABV) to go with it. There's also another option for night owls on Fridays and Saturdays: share an appetizer plate to quiet your stomach and then stay until just before closing time to get a slice and a beer for under seven bucks. Elsewhere in Philadelphia, the restaurant, bar, and music venue called Johnny Brenda's (215-739-9684; www.johnnybrendas.com) keeps Dock Street beers in their mix of all-draft, all-local beer.

Sure, you can wait in line to see the Liberty Bell and Independence Hall, but there's more to Philadelphia's colonial history than State Houses and musical instruments.

As it turns out, the Founders liked their ale, too. So don't miss the City Tavern Restaurant (215-413-1443; www.citytavern.com) at Second Street and Walnut. During the First Continental Congress in 1774, the original tavern, which was partially destroyed by fire and then demolished in the nineteenth century, served as the unofficial meeting place for the delegates. Stop in for a break during a visit to some of the other highlights in the Center City. Overlooking the Schuylkill River, the Philadelphia Museum of Art (215-763-8100; www.philamuseum. org) and the associated Rodin Museum (www.rodinmuseum.org) are two of the city's biggest magnets for art lovers. From the second-largest collection of arms and armor in the United States to three centuries of American art, and numerous special exhibitions every year, the Philadelphia Museum of Art has some of the most impressive visual art galleries on the East Coast. When you start to feel as if you've spent too much time indoors, seek out Fairmount Park (215-683-0200; www. phila.gov/parksandrecreation), more than 9,000 acres of green space.

CONTACT

701 South 50th Street
Philadelphia, PA 19143
215-726-2337
www.dockstreetbeer.com
@DockStreetBeer

TASTING ROOM HOURS:

Mon-Thu, 3-11pm;
Fri-Sat, Noon-1am

LODGING:

Cornerstone Bed & Breakfast
3300 Baring Street
Philadelphia, PA 19104
215-387-6065
www.cornerstonebandb.com

EAST END
BREWING COMPANY

YEAR FOUNDED: 2004

FOUNDER:
Scott Smith

ANNUAL PRODUCTION:
2,500-3,000 barrels

**YEAR-ROUND &
SEASONAL BEERS:** Monkey Boy,
Session Ale, Big Hop IPA, Fat Gary Nut
Brown Ale, Black Strap Stout, East End
Witte, Pedal Pale Ale, Big Hop Harvest
Ale, Snow Melt Winter Ale, The Bitter End,
Honey Heather, Gratitude Barleywine,
Coffee Porter, Steelcut Oatmeal Stout

LOCAL FLAVOR: East End's
brewhouse comes from the Foundry Ale
Works, another small Pittsburgh brewery
that went out of business in 2004.

When Scott Smith first tried to sell kegs of his Big Hop IPA to restaurants and bars in Pittsburgh, he often heard some version of the same basic tune: we're not really into food beers. He had worked long hours at a Fortune 500 company for years, but when he moved back to his hometown, he decided his future was with beer. Armed with nine years of homebrewing experience and a background in engineering, he dove headfirst into his new occupation, building out much of his first brewhouse on his own when he couldn't get contractors to show up. In his words, the initial phase of the East End Brewing Company involved a lot of long, dark days. At the time, Penn Brewing and Church Brew Works were about the only craft brewers in the city, and a few brewpubs had recently closed. He stuck by his IPA, though, and poured his energy into educating people until they came around to his (at the time) draft-only products. Now he has a small staff, a larger brewing space, a range of beers that exceeds thirty varieties, and bars and restaurants that are coming to him.

Before moving to Julius Street and adding the tasting room in 2012, a visit to East End to pick up a growler was an unglamorous affair. His brewery's new home isn't vastly more attractive from the outside, but it is somewhat easier to find and the interior is a huge improvement. Smith shares the space with The Common Place Coffee Company so the low-ceilinged room actually has two bars, one for coffee and another for beer. For a $3 deposit, you can have your own East End growler, and for another $9-$18, Smith or one of his employees will fill it with your beer of choice; taste as much as you want before parting with your hard-earned cash. Without food of some kind, which he doesn't want to deal with, Smith can't sell full pints, and without seating, you probably aren't going to linger for hours anyway. Pick up a bag of Black Strap Stout cake mix, ask for a growler of the same or even Snow Melt Winter Ale, and do a little beer baking when you get home. Adding to the fun, visitors will usually find four or five brewery-only beers on tap in the Tasting Room.

Smith brews five beers year-round, including Big Hop IPA (5.8% ABV). A big part of its appeal is lots of citrusy (think grapefruit, pomelo, or even kumquat) flavor without a distracting amount of bitterness. It has become East End's most popular offering. Rounding out the starting five is a session ale, a nut brown, a stout, and Monkey Boy (5% ABV), a Hefeweizen brewed with floral, delicately spicy Saaz hops, a pale Pilsen malt and flaked wheat to give it color and body, as well as a German yeast strain that makes it smell like, well, bananas. Alongside these core beers he mixes in half a dozen seasonal releases, ales like Snow Melt (7% ABV), a dark drink with a medium body, a nip of woody hop flavor, and a mystery spice. But the best reason to turn up in Pittsburgh is the chance to try the things that don't get bottled, beers like Honey Heather (4% ABV), made with heather tips and local honey that give it an aroma akin to a field of wildflowers.

Even if food critics on either coast usually leave it off of their "Where to Eat" lists, Pittsburgh does have an interesting restaurant scene, and a thriving one at that. Salt of the Earth (412-441-7258; www.saltpgh.com) on Penn Avenue is one of the more recent additions, offering dishes like duck pho and soft shell crab with tomatillo, hominy, and hot sauce. Try the latter with Pedal Pale Ale (5.4% ABV) or The Bitter End (3.8% ABV), a small or session beer with lots of piney, grapefruity bitterness minus the boozy wallop of bigger IPAs. In Lawrenceville, Cure (412-252-2595; www.curepittsburgh.com) relies on Pennsylvania farmers and food producers for a menu that leans Mediterranean. What this means for the diner is a different list of starters and mains nearly every week. For excellent wood-fired pizza, handmade pasta, and just about any East End beer you might want to drink, look no further than Piccolo

Forno (412-622-0111; www.piccolo-forno.com) near Arsenal Park. The BYOB policy at this popular Tuscan-style ristorante means you can (and should) fill a growler with Fat Gary Nut Brown (3.7% ABV) and ask for a Salsiccia e Cipolle pie: crushed tomatoes, fresh mozzarella, sausage, onions, and roasted fennel. If you're going to order tiramisu for dessert, you'd better pick up a bottle of Eye Opener (5.6% ABV), East End's roasty coffee porter, too.

With a limited amount of time to spend, Point State Park (412-565-2850; www.dcnr. state.pa.us/stateparks) at the confluence of Pittsburgh's Three Rivers is a pleasant spot to stretch out on the lawn, stroll along the waterfront, or toss a Frisbee. The Fort Pitt Museum and the Fort Pitt Blockhouse, the oldest structure in western Pennsylvania, fall within the boundaries of the park, too. Another great place for views is from the top of Mount Washington, a neighborhood once known as Coal Hill when there was nothing here but mines and rock quarries. You can drive to an overlook, but a fun way to reach the low summit is to ride the historic Dusquene Incline (412-381-1665; www.duquesneincline.org) or the nearby Monongahela Incline, the oldest continually operating funicular in the country. Those fascinated by building design might want to look into a guided or self-guided Architectural Walking Tour with the Pittsburgh

History & Landmarks Foundation (412-471-5808; www.phlf.org/phlf-tours-events). Trips cover specific neighborhoods or architects, various landmarks around the entire city, or a short, one-hour tour of H. H. Richardson's Allegheny County Courthouse, built in 1888. And of course, in this sports-loving "City of Champions", you always have the option of a football, baseball, or hockey game. 🍾

ROY PITZ
BREWING COMPANY

YEAR FOUNDED: 2008

FOUNDERS:
Jesse Rotz and Ryan Richards

ANNUAL PRODUCTION:
3,000 barrels

**YEAR-ROUND &
SEASONAL BEERS:** Old Jail Ale, Best Blonde Ale, Gobbler Lager, Lovitz Watermelon Lager, Ludwig's Revenge, White Horse Hefeweizen, Ichabod Crane's Midnight Ride, Daddy Fat Sacks, Truly Honesty Ale, Laydown Stay Down, Mind Your P's and Q's, Doc's Double Pale Ale, Ouimet Lager

LOCAL FLAVOR: In July of 1864, Confederate forces set fire to Chambersburg, burning much of the town center. The "Old Jail," a short five-minute walk from the brewery, is one of the few buildings that survived the destructive raid.

In the nineteenth century, the town of Chambersburg, Pennsylvania, had six breweries. Rumor has it that conjoined twins owned one of these businesses, a pair of brothers named Roy and Pitz. When friends Jess Rotz and Ryan Richards moved back to their hometown with the intention of starting a brewery, they looked to the past. Chambersburg lacked anything resembling a beer scene at the time, and they wanted to bring some life back to their community—they wanted to put it on the craft beer map. So they wrote a business plan, found a suitable site, and chose a name: Roy Pitz Brewing Company. Rotz and Richards had already been brewing for close to a decade, beginning in college when they had to lock friends out of their apartment to keep them away from their homebrews. But selling beer proved to be a challenge. For close to a year they went door to door at area bars, pitching their new brand and trying to convince people to buy their beer. Sales were slow at first, but quality and persistence paid off. Roy Pitz is now one of the fastest growing breweries in the state.

Built in 1906, the stocky brick building that now contains a brewery, a dance studio, and a church once functioned as a factory that made hosiery and other nylon products. Roy Pitz occupies the entire basement level, and when they carved out a tiny shop and tasting bar for visitors, it too was down the same staircase at the back of the building. A bell on a rope hangs from the ceiling in this room with instructions reading: "Ring for a Brewer." In the early days, when Rotz and Richards were busy brewing on the other side of the basement, this was the only way they knew when they had a customer. You can still sample

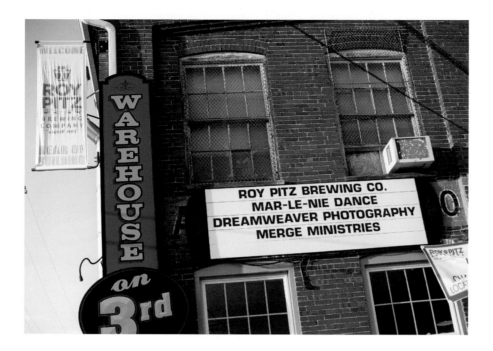

beers, make your own six-pack, or fill a growler ($10-$15) down here, but these days most of the action has moved upstairs to the Beer Stube. Designed as a place for people to sit down with a pint, the Stube serves Pennsylvania wines along with Roy Pitz beers from eight tap lines. Wood floors, tractor seat stools, and some of the original oil paintings that show up on their beer labels lend an air of rural American charm, while a Double Dragon reminds visitors to have fun, too. The pub also serves brats, paninis, and pretzels made by Richards's brother.

Rotz and Richards made their reputation brewing lighter German styles. Their first two beers were Lovitz Watermelon Lager (4.9% ABV) and White Horse Hefeweizen (5.2% ABV). Knowing Chambersburg didn't have a built-in market for craft beer, they hoped to entice crossover drinkers by brewing malt forward, sessionable beers, sneaking in a few unexpected styles later on. Ludwig's Revenge (5.2% ABV) is one such beer. Slowly pouring it into a glass shows off its deep black body and its thick head of foam—nothing too out of the ordinary here. But with the first sip, your taste buds will be greeted by a prickle of earthy hops and in the finish, a slight smokiness; two telltale signs that you're drinking a smoked porter. Their IPA, Daddy Fat Sacks (7.5% ABV) is not for timid palates, either. Rust colored with the smell of wet grain and buckwheat honey, this beer starts malty and then increases in bitterness as you work your way to the bottom of the glass. Now that they've established a following locally, Rotz and Richards have also had the freedom to introduce more challenging beers, like Mind Your P's and Q's (9% ABV), a triple-hopped Belgian-style tripel.

You'll find light fare (and local wine) at the Beer Stube, the fifty-seat brewpub above the brewery itself, but this casual spot is far from the only place in town to track down a pint of Roy Pitz. EJ's Grill (717-263-1137; www.ejsgrill.com) is a short walk from the brewery and frequently pours Best Blonde Ale (4% ABV), Ludwig's Revenge, or both. The smoky character of the latter lends itself to a pairing with one of the beef dishes on the menu. For example, try this German-style rauchbier alongside the tenderloin kabobs grilled with sweet onions, red peppers, mushrooms, and zucchini. Grilled pork chops could be a successful pairing, too. On the south side of town, the Orchards Restaurant (717-264-4711; www.orchardsrestaurant.com) offers guests more of an upscale dining experience including a full menu in the main dining area and small plates in their Civil War lounge. Request a glass of the sweet, nutty Old Jail (4.3% ABV) with a hearty entrée such as the rack of lamb. A third possibility is the Cottage Pub & Restaurant (717-264-8543; www.cottagepubandrestaurant.com), a neighborhood joint with a draft list split between macro lager and craft ale. When Best Blonde Ale, a light-bodied beer with a cracker-like taste and a hint of lemony citrus is on tap, drink it with a seafood plate like broiled haddock seasoned with Old Bay and lemon pepper.

The closest place for outdoor recreation is Caledonia State Park (717-352-2161; www.dcnr.state.pa.us/stateparks), more than a thousand acres of undeveloped land at the northern edge of the Blue Ridge Mountains. Camp overnight, swim in the outdoor pool, hike ten miles of footpaths including a section of the Appalachian Trail, or hit the links on the eighteen-hole, par 68 public golf course. Drive a little farther east and you'll reach Gettysburg National Military Park (717-334-1124; www.nps.gov/gett), the site of the bloodiest fight in the Civil War. Start at the visitor center to get an overview of the battle, and then set off on foot or by car, to see more. Book a trip with GettysBike Tours (717-752-7752; www.gettysbike.com) if you'd rather pedal your way around the park, or contact one of several local stables to tour the battlefield on horseback. Learn about Chambersburg's history at the Heritage Center (717-264-7101; www. chambersburg.org/pages/HeritageCenter) in the renovated marble bank building on Memorial Square. Admission is free and guided walking tours begin here in the summer. 🍾

CONTACT

140 North Third Street
Chambersburg, PA 17201
717-496-8753
www.roypitz.com
@roypitz

GROWLER ROOM HOURS:

Wed-Fri, 4-8pm; Sat, 1-5pm
(Tours on request)

BEER STUBE HOURS:

Tue and Thu, 3-10pm;
Fri, 3-Midnight;
Sat, Noon-Midnight;
Sun, Noon-5pm

LODGING:

The Inn at Ragged Edge
1090 Ragged Edge Road
Chambersburg, PA 17202
717-496-8372
www.theinnatraggededge.com

TIRED HANDS
BREWING COMPANY

YEAR FOUNDED: 2001

FOUNDER:
Jean Broillet IV

ANNUAL PRODUCTION:
1,000 barrels

**YEAR-ROUND &
SEASONAL BEERS:** FarmHands, HopHands, Tabel, Guillemot, Desert, Thesaurus, Foliage, Aloysius

LOCAL FLAVOR: Before Brolliet came along with his beer plans, 16 Ardmore Avenue was the offices of a doctor and a chiropractor.

In some ways, it's easier to explain what Tired Hands isn't than to explain what it is. There are no televisions, beer signs, or mugs. They don't have a rowdy beer garden out back although on warm, breezy days, they might open the windows. Founder and brewer Jean Brolliet IV refers to Tired Hands as a brewery first and foremost, but by baking their own bread, serving up local cheese, meat, and produce, and brewing just six barrels at a time, this unique spot in the Philadelphia suburbs can seem like a café with beer.

Unless you turn up twice in the same week, you'll probably be trying different beers every time you visit. Even before their first anniversary, this little brewery already had a voracious following, and you can count on eight enticing new ales on tap (plus a new cask on Fridays) each time you darken their doorstep on Ardmore Avenue. The first floor only has a few tables and bar seating. Climb the front staircase for additional seating and a second bar. Tired Hands doesn't do tasting flights but instead serves beer by the growler, in 16-ounce glasses, in 8-ounce glasses, and in 4-ounce samplers.

Brolliet does occasionally brew the same beer twice but not back to back unless it's one of his two perennials, HopHands (4.8% ABV), a pale ale with a fresh bouquet and a pronounced hoppiness, and FarmHands (4.8% ABV), a bright, dry, and expressive saison brewed with oats, rye, and wheat. For those who find HopHands too mild-mannered, check their tap list before you arrive to see if they'll be pouring Carpathian Kitten Loss (8.8% ABV), a double IPA. Mango, marmalade, and pine jump out in this beer brewed with rye malt for added spiciness. Tired Hands likes to brew single-hop beers almost as much as they enjoy releasing beers that defy categorization. 5 Out of 5 (10% ABV) turns an imperial stout on its head by adding coffee, chocolate, peanut butter, vanilla, and marshmallow. And the rare Everything Was Beautiful and Nothing Hurt (6.9% ABV) is an intriguing, full-bodied saison with a sour nose and layers of black currant and coffee flavor.

Beer is food, and the food they serve at Tired Hands is well-suited to the rustic and often barrel-aged creations that emerge from the basement. Nothing is fried or microwaved, and everything is sourced from within a hundred miles or less. Think Alpine-style cheese, duck prosciutto, spring asparagus, half-sour whiskey dill pickles, and crusty loaves of bread fermented with their own ale yeast and baked fresh daily. The thick cuts of candied bacon, double-smoked and brushed with local maple black walnut butter, are hard to resist and sell out almost every day. They also feature a handful of different toasted sandwiches, one of which is named after Broillet: Jeano's Panino. A memorable yet meatless creation well suited for the four-grain saison FarmHands, it layers young Swiss, blue cheese from Birchrun Hill Farm, a blend of haricots verts, and baby greens between two pieces of delicious bread. To satisfy your sweet tooth, order the crème brulee with Meyer lemon and mint and then pair it with something like Our Berry Vest (11.5% ABV), a strong brown ale conditioned, or brought to maturation, on copious amounts of fresh strawberries.

Northwest of Ardmore, Valley Forge National Park (610-783-1099; www.nps.gov/vafo) offers guided tours, living history demos, and a museum gallery. Around the corner from the brew-café, Human Zoom Bikes & Boards (610-649-9839; www.humanzoom.com) rents bikes by the hour, day, or weekend. Pedal around Ardmore, Bryn Marr, Haverford, and Narbeth, or take a longer ride through Fairmount Park to link up with the multi-use Schuylkill River Trail (484-945-0200; www.schuylkillrivertrail.com). Port Providence Paddle (610-935-2750; www.canoeandkayak. biz) rents canoes, kayaks, and inner tubes from the village of Port Providence. For evening entertainment head to Malvern, where the People's Light & Theater (610-644-3500; www.peopleslight.org) produces seven to nine plays each season. 🍾

CONTACT

16 Ardmore Avenue
Ardmore, PA 19003
610-896-7621
www.tiredhands.com
@tiredhandsbeer

TASTING ROOM HOURS:

Tue-Thu, 4-Midnight;
Fri, 4pm-1am; Sat, Noon-1am;
Sun, Noon-Midnight

LODGING:

Wayne Hotel
139 East Lancaster Avenue
Wayne, PA 19087
610-687-5000
www.waynehotel.com

TRÖEGS BREWING COMPANY

YEAR FOUNDED: 1997

FOUNDERS:
Chris and John Trogner

ANNUAL PRODUCTION:
50,000 barrels

**YEAR-ROUND &
SEASONAL BEERS:** JavaHead Stout,
Pale Ale, HopBack Amber, Troegenator
Double Bock, Dreamweaver Wheat,
Perpetual IPA, Nugget Nectar, Flying
Mouflan, Sunshine Pils, Dead Reckoning
Porter, Mad Elf

LOCAL FLAVOR: Before the
Trogner brothers turned it into a brewery,
the building at 200 East Hersheypark
Drive held the famous chocolatier's mail-
order division.

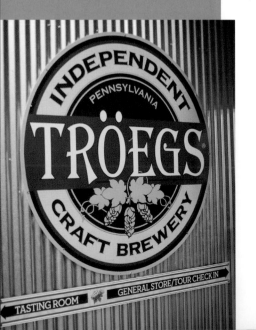

When most people hear the word Hershey, they think of chocolate. But to Chris and John Trogner, the Sweetest Place on Earth needed a small improvement. In their opinion, it lacked a certain amount of bitterness. In 2011 the brothers moved their Tröegs brewery from Harrisburg to the industrial community turned vacation destination. Today, the town that chocolate built is making its own beer. By any measure, the brothers have come a long way since their first steps into the world of beer on a little five-gallon system in Boulder, Colorado.

They now employ one hundred people, and keep their German-made brewing equipment busy seven days a week— the modern bottling line at their expanded facility fills 300 bottles a minute with the seasonal, year-round, and one-off beers bearing the Tröegs label. Equally, if not more impressive is the spacious tasting room, a soaring hall filled with long communal tables, a gourmet snack bar, and a front-row view of the gleaming stainless-steel brewhouse. Take a self-guided tour anytime during regular hours or, for $5, reserve a spot on a guided tasting tour (Tuesday through Saturday), which includes samples and a souvenir glass. And don't miss the chance to try the food. From cornmeal fried Chesapeake oysters and fondue made with their Mad Elf Ale to house-cured charcuterie and seasonal cobbler, the snack bar menu is several steps ahead of your run-of-the-mill pub grub.

The focus at Tröegs, though, will always be beer. Get a flight of all six year-rounds for $7, or try samples of any three on tap for $5. HopBack Amber Ale (6% ABV) is a bold, spicy beer that receives additional flavor when it is filtered through whole flower hops held in a straining vessel. JavaHead Stout (7.5% ABV) also passes through the hop back, but is filtered through hops and ground coffee beans from St. Thomas Roasters in

CONTACT
200 East Hersheypark Drive
Hershey, PA 17033
717-534-1297 x102
www.troegs.com
@TroegsBeer

TASTING ROOM HOURS:
Sun-Wed, 11am-9pm;
Thu-Sat, 11am-10pm

LODGING:
The Inn at Westwynd Farm
1620 Sand Beach Road
Hummelstown, PA 17036
717-533-6764
www.westwyndfarminn.com

Harrisburg. Besides the figgy, full-bodied Mad Elf Ale, Nugget Nectar (7.5% ABV), a bigger, badder version of their amber ale, tends to be the other popular seasonal release. The Scratch series, meanwhile, is an ongoing range of experimental beers made in very small batches. Impending Descent (10.9% ABV), a thick, bittersweet, midnight-black Russian imperial stout brewed to coincide with the world's end on 12/12/12 is one such memorable example. Pick one you like and fill up a growler ($16 empty) or grab a six-pack in the gift shop.

If you're in the area for more than just a brewery visit, linger over a meal or two in Hershey, Harrisburg, or maybe little Hummelstown. Just over a mile from Tröegs, Harvest restaurant at the historic Hotel Hershey (717-533-2171; www.thehotelhershey.com) offers a menu featuring local ingredients and always has something from their beer-brewing neighbor on draft. On Thursdays, the more casual Gas Station Kitchen and Bar (717-566-5086; www.thegasstation.us) in Hummelstown gives diners the chance to try Tröegenator Double Bock (8.2% ABV) with smoked prime rib and smashed potatoes for a reasonable $10. In downtown Harrisburg, Home 231 (717-232-4663; www.home231.com) relies on small farmers for their meat, eggs, and seasonal produce.

A visit to Hershey obviously offers the chance to have a similar experience with one of the most famous candy brands on the planet. At Hershey's Chocolate World (717-534-4900; www.hersheys.com/chocolateworld), take a Chocolate Tasting Adventure, create your own candy bar, or ride through Chocolate Town on a trolley tour. In Harrisburg, history buffs will find it easy to spend hours wandering through the National Civil War Museum (717-260-1861; www.nationalcivilwarmuseum.org) while across the Susquehanna River in York County, Roundtop Mountain Resort (717-432-9631; www.skiroundtop.com) has skiing, snowboarding, and snow tubing in the winter, and paintball, ziplining, and chairlift rides in the spring, summer, and fall. 🍾

TURKEY HILL
BREWING COMPANY

YEAR FOUNDED: 2011

OWNER:
Andrew Pruden

ANNUAL PRODUCTION:
600 barrels

YEAR-ROUND & SEASONAL BEERS: Barn Dance Blonde Ale, Urban Abbey Apricot Wheat, St. Abban's Irish Red Ale, Fort Wheelers Stronghold Ale, Revelation Pale Ale, DortMoose Exchange, Journeyman IPA, 60 Schillings Scottish Ale, Iron Street Porter, Group Therapy ESB

LOCAL FLAVOR: The Inn at Turkey Hill has grown over the years to include several buildings, beginning with the 1839 farmhouse that contains the original rooms.

Outside of greater Philadelphia, beyond the edges of Amish country, and west of the Delaware River, Pennsylvania's breweries and brewpubs begin to thin out a bit. Even on a carefully mapped beer tour you might drive an hour or two between stops. You might even need somewhere to stay overnight. Enter Turkey Hill. A short detour from the interstate in the town of Bloomsburg, this young brewpub is an extension of the Inn at Turkey Hill next door. The planning and construction of the brewery took longer than expected, complicated by a windstorm that flattened the 1839 barn intended to be the nucleus of the new operation. When the replica barn that took its place was finally finished though, diners and beer enthusiasts flocked to Turkey Hill, eager to sample its food and drink. When it comes to the beer, Donny Abraczinskas is in charge. A former college linebacker and a fourth-generation Christmas tree farmer, he had been a homebrewer for about twenty-five years when Turkey Hill's owners approached him about helping to establish a small brewery. If you happen to be there on a weeknight and spot a tall gray-haired guy at the bar with his nose in a glass, it's probably Donny. Go say "hello."

At a glance, the brewpub almost looks like it's in the historic barn after all. Large timbers and plank flooring were saved from the original structure and utilized in the rebuilding. Downstairs, the beer taps are resting on a replica of the original grain bin. The tabletops were created using reclaimed wood planks from the horse stable doors and a large antique wheat thresher sits next to the main entrance. Horseshoe coat hangers, little lanterns on each table, and other folk art accents continue the rural theme. A 180-seat restaurant, Turkey Hill has a bar with ten taps and a beer engine on the lower level and another bar with ten tap lines in the main dining area upstairs. A taste alone won't cost anything, but a six-beer sampler with a more substantial pour is just under $7. They don't bottle their beers, but you can fill a growler to go for $12-$16. In the upper restaurant, musicians playing jazz, folk, bluegrass, and blues often provide entertainment. For visitors who might want to take advantage of the accommodations, the Inn at Turkey Hill offers a Room and a Brew (add $65) package throughout the year.

Abraczinskas's beer journey began at a wedding in the 1980s when he tasted his first English bitter. When he got home after the reception, he tracked down a brewing magazine and took the proverbial plunge. At Turkey Hill his philosophy is to introduce people to unfamiliar styles without being heavy handed with hops, specialty grains, or alcohol content. With ten taps to work with, he and assistant brewer Jim Coulter have some flexibility, but always devote fermenter space to Revelation Pale Ale (5.4% ABV), Barn Dance Blonde (4.5% ABV), and Journeyman IPA (7.7% ABV). Their most sessionable beer, Barn Dance has a grassy aroma, a biscuity malt character, and some faint bitterness in the finish. Journeyman turns the hop channel up a few notches, perhaps appropriately so given that it takes its name from a song by Jethro Tull, Abraczinskas's favorite band. Other beers that pop up regularly include a hazy, unfiltered German Hefeweizen called Token to Hoboken (5.7% ABV) and an amber Vienna lager (5.2% ABV).

In the Pub and Grille at Turkey Hill, beer is anything but an afterthought. Besides the offerings on draft in the main dining area and at the downstairs bar, beer turns up on the menu, appearing in the queso sauce and chipotle mustard that accompany the soft pretzels, adding a little extra character to the broccoli, bacon, and cheddar soup, and even serving as an ingredient in their pizza dough. For a pairing that's big on flavor and well suited to those who like a little bite to their daily bread, match the Five Spice Sweet Potato and Duck Flatbread with a pint of Revelation, a medium-bodied beer that brings plenty of hop flavor and aroma without going overboard. A Midsummer Night's Saison (6.8% ABV), with a touch of orange peel and suggestion of spice, could be nice with this pizza, too. On cooler evenings in Bloomsburg, the Shepherd's Pie filled with ground beef and lamb, onions, peas, carrots, and mashed potatoes in a wild mushroom and porter gravy is hard to pass up on. In this case, the obvious match is Lightstreet Porter (4.9% ABV), but you might decide to compare this pairing against the bolder American Extra Stout. Turkey Hill doesn't currently distribute their beer, although following Route 11 south along the Susquehanna will lead you to two other brewpubs: Old Forge in Danville (570-275-8151 ; www.oldforgebrewingcompany.com) and Selin's Grove Brewing in Selinsgrove (570-374-7308; www.selinsgrovebrewing.com).

Of the variety of reasons to visit central Pennsylvania, one of the best is to simply escape for a couple of days. Drive to the country, slow down, and appreciate the scenery. In this rural part of the state, no fewer than twenty-five covered bridges survive more than a century after their construction, scattered across Columbia and Montour counties. One of them, a short distance from the brewery, is especially remarkable. The East and West Paden Bridges stand as one of two remaining twin covered bridges in the country. Find your way to this historic structure and others like it by using the free driving map published by the Columbia-Montour Visitors Bureau (800-847-4810;

www.itourcolumbiamontour.com). But if waterfalls hold more appeal than bridges, continue driving north from Bloomsburg to Ricketts Glen State Park (570-477-5675; www.dcnr.state.pa.us/stateparks). Here, within thousands of acres of protected forest, twenty-four named waterfalls along Kitchen Creek splash and crash their way south from the Allegheny Plateau. Go for a swim, rent a boat to take out on Lake Jean, or set off on one of the park's many trails. For a little culture, try the Weis Center for the Performing Arts (570-577-1000; www.bucknell.edu/WeisCenter.xml) at Bucknell University.

CONTACT

991 Central Road
Bloomsburg, PA 17815
570-387-8422
www.turkeyhillbrewing.com

BREW PUB HOURS:

Mon-Thu, 4-11pm;
Fri-Sat, 4pm-Midnight;
Sun, 4-9pm

WEYERBACHER
BREWING COMPANY

YEAR FOUNDED: 1995

FOUNDERS:
Dan and Sue Weirback

ANNUAL PRODUCTION:
18,000 barrels

YEAR-ROUND & SEASONAL BEERS: Last Chance IPA, Double Simcoe IPA, Blithering Idiot, Old Heathen, Tiny, Verboten, Merry Monks, White Sun Wit, Riserva, Heresy, Insanity, Quad, Winter Ale, Imperial Pumpkin Ale, AutumnFest, Blasphemy

LOCAL FLAVOR: Sue and Dan's stable brewery was on Sixth Street, across the Lehigh River from their current location. Almost twenty years later, a group of friends has opened a brewpub on the corner of Sixth and Northampton Streets.

Whether or not it qualifies as a religious experience, the fact still remains: Weyerbacher was born in a stable. While on vacation in Vermont, Dan and Sue Weirback paid a visit to a then very young Long Trail Brewing Company. On the drive home, the gears began to turn. Dan, a homebrewer, had been looking for a career change, and was excited after seeing a craft brewery from the inside. When Sue floated the idea of starting their own brewery, he agreed immediately. When they began selling their beers two years later as Northampton County's first microbrewer, they played it safe, sticking to English styles. Another two years went by before they released a big beer, a Raspberry Imperial Stout. The decision turned out to be a pivotal moment. Blithering Idiot Barleywine came next, and they were off to the races, carving out a niche as a brewer of strong, full-flavored beers.

Today Weyerbacher occupies a modern production facility. For a time, visitors got an unembellished look into the business of beer. Lacking a dedicated public space, Weyerbacher's visitor center essentially consisted of a little bar and a desk in one of their receiving bays. With their most recent expansion however, they've added a large tasting room and retail shop with a bigger bar, seats, and snacks. For those who want to step over hoses, dodge forklifts, and ogle racks of barrel-aging beers, they still offer tours on a regular basis. Any of the ten to fifteen beers on tap in the tasting room can be purchased in a growler ($11 to $28), but this is also a good place to track down elusive bottles of Brewer's Select Beers.

This is not a brewery to visit if you're hunting for light-bodied session beers. Blithering Idiot (11.1% ABV) pours with a reddish or mahogany body and offers wine-like tannins, tart cranberry, alcohol heat, and a slight nuttiness in the nose. And if this isn't a bold enough beer for you, try Insanity (11.1% ABV), Blithering Idiot Barleywine aged in bourbon casks. After Merry Monks, Imperial Pumpkin (8% ABV) is their most popular offering. An opaque orange with a thin off-white head, this sweet, squashy beer has cinnamon and nutmeg aromas and relies on earthy hops and cardamom to prevent it from drifting into cloying territory. Every year Weyerbacher also releases a dependably interesting anniversary beer.

Given the high ABV of many of Weyerbacher beers, a food pairing is a good idea for those who have made plans for later in the day. At Pearly Baker's Alehouse (610-253-9949; www.pearlybakers.net) in Easton's Centre Square, you might find a year-round offering like Merry Monks or the occasional Brewers' Select beer such as Zulu (3.4% ABV), a light-bodied wheat ale with a tart character and dry finish produced by the introduction of lactic acid bacteria. On the other side of Northampton Street, Valenca Restaurant (610-923-5142; www.valencaonthesquare.com) has held beer vs. wine pairing dinners with Weyerbacher in the past. The more casual Porter's Pub (610-250-6561; www.porterspubeaston.com) regularly taps kegs from Easton's own, too.

On a hot and humid summer day, head northwest to the Lehigh River where Whitewater Rafting Adventures (800-876-0285; www.adventurerafting.com) and Pocono Whitewater (570-325-3655; www.poconowhitewater.com) offer guided rafting, kayaking, and biking trips in Lehigh Gorge State Park. During the winter months, the Blue Mountain Ski Area and Camelback Mountain Resort (570-629-1661; www.skicamelback.com) are two of the closest places to hit the slopes. And in Nazareth, not much more than a twenty-minute drive from the brewery, C. F. Martin & Co. (610-759-2837; www.martinguitar.com), one of the country's oldest manufacturers of musical instruments, conducts factory tours five days a week. 🍾

CONTACT

905-G Line Street
Easton, PA 18042
610-559-5561
www.weyerbacher.com
@Weyerbacher

TASTING ROOM HOURS:

Mon-Sat, Noon-7pm
(Tours Fri & Sat)

LODGING:

Lafayette Inn
525 West Monroe Street
Easton, PA 18042
610-253-4500
www.lafayetteinn.com

PROVIDENCE
The Trinity Brewhouse

NEWPORT
Newport Storm Brewery

WESTERLY
Grey Sail Brewing

RHODE ISLAND

GREY SAIL
BREWING

YEAR FOUNDED: 2012

FOUNDERS:
Jennifer and Alan Brinton

ANNUAL PRODUCTION:
1,500 barrels

**YEAR-ROUND &
SEASONAL BEERS:** Flagship Ale,
Flying Jenny Extra Pale Ale, Hazy Day
Belgian Wit, Autumn Winds Fest Beer,
Leaning Chimney Smoked Porter

LOCAL FLAVOR: In 1892, more
than half of Westerly's 7,000 residents
were involved in the granite industry,
quarrying and sculpting blue, pink, and
red stone into monuments and statues
that still stand in parks and cemeteries
in forty-two states.

If you turn up in Westerly with a thirst for beer, try the old macaroni factory first. As a single-story brick building on Canal Street, it doesn't necessarily stand out from its surroundings, but the large, floor-to-ceiling windows on either side of the entrance allow passers-by to see right in. The first thing you might notice is the large, colorful mural depicting a pair of brewers at work, and then, as your eyes slowly absorb the scene, you'll probably see the small bar in front of it, perhaps with a few thirsty visitors gathered around. This is Grey Sail Brewing. Noticing the relative lack of craft beer produced in Rhode Island and realizing that Westerly's summer community presented an opportunity for a new business, Jennifer and Alan Brinton decided to open their brewery in a town that has previously been an important center of fishing and later, granite quarrying. So while Grey Sail's approachable cream ale might have appealed to a working population in the past, today it's a light and somewhat sweet beer for Westerly's seasonal beachgoers.

Although the tasting area at the brewery isn't a gigantic one, this cheery, light-filled space is a relaxing environment in which to sample the beers on tap. In the late afternoon the room glows with the setting sun, and a handful of seats offer an alternative to standing at the bar for the duration of your visit. Separated from the production space by a low wall and somewhat elevated above the street level, it also affords a good view of the conical fermenters, the stainless-steel brewhouse, and even the leaning chimney that inspired the name of Grey Sail's smoked porter. They probably won't charge for a sip or two, and short casual tours are free of charge, but if you want to taste your way through their full range of beers, be prepared to spend $5. And until the state changes its liquor laws, visitors have to head to one of the bottle shops in town to buy something they liked—breweries in Rhode Island can't yet sell directly to consumers. You will, however, find T-shirts, golf shirts, hats, and koozies for sale if you happen to like the look of Grey Sail's stylized, maritime-themed logo.

Light- to medium-bodied with a deep gold or metallic orange color, a Honey Nut Cheerios aroma, and an herbal finish, Autumn Winds (5.8% ABV) is a well-executed example of a German Oktober-fest beer with a low level of bitterness and a measured degree of malt sweetness. In contrast, Flying Jenny Extra Pale Ale (6% ABV) is a beer that puts hops first. Goldenrod or pale copper color with a rocky, off-white head, lots of pine and fruit on the nose, and flavors of pineapple, star fruit, and pomelo, this is a very drinkable, medium-bodied ale with a round, citrusy bitter side, not unlike a tart key lime pie. Bolder still, Leaning Chimney Smoked Porter (6% ABV) smells like chocolate and peat and will probably impress fans of Laphroaig single malt whisky. Rich and full-bodied, this sepia-colored beer leaves a slightly bitter aftertaste. Grey Sail has also done some experimenting already, releasing a sour pumpkin ale

called Gourdemyces (a creative example of this style) as well as a Flanders-style red made with sour cherries called Ciel Rouge a Nuit (5% ABV). Other successful one-off beers include Bring Back the Beach, a hoppy blonde ale with a peachy aromas.

Walking distance from the brewery on High Street, the Malted Barley (401-315-2184; www.themaltedbarleyri.com) can be counted on for fresh pints of Flying Jenny. They also serve seven different kinds of pretzels made in-house along with pretzel sandwiches and even a few pretzel desserts. Order a warm, salted knot of baked dough with apricot butter and notice how well it pairs with the snappy extra pale

ale and its pithy, citrusy bitterness. A block away, 84 Tavern on Canal (401-596-7871; www.84highstreet.com) features a handful of shandies and beer cocktails as well as twenty-four draft lines—half a dozen of which are usually devoted to breweries from Connecticut and Rhode Island. When Flagship Ale (4.5% ABV) is on tap, try this light-bodied and honey sweet cream ale with one, two, or three deep-dish Dutch apple pancakes for brunch. If you need an appetizer, share an order of salty, crispy, fried oysters. Overlooking the Pawcatuck River, Bridge Restaurant & Bar (401-348-9700; www.restaurantinri.com) is the place to seek out in Westerly for a fine dining experience. Find a shady table outside at the Duck Bar and snack on clam and corn fritters or shrimp tacos with an unfiltered Hazy Day (4% ABV).

Located just off the interstate on the Connecticut State line, Grey Sail is within easy striking distance from Mystic Seaport (860-572-0711; www.mysticseaport.org).

Founded in 1929 as one of the country's first living history museums, Mystic centers on a recreated nineteenth-century fishing village and is famous for its impressive collection of historic vessels, including the world's last surviving wooden whaling ship. The museum also hosts a seaport music festival every June. To see Westerly from the seat of a bicycle, stop at Napatree Bikes (401-348-6317; www.napatreebikes.com) to rent a beach cruiser for the day. Point your borrowed wheels south and follow the Watch Hill Road to Watch Hill Beach and Napatree Point. Stretching for approximately two miles along the Block Island Sound, this beach features an antique carousel, and out on the point, the Watch Hill Lighthouse (www.watchhilllighthousekeepers.org), a granite tower that has aided ships at sea since 1856. A small museum is open on Tuesdays and Thursdays between July first and Labor Day. To explore the Ocean State's scenic coastline from the water, head to the Kayak Center of Rhode Island (401-364-8000; www.kayakcentre.com) in Charlestown Beach and rent a boat or join a guided tour. 🍶

CONTACT

63 Canal Street
Westerly, RI 02891
401-315-2533
www.greysailbrewing.com
@GreySail

TASTING ROOM HOURS:
Sat, 1-5pm

LODGING:
Villa Bed and Breakfast
190 Shore Road
Westerly, RI 02891
401-596-1054
www.thevillaatwesterly.com

NEWPORT STORM BREWERY

YEAR FOUNDED: 1999

FOUNDERS:
Brent Ryan, Derek Luke, Mark Sinclair, and Will Rafferty

ANNUAL PRODUCTION:
4,000 barrels

YEAR-ROUND & SEASONAL BEERS: Hurricane Amber Ale, Rhode Island Blueberry Ale, India Point Ale, Summer Hefeweizen, Winter Porter, Marzen Lager Oktoberfest, Spring Irish Red Ale

LOCAL FLAVOR: In 1769, Newport County had twenty-two distilleries, giving it a reputation as a rum capital. When the brewery decided to launch the Thomas Tew Rum brand, they became the first distillery to operate in Rhode Island since 1842.

Good friends and good beer. Simple and satisfying, this time-tested combination dates back centuries upon centuries and by no mere accident has ended up in the advertising language of many a brewery, too. It also happens to be the shortest way to tell the story of Newport Storm. Four friends met at college in Maine (three of whom were New Englanders, with the fourth hailing from the West Coast), began homebrewing, and then, shortly after graduating from Colby with science degrees, decided they should probably keep making beer and go into business together. When they weren't studying or working on their own recipes, they found inspiration in pints of handcrafted ale from some of the forerunners of Maine's beer scene: Shipyard, D. L. Geary's, and Gritty McDuff's. Things got off to a modest start, with the foursome running their fledgling company from a pair of bays in a Middletown industrial park, but after two years of brewing nothing but amber ale for a growing number of draft accounts, they could say they'd built a loyal following and created demand for what is still their most popular beer.

Since moving to their current location in 2010, Newport Storm has become a much more welcoming place for beer fans with a small gift shop, a handsome tasting bar, and a second-floor balcony overlooking the brewhouse. Two oversized nautical charts of Narragansett Bay hang next to the bar, adding a bit of maritime flare to the otherwise subdued décor. A large window in the back wall also looks out on the action on the production floor, whether it's bottling, kegging, or the most important step at any brewery: cleaning. Here at the Nutmeg State's largest brewery, $7.49 buys visitors a souvenir glass and a sample of four beers on tap. For another $9.63, you can also

sample Thomas Tew Rum at all three stages of the distilling process. On quieter days, one of the brewers might even pop in to field questions for a little while. Guided tours begin at 3 p.m. and include a brief history of the brewery, a bit of background on the founders, and additional information about the beers themselves. Plus, Newport Storm has continued their tradition of holding an open house of sorts called Fridays at Six. Be one of the first fifty people to sign up online, arrive early, and hand over your ID at the door for a free, ninety-minute beer tasting each week.

Hurricane Amber Ale (5.2% ABV) paved the way—or perhaps, cleared a path—for Newport Storm, relying on a trio of malt varieties to give it a medium body, a toasty aroma, and a caramel sweetness moderated by a light-handed dose of hops. While other beers dazzle with their individuality, this ale is meant to be a sessionable companion for any occasion. Which makes India Point Ale (6.5% ABV) the yin to Hurricane's yang. Six types of hops, including a locally grown portion of the piney Chinook variety, end up lending their flavors and aromas to this pungent pale ale. Rhode Island Blueberry (4.6% ABV) is the third member of their core range, a fruity, light-bodied beer brewed with malted wheat and juice pressed from berries grown at Schartner Farms in Exeter. For a number of years now, Newport Storm has also released various one-off beers in limited quantities that they refer to collectively as the Cyclone Series. Alternating between boys' and girls' names, they've already made it through the alphabet once, and ended up with a number of popular releases in the process. Tim (6.3% ABV) for instance, was a dark wheat beer with a deep brown tone and ruby highlights. Sweet and malty with a brush of earthy bitterness in the finish, this chewy German-style Dunkleweizen had molasses aromas and a raisin bread flavor.

One of the best places to go for craft beer and food in town is Pour Judgement Bar & Grill (401-619-2115; www.pourjudgement.com) on Broadway. Drop in for lunch and have the soup du jour or a bowl of turkey chili with herb sour cream. Large and warming on a windy afternoon, the latter is improved when accompanied by Newport Storm's Winter Porter (5.9% ABV), a dark, roasty ale with a subtle hop character. On the other side of Eisenhower Park, Brick Alley Pub & Restaurant (401-849-6334; www.brickalley.com) also keeps Coastal Extreme beers in their regular rotation. At dinnertime, ask for the Cajun-seasoned T-bone pork chop on a bed of brown rice with a mustard cream sauce. To drink, have a pint of Hurricane Amber Ale. Bready with a caramel-like sweetness and a delicate level of hop spiciness, it's a versatile beer that will work with many other items on the Brick Alley menu, too. To get your seafood fix in town, look no further than Benjamin's Raw Bar (401-846-8776; www.benjaminsrawbar.com), a three-story restaurant with an open-air dining area called the Crow's Nest that offers views of the harbor. Bring a friend and some spending money and order the Mother Shucker, a platter including a dozen each of oysters, shrimp, and littlenecks in addition to a pair of lobsters and two Dungeness crabs. Pair with a refreshing Summer Hefeweizen (4.9% ABV).

From the late 1800s through the turn of the twentieth century, a period known as the Gilded Age, wealthy industrialists turned Newport into the nation's social capital, constructing enormous mansions along Bellevue Avenue. Visit some of the Newport Mansions, including the Breakers, the seventy-room "summer cottage" built by Cornelius Vanderbilt II, on a tour led by the Preservation Society of Rhode Island (401-847-1000; www.newportmansions.org). The other way to get a taste of architectural history, as well as a little fresh air, is to follow part or all of The Cliff Walk (401-845-5300; www.cliffwalk.com), a 3.5-mile National Recreational Trail that winds its way along the rocky coastline. A cruise around Newport Harbor and Narragansett Bay is another apropos activity in a town with such a rich maritime history. Operating out of Bannister's Wharf, Classic Cruises of Newport (401-847-0298; www.cruisenewport. com) runs afternoon and cocktail cruises aboard a two-mast schooner called the *Madeline* and a restored motor yacht called *Rum Runner II*, which was built in 1929 for two New Jersey mobsters. Newport is also home to the International Tennis Hall of Fame (401-849-3990; www.tennisfame.com). 🍾

CONTACT

293 JT Connell Road
Newport, RI 02840
401-849-5232
www.newportstorm.com
@NewportStorm

TASTING ROOM HOURS:

Sun-Mon & Wed-Sat, Noon-5pm
(Guided tours daily at 3pm)

LODGING:

The Attwater
22 Liberty Street
Newport, RI 02840
401-846-7444
www.theattwater.com

THE TRINITY BREWHOUSE

YEAR FOUNDED: 2012

OWNER:
Joshua Miller

ANNUAL PRODUCTION:
1,500 barrels

YEAR-ROUND & SEASONAL BEERS: Kolsch, Hefeweizen, Larkin's Irish Stout, Belgian Saison, Extra Special Bitter, Rhode Island IPA, Belgian Witbier, Mercy Brown Imperial Brown Ale, Imperial October Fest, Tommy's Red, Decadence Imperial IPA, Redrum Imperial Red, People's Porter, Scotch Ale, Russian Imperial Stout, Chocolate Milk Stout, Pumpkin Spice, Sir Perry's Pear Cider

LOCAL FLAVOR: From the late nineteenth century until 1957 when competition from national beer brands forced them to close, the James Hanley Brewing Company produced ale at the corner of Fountain and Jackson Streets in Providence.

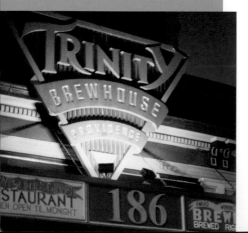

Before he got hooked on good beer, Joshua Miller was into good music. In 1975, while still in college studying for an art history degree, he and a pair of childhood friends opened The Met Café near the water in downtown Providence. Booking local musicians initially and then national acts, they worked late and partied hard. After that came the Hot Club, and then in 1994, Miller became the owner of the Trinity Brewhouse, one of the early brewpubs in New England. For almost two decades now, it's been an anchor for Rhode Island's beer scene. One of Miller's first hires was Sean Larkin, a recent graduate of the College of Culinary Arts at Johnson and Wales University. Starting in the kitchen, Larkin soon gravitated to beer side of the business and took over as head brewer in 1996. Today, in addition to continuing to serve as brewmaster, he also consults for Narragansett Brewing Company and recently helped launch Revival Brewing Company as chief brewing officer.

Great beer has the tendency to attract a following—the brewpub recently took home a bronze medal from the Great American Beer Festival for their Decadence Imperial IPA—but Trinity's central location has also been a key to its success. Midday can be quiet, but most evenings tourists and locals crowd around the bar just inside the entrance, waiting for a sample, a pint, or a refill. When it comes to décor, beer history collides with Miller's background in art and music, from cartoony, brightly colored banners imploring visitors to "Think Globally, Drink Locally," to the vintage beer serving trays on the walls and the Last Supper–inspired mural featuring Bob Marley, Beethoven, and Kurt Cobain. Start with the six-beer sampler to find your favorite Trinity beer, and then on your way out, grab a growler to go for $12 or $15, depending on which beer you choose. Any night is a good night for a pint of Providence Pilsner or Rhode Island IPA, but various weekly events make it hard to choose. On Tuesdays, Trinity hosts pub trivia in the Basement Bar; a beer, a burger, and an Irish coffee are $20 on Wednesdays; and pool is free on Sundays from 7:00 p.m. until close.

The first beers Trinity brewed were a pale, smooth, palate-pleasing kölsch and Rhode Island IPA (7.4% ABV), also referred to as Trinity IPA. The first IPA available in Rhode Island since the demise of Ballantine, this ale doesn't pull punches when it comes to bitterness. Its fruity aroma is immediately followed by a wallop of prickly, piney hops and a finish that sticks around after your glass is empty. Building on this base, Larkin has steadily added to the lineup over the years and has now released somewhere in the neighborhood of sixty different beers. The creamy, ink-black Larkin's Irish Stout (3.4% ABV), has also long been a popular favorite and delivers waves of roasted barley, cocoa powder, and the slightest pinch of charcoal to your taste buds. More recently, the brewpub has also ventured into imperial waters, creating an imperial stout, imperial brown, imperial porter, imperial red, and imperial pumpkin ale. With

nine taps to work with, Trinity always keeps lighter and darker, stronger and more sessionable beers on tap, however.

Seafood lovers will want to begin a meal at Trinity with Zuppa di Brew, a steamy helping of chorizo, onions, roasted garlic, and black shell mussels simmered in a pilsner-seafood broth. Pair it with a sample-sized pour of the tangy, medium-bodied Belgian Saison (6.5% ABV). From there, move on to a main dish like the lobster mac and cheese, penne pasta in a creamy sherry lobster sauce with sharp cheddar and chunks of succulent tail and claw meat. Crisp and balanced Tommy's Red (6.5% ABV) would be a nice pairing. The vegetarian gumbo with smoked paprika tofu is an equally delicious and arguably healthier option from the list of entrees. Unless you plan to return the following day to sample other menu items, make sure to save room for dessert. The stout brownie sundae, peanut butter pie, and chocolate truffle cake all deserve to be teamed up with Larkin's Irish Stout (3.5% ABV), a velvety, black-as-night ale with a chocolate aroma and just enough of a bitter edge in the finish. Another thought is to splurge on dessert at Local 121 (401-274-2121; www.local121.com), a newer restaurant owned by Miller that focuses on agricultural and ecological sustainability. The flavors in Mercy Brown (9% ABV) should mingle wonderfully with the spiced pear brioche bread pudding topped with walnut cream and golden raisin compote.

Because the downtown area is so compact, it's possible to get to several attractions and still have time for beer tasting during a weekend in Providence. Foodies might want to start at the Culinary Museum (401-598-2805; www.culinary.org) near Roger Williams Park. Open from Tuesday to Sunday, it houses a collection of food-related items from old photographs and menus to restaurant equipment and more than 60,000 cookbooks. When you've had enough history, stroll around the park (401-785-9450; www.providenceri.com/parks-and-rec) or see its highlights: the zoo, the botanical center, the Museum of Natural History, and Planetarium. On the same block as the brewpub, the Trinity Repertory Company (401-351-4242; www.trinityrep.com) produces a variety of theatrical performances each year, from programs with Brown University's Department of Theatre Arts to shows by Sam Shepard, Shakespeare, and Lynn Nottage. Across Fountain Street the Providence Bruins (401-273-5000; www.providencebruins.com) host their American Hockey League opponents at the 12,000-seat Dunkin Donuts Center.

CONTACT

186 Fountain Street
Providence RI 02905
401-453-BEER (2337)
www.trinitybrewhouse.com
@TrinityBrew

TASTING ROOM HOURS:

Mon-Thu, 11:30am-1am;
Fri 11:30am-2am; Sat Noon- 2am;
Sun Noon-1am

LODGING:

Christopher Dodge House
11 West Park Street
Providence, RI 02908
401-351-6111
www.providence-hotel.com

St. Albans
14th Star Brewing Co.

Greensboro
Hill Farmstead

Morrisville
Rock Art Brewery

Waterbury
The Alchemist

Shelburne
Fiddlehead
Brewing Co.

The Norwich Inn
Norwich

Bridgewater Corners
Long Trail Brewing Co.

VERMONT

14TH STAR
BREWING COMPANY

YEAR FOUNDED: 2012

FOUNDERS:
Steve Gagner and Matt Kehaya

ANNUAL PRODUCTION:
400-500 barrels

**YEAR-ROUND &
SEASONAL BEERS:** Harvest Brown,
1493 Pale Ale, Valor Ale, Honey IPA,
Roasted Porter, 802 Ale (Golden Wheat)

LOCAL FLAVOR: The Vermont Maple
Festival takes place in St. Albans each
spring, and 14th Star has the only maple sap
collection tanks in the brewing business.

The drive to Quebec is only twelve miles from St. Albans, Vermont. Canada is closer than Burlington's small but thriving beer scene. Which might explain why, in this community of 7,000 people, Steve Gagner decided to open a nanobrewery: the state's original craft brewery, the Vermont Pub & Brewery, was just too far from home. Or maybe he didn't realize that Vermont already holds the national record for most breweries per capita. Believe it or not, neither of these things affected the decision that he and friend Matt Kehaya made while they were finishing a tour of duty in Afghanistan. They knew that they both loved brewing. And they knew that they would need something to do when they got back to the United States. So, on a little green Army-issue notebook, the two soldiers sketched out the business plan that would become the blueprint for 14th Star Brewing Company.

With Kehaya's welding experience and Gagner's sheer determination to be part of a St. Albans renaissance, the two put together a one-barrel system in time to debut their beer at the annual Vermont Brewer's Festival. But first they sought advice from a few beer veterans in the fourteenth state: Vermont Pub & Brewery owner Steve Polewacyk and Zero Gravity Craft Brewery owner Paul Sayler. And they decided not to advertise, figuring if they put out the best possible product, word would eventually get out. News about 14th Star did in fact spread quickly, and almost immediately they found themselves selling out each batch days after it went on tap in their tasting room. Decorated with folk art stars and a small collection of German beer steins, the cheery space isn't big, but there is room enough for a handful of visitors to crowd in for a sixty-four-ounce growler ($3 deposit, $9 to fill) or a smaller growlette ($2 deposit, $5 to fill).

If beer is flowing from all four taps when you turn up, start with their Pale Ale (5.5% ABV), a malty example of the style that starts with a honey-like sweetness but finishes with a biscuity dryness. Next, try Valor Ale (5.5% ABV), a slightly hoppy amber ale with a crisp snap in the aftertaste. A portion of the proceeds earned from the sale of Valor Ale growlers will benefit Purple Hearts Reunited, a non-profit organization that locates and returns lost or stolen valor medals to combat veterans and their families. Harvest Brown (4.5% ABV) is the most robust beer of the bunch, with a smooth mouthfeel, a caramel sweetness, and a hint of dark chocolate. It is Honey IPA (6.6% ABV), however, made with pure Vermont honey of course, that found a local fan base the fastest.

A bit of luck might be required to find 14th Star's Harvest Brown or Honey IPA on tap in St. Albans. Check out One Federal Restaurant & Lounge (802-524-0330; www.onefederalrestaurant.com) at the corner of Federal and Lake streets. At least half of the eight taps at the bar tend to be local. Outside of St. Albans, another safe bet for eventually finding 14th Star on draft is the Farmhouse Tap & Grill in Burlington (802-859-0888; www.farmhousetg.com), a gastropub that sources most of its food from Vermont farmers and producers and also pours twenty or more draft beers.

With close to forty cheesemakers scattered across its fourteen counties, Vermont might also have more creameries per capita than any other state. Between St. Albans and Burlington in Milton, Willow Hill Farm (802-893-2963; www.sheepcheese.com) plank-ages its award-winning sheep milk cheeses in small underground caves. To burn off the beer and cheese calories, lace up a pair of hiking boots and head east to the Long Trail. A 273-mile footpath maintained by the Green Mountain Club (802-244-7037; www.greenmountainclub.org), it starts at the Massachusetts state line and continues north to Canada. 🍾

CONTACT
41 Lower Newton Street
St. Albans, VT 05478
802-393-1459
www.14thstarbrewing.com
@14thStarBrewing

TASTING ROOM HOURS:
Thu-Fri, 5-9pm;
Sun, 9am-Noon

LODGING:
The Inn at Grace Farm
117 Highbridge Road
Fairfax, VT 05454
802-242-4043
www.theinnatgracefarm.com

THE ALCHEMIST

YEAR FOUNDED: 2011

FOUNDERS:
John and Jen Kimmich

ANNUAL PRODUCTION:
9,000 barrels

**YEAR-ROUND &
SEASONAL BEERS:** Heady Topper
Double IPA

LOCAL FLAVOR: Some of the original Alchemist beers took their names from the landscape—Thatcher Brook Blonde refers to the small stream passing through Waterbury while Onion River Rye refers to the first name given to the Winooski.

For years and years, almost everyone who took Exit 10 off Vermont's Interstate 89 was either heading to the Ben and Jerry's factory or Stowe Mountain Resort, depending on the season. Since 2011, however, a steady stream of traffic has found its way to a newer attraction just off the highway, The Alchemist, a small craft brewery that has steadily accumulated a legion of fans based on the merits of a single beer. The story of the Alchemist begins in late 2003, when John Kimmich and his wife, Jen, turned a former blacksmith shop and post office into a seven-barrel brewpub after working for years at the Vermont Pub & Brewery in Burlington. Relying on cobbled-together used equipment from around the county, Kimmich tinkered with his recipes until he was completely satisfied with each beer's appearance, aroma, and taste. Soon after opening, they won their first awards, and pilgrims began turning up in Waterbury, occasionally attempting to secretly fill bottles with draft-only Heady Topper in the days before John and Jen built a cannery. At the time, Donovan's Red was their flagship beer, the double IPA one of several seasonals. When Tropical Storm Irene destroyed the brewpub in 2011, the couple chose to focus exclusively on this production brewery.

Even after a recent expansion that tripled capacity at the cannery, The Alchemist continues to sell out of their double IPA on a regular basis. This in spite of the fact that Heady Topper remains the only beer they can and distribute. Turn up on Mondays or Wednesday for your best chance to go home with a four-pack ($12) or a case (three per person) of this sought-after brew. If you're lucky enough to leave with some quantity of your quarry, pose for quick photo with your face in the can sign out front. Inside, the tasting room itself isn't large, and if you haven't tried the hoppy flagship, you'll probably want to get a free two-ounce taste before you look around. A second

tap varies from month to month, and pours beers from the pub and brewery "archive." The décor, much like the beer itself, is all about hops, right down to the hop flower light covers on the overheads that bathe the room in a greenish glow. Tours are self-guided and entail wall-mounted exhibits on the history of IPA and low-impact brewing. In the corner, a video on a seven-minute loop shows Kimmich crafting beer in the basement of his former brewpub.

Unfiltered, uncommon, and unbelievably popular, Heady Topper (8% ABV) has an apricot color, and, as advertised, quite an impressive head of foam. With six hops combining to contribute flavor and aroma, it's a juicy, unforgettable beer with notes of pink grapefruit, pine, orange zest, and passion fruit. The other year-round product made by the Alchemist isn't actually made at the Alchemist. Celia Saison (6.5% ABV), a gluten-free beer, is contract brewed off-site with sorghum, Curacao orange peel, and a hop variety from Slovenia called Celia. In the past, Celia Pale Ale and Celia Framboise took gold medals in the gluten-free category at the Great American Beer Festival. Now that Kimmich is revisiting some of his pub beers on a monthly basis, early Alchemist's fans might arrive in Waterbury to find one of their favorites on tap. Uncle Daddy (7.5% ABV), a Hefeweizen brewed with local sugar pumpkins could appear in the fall, winter might bring El Jefe (6.2% ABV), a black IPA with bite, or he could decide to reintroduce Sterk Wit (7.3% ABV), his award-winning Belgian-style double white beer with coriander.

Hard as it might be to come by across much of New England, Waterbury is always a reliable place to track down a can of Heady Topper. Prohibition Pig (802-244-4120; www.prohibitionpig.com) occupies the spot where The Alchemist brewpub once

stood, and continues to serve some of the best beers available in North America. Fresh food is made in-house daily and leans toward Southern cuisine, especially barbecue. Go whole hog and order the beef brisket—smoked for twelve hours and served with a bacon barbecue sauce—or select the healthier option, BBQ tempeh in a sweet potato sauce. Don't worry if you can't get a table at the Pig, just head down Main Street to The Reservoir (802-244-7827; www.waterburyreservoir.com), another member of the Vermont Fresh Network, with generous portions and no fewer than thirty-eight beers on tap. When Heady Topper is one of them, pair it with the tacos: fried haddock or pulled pork topped with red cabbage, pickled jalapeño, cilantro lime onions, and creamy chipotle aioli.

Good beer is worth traveling for, but there's more to Vermont than ales and lagers. Like ice cream, for instance. From the Alchemist, you can practically walk to Ben & Jerry's (802-882-1240; www.benjerry.com), the world famous cow-to-cone company known for funky flavors like Cherry Garcia and Chunky Monkey. Learn all you ever wanted to know on one of their factory tours. Turn up on a snowy day before the end of March, and you can have your ice cream and a snowshoe tour, too. On Saturday nights in July and August, they screen free movies outside. Hikers and backpackers will want to stop by the Green Mountain Club's visitor center (802-244-7037; www.greenmountainclub.org) to pick up maps, find the ideal hiking book, or admire the view of the mountains themselves with a free cup of coffee. This nonprofit organization regularly hosts educational programs and workshops, and also organizes guided hikes and backpacking trips. If kayaking or stand-up paddle boarding is more of your speed, however, visit Umiak Outdoor Outfitters (802-253-2317; www.umiak.com) to register for a river trip or an ice cream float tour.

CONTACT

35 Crossroad Road
Waterbury, VT 05676
802-244-7744
www.alchemistbeer.com
@alchemistbeer

TASTING ROOM HOURS:

Mon-Sat, 11am-7pm
(Tours self-guided)

LODGING:

The Old Stagecoach Inn
18 North Main Street
Waterbury, VT 05676
802-244-5056
www.oldstagecoach.com

FIDDLEHEAD
BREWING COMPANY

YEAR FOUNDED: 2011

FOUNDER:
Matt Cohen

ANNUAL PRODUCTION:
2,000 barrels

YEAR-ROUND & SEASONAL BEERS: Fiddlehead IPA

LOCAL FLAVOR: For a taste of fiddleheads, track down a jar made by Vermont Pickle at the Shelburne Farmer's Market or occasionally at the brewery itself.

To hear Matt Cohen tell it, he wanted to own a brewery the moment he first set foot in one. After graduating from Ithaca College with an anthropology degree, he moved to Vermont and set to work learning the beer business. Beginning at the now-defunct Shed Restaurant & Brewery in Stowe, he started off washing growlers, and then landed a job filling kegs at Magic Hat in Burlington. As the company quickly grew to become one of the largest in the country, Cohen worked his way up to the position of head brewer. But all along, he hung on to the dream of making the beers he wanted to, so he left Magic Hat in 2010 to strike out on his own. Planning to brew for the local market, he chose the name Fiddlehead, after the scroll-shaped young ferns that appear in spring in New England cuisine.

The tasting room at Fiddlehead is inviting, if not enormous, with lots of blonde wood, pale green walls, and big windows looking out onto the brewhouse. Expect two different beers on tap, both of which are available in growlers ($10 plus a $3 glass deposit) and thirty-two-ounce growlettes ($6 plus a $3 deposit). Save two bucks on growler fills every Monday. As an avid disc golfer, Cohen naturally sells Fiddlehead Frisbees alongside T-shirts, tank tops, baseball hats, and can-shaped pint glasses. He'll probably be willing to tell you how to get to the nearest course in Vergennes if he isn't busy brewing when you turn up.

Rather than designing a large portfolio of ales and lagers, Cohen has decided to concentrate on producing one year-round draft beer: a mainstream, accessible India pale ale. Fragrant with an orange blossom aroma, his Fiddlehead IPA (6.2% ABV) pours a medium amber color with an impressive head of foam. Medium-bodied with an understated bitterness, Fiddlehead IPA has a juicy character and a dry finish. Drinkability, however, is its defining quality. Yet Cohen's dedication to this beer hasn't

CONTACT

6305 Shelburne Road
Shelburne, VT 05482
802-399-2994
www.fiddleheadbrewing.com
@fiddleheadbrew

TASTING ROOM HOURS:

Mon-Sat, Noon-9pm;
Sun, Noon-7pm

LODGING:

Heart of the Village Inn
5347 Shelburne Road
Shelburne, VT 05482
802-985-9060
www.heartofthevillage.com

prevented him from brewing a variety of other styles since launching his small company. With a few exceptions, he sticks to lower-gravity beers—that is beers under 7 percent alcohol by volume. His clean, crisp Bavarian-style Helles lager remains the most sessionable beer he's brewed to date, with only 4.6% ABV. Which isn't to say he always plays it safe. In 2012, the Vermont Folklife Center approached Cohen to brew Frog Run Sap Beer (6.5% ABV), a lightly hopped historical style whereby farmers substituted the final run of maple tree sap in the spring for water.

Folino's Wood Fired Pizza (802-881-8822; www.folinopizza.com), the restaurant that shares the building with Fiddlehead, is the closest place to go to enjoy one of Cohen's beers with food. Their BYOB policy means diners can fill up a growler with Fiddlehead IPA or the current limited release on tap in the tasting room. Meanwhile, at the center of pint-sized Shelburne, the Bearded Frog (802-985-9877; www.thebeardedfrog.com) serves eclectic American fare with an emphasis on seasonality; the drinks list, as one might expect, heavily favors Vermont craft brewers.

A visit to Vermont can hardly be considered complete without a visit to one of the state's numerous parks. Mount Philo (802-425-2390; www.vtstateparks.com) is roughly eight miles south of Fiddlehead. Drive to the top if you're in a hurry, or park at the base and hike less than a mile to the summit. In the other direction, Shelburne Farms (802-985-8686; www.shelburnefarms.org) on Harbor Road is a National Historic Landmark and working farm with ten miles of walking trails, cheesemaking demonstrations, guided property tours, and farm-grown lunches. Southeast of Shelburne, Mad River Glen (802-496-3551; www.madriverglen.com) on General Stark Mountain offers downhill skiers more than forty runs. A network of snowshoe trails is also open throughout winter and links to the Kent Thomas Nature Center. 🍾

HILL FARMSTEAD
BREWERY

YEAR FOUNDED: 2010

FOUNDER:
Shaun Hill

ANNUAL PRODUCTION:
3,000 barrels

**YEAR-ROUND &
SEASONAL BEERS:** Edward Pale
Ale, Abner Double IPA, Ephraim Imperial
Pale Ale, Earl Coffee Oatmeal Stout,
Florence Wheat Saison, Clara Grisette,
Arthur Saison, Foster Black IPA, George
American Brown Ale, Harlan IPA, James
Black Ale, Anna Saison, Edith Black Saison,
Everett Porter, Susan IPA, Vera May
Saison, Mary Pilsner, Civil Disobedience,
Fear & Trembling, Life Without Principle,
Madness & Civilization, Society & Solitude,
Twilight of the Idols

LOCAL FLAVOR: The Hill Farmstead
logo is loosely based on an old design that
appeared on the sign hanging in front of
Shaun's great-great-great-grandfather
Aaron's tavern in the early 1800s.

Based on reputation alone, you might expect Hill Farmstead to be a lot bigger. Disciples of owner-brewer Shaun Hill's uncommon beers talk of pilgrimages to his property in Vermont's Northeast Kingdom and rate his work as among the best in the world. Not bad for a guy who started a brewery to help diversify and preserve his family's small farm— land that they've owned for close to 250 years. Which is why Hill likes to say he's still a homebrewer, just one who produces much larger batches. Larger maybe, but visitors shouldn't expect a massive multi-story brewhouse or a sprawling parking lot blanketed in cars. Hill's brewery occupies a shingled barn that stands next to his weather-worn farmhouse. He's expanded the gravel driveway in front of the retail location once, but the solution for overflow parking is simply to use the adjacent field. Hill first became interested in fermentation in high school; at fifteen, he made it the subject of a science project. Years later he secured a job washing kegs at the Shed Restaurant and Brewery in Stowe that led to a stint as head brewer. Taking this experience with him to Copenhagen, he then worked at Nørrebro Bryghus and won three World Beer Cups. This was his last brewing position before opening Hill Farmstead.

In Vermont, perhaps more than in other states, breweries do much of their business on-site. Hill's is no different, and he's OK with that—he likes people to realize why it's called Hill Farmstead. Follow the winding country roads that lead past old barns and twisting brooks, and eventually you'll see the banner with brewery's logo, a red goblet against a black and orange background, hanging on the side of the building. The retail shop and tasting room isn't particularly large, and depending on the season and time of day, might be busy. Everything here has a handmade look and feel, right down to the Gaudi-esque doorframes inspired by a trip to Barcelona. Five to six taps pour a rotating selection of beers; a taste of four is $5. There isn't much in the way of seating, but you can wander outside to soak up the view. Hill Farmstead sells refillable bottles instead of growlers for $10 (750 ml) or $28 (two liters). Prices include tax and the cost of the container. All sales are cash only. In May, August, and September, the brewery also hosts small festivals with live music, camping, and food from local vendors.

Every beer brewed at Hill Farmstead has a strong sense of place, whether it's the well water, one of their house yeasts, or wildflower honey, organic Vermont spelt, and dandelion flowers in the Vera Mae Saison (6% ABV). Given that his beers are an expression of himself and Greensboro, Hill names each release in the Ancestral Series after one of his relatives. Edward (5.2% ABV), an unfiltered, aromatic, and naturally carbonated pale ale serves as a flagship of sorts, highlighting the flavors and aromas of five different American hop varieties. Regardless of style, each beer in the series has multiple dimensions and a degree of elegance; the flavors you perceive in Anna (6.2% ABV) for instance, a Bière de Miel or honey saison, evolve as you drink. An extensive barrel program is also an important part of the brewery that informs many of the beers in their Philosophical Series. Twilight of the Idols (7.2% ABV), a winter porter brewed with coffee and aged on vanilla beans, is inky black with a thin brown head. Released annually, it's full of round, roasted coffee character and rich bourbon vanilla notes. In

the future, Hill also hopes to plant fruit trees and release more wild ales with Vermont cherries and blueberries.

It's a decent drive from Hill Farmstead to anyplace serving food as well as their beer. Among the nearest, thirty minutes away by car, the Parker Pie Company (802-525-3366; www.parkerpie.com) in West Glover might have as many as six of Hill's beers on tap. The "pies" here are of the savory, Italian variety, and come in three sizes. They'll make you a Margherita if that's what you really want, but a pizza like the Green Mountain Special topped with fresh garlic, cheddar, baby spinach, red onion, bacon, and apple, and drizzled with maple syrup sounds more like something befitting of a piney, complex pale ale like Edward. To reach the Three Penny Taproom (802-223-TAPS; www. threepennytaproom.com) another one of Vermont's well-regarded restaurant pubs, head south from Greensboro and don't stop until you reach Montpelier, the state capital. On occasion, all twenty-four taps here will be pouring Vermont beer. The entire menu, from starters like pickled beet and egg to a simple dessert of vanilla custard and rhubarb, wants to partner with something special. Edith (6% ABV), a tart, slightly funky black saison with a trace of cocoa might be nice with the latter. Among the entrees, a Geuze braised rabbit and spaetzle stands out as a candidate for one of Hill Farmstead's more adventurous blends from their ongoing Philosophical Series of beers.

Greensboro is located in the three-county region known as the Northeast Kingdom. Heavily forested and lightly populated, it's a beautiful part of the state that, like Hill Farmstead, rewards people who make the drive. Adventure seekers might want to try a morning or afternoon of recreational climbing with Twin Pines Tree Climbing (802-684-2164; www.newenglandtreeclimbing.com/vermont.html). If you really have a good time in the canopy, the on-site treehouse doubles as lodging. But for those who'd rather stay on the ground, there are other things to see and do. Many maple sugar houses are open to the public, for example. Visit one like Chandler Pond Farm

(802-626-9460; www.chandlerpondfarm.com) in late March and you can even help collect sap and watch the boiling process. Once a year the Vermont Maple Sugar Makers Association also has an open house weekend. To the south in Hardwick, Caledonia Spirits and Winery (802-472-8000; www.caledoniaspirits.com) offers tastings and tours of their artisan distillery six days a week. Using local honey and organic grains, they produce gin, honey vodka, and elderberry cordial as well as several different types of mead. And of course, if the pleasure of being outdoors is your aim, a swathe of green like Ricker Pond State Park (802-584-3821; www.vtstateparks.com/htm/ricker.htm) in the 26,000-acre Groton State Forest should fit the bill. Lace up your boots, grab a map, and hit the trail.

CONTACT

403 Hill Road
Greensboro, VT 05842
802-533-7450
www.hillfarmstead.com
@HillFarmstead

TASTING ROOM HOURS:

Wed-Sat, Noon-5pm)

LODGING:

The Kimball House
173 Glenside Avenue
Hardwick, VT 05843
802-472-6228
www.kimballhouse.com

LONG TRAIL
BREWING COMPANY

YEAR FOUNDED: 1989

FOUNDER:
Andy Pherson

ANNUAL PRODUCTION:
120,000 barrels

**YEAR-ROUND &
SEASONAL BEERS:** Long Trail
Ale, Blackberry Wheat, IPA, Pale Ale,
Double Bag, Pollenator, Belgian White,
Harvest, Pumpkin Ale, Hit the Trail, Triple
Bag, Coffee Stout, Double IPA, Imperial
Porter, Centennial Red, Double White,
Imperial Pumpkin

LOCAL FLAVOR: About six miles up
the road from the brewery in Plymouth
Notch, Calvin Coolidge was sworn in by his
father as the 30th president of the United
States on August 3, 1923.

All around the region, and in fact, across the country, breweries often choose names associated in some ways with their place of origin: Moat Mountain, Grey Sail, Cape May, Milkhouse. When it comes to Vermont brewery names, Long Trail benefitted from its head start on the craft beer boom. When Andy Pherson first started the business in the basement of the Bridgewater Woolen Mill, he called it Mountain Brewers, later changing it to Long Trail linking it to the 270-mile hiking trail, the Green Mountains, and the state's identity as a place for hiking, camping, and climbing. In 1994, Long Trail moved down the road and built a new facility in a former hay field on the banks of the Ottauquechee River. With a background in mechanical engineering, Pherson actually built much of the original equipment by hand, using it up until his retirement in 2006. Today, the privately owned company he started continues to grow and has since acquired three other Vermont beer brands: The Shed, Otter Creek, and Wolaver's.

The visitor center and Pub at Long Trail is intended to evoke the feel of a German bierhall, an appropriate choice given the historical origins of their flagship beer. Inside the entrance, a retail shop sells all manner of Long Trail accessories, from bike jerseys to bandanas to tank tops and beach towels. The pub area has seating at picnic tables grouped around a wood-burning stove that keeps things warmer during the winter months. Although a local or two can almost always be found at the bar, people from all over world find their way to Bridgewater Corners; a world map covered with pushpins left by visitors from dozens of countries attests to that fact. As a result, you should expect to wait for a table on summer weekends. Adirondack chairs and a few additional tables can

be found outside on the riverside deck, a relaxing place for a pint after a hike or a bike ride. Back inside, the beer can collection on display is Pherson's own and surrounding the room, posters of the brewery's cartoony beer labels cover the walls. Tours are self-guided. Down the road, Long Trail might also turn the farmhouse where they currently brew pilot batches into a bed and breakfast.

As one of the first breweries in the state of Vermont, Long Trail can be seen as a pioneering craft brewery. And while they continue to experiment with styles and introduce new beers with some frequency, they have long produced a range of beers intended to offer something for everyone. From the flavorful, easy drinking Long Trail Ale (4.6% ABV) they debuted with in 1989, which has seen its recipe change very little since, to something newer like the strong Triple Bag (9.2% ABV), a beer that appeals to the well-versed palates of today's drinkers, this brewery favors breadth and variety. After launching with a German-style altbier, Pherson branched out, adding an approachable English-style brown ale and a malty, ruby-colored Scottish ale before arriving at a beer that for many New Englanders signals the return of warmer weather: Blackberry Wheat (4% ABV). Substituting fruity tang for loads of hop bitterness, this golden-hued drink is a refreshing choice on a hot day. More recently still, a Brewmaster's series that debuted in 2008 introduced the world to a bolder version of Long Trail, and includes releases such as their Imperial Porter (8.3% ABV), a jet black ale with a thin tan head, dark roasted malt and coffee in the nose, and an earthy, full-bodied taste that brings to mind tobacco, espresso, and dark chocolate or mocha.

Although beer is obviously the main draw at Long Trail, the brewery also contains a small pub with outdoor seating, label artwork on the walls, and a wood-burning

stove for the winter months. The kitchen keeps things simple with soups, salads, and sandwiches. Vegetarian options include a roasted red pepper hummus wrap and for the healthy eater with a sense of humor, the Hippie Burger. Cheddar ale soup makes for a nice warming snack with a pint of Hit the Trail (4.2% ABV), a malty English-style brown ale with a relatively low level of bitterness. To quiet a grumbling stomach, though, pair the bratwurst topped with maple mustard and grilled onion with a foaming pint of Long Trail Ale. Sit riverside on the deck outdoors, rest your elbows on the horseshoe-shaped bar, or grab a spot at one of the picnic tables scattered around the pub inside. Traveling east on Route 4, the Woodstock Inn (802-457-1100; www.woodstockinn.com/Dining) contains two restaurants on-site: the Red Rooster and Richardson's Tavern. Choose the latter for a more casual atmosphere and less expensive entrees. Port, sherry, and scotch are typically offered with the dessert course at most restaurants, which isn't to say that the right beer couldn't work, too. For example, the creamy, chocolate character of Long Trail's bold Coffee Stout (8% ABV) would harmonize well with the tavern's Tahitian Vanilla Bean Crème Brulee.

In addition to beer, Vermont is known for its cheese, butter, milk, and ice cream. Visit a working dairy farm and learn something about the state's rural heritage at the Billings

Farm & Museum (802-457-2355; www.billingsfarm.org) in Woodstock. Peek inside the restored nineteenth-century farmhouse, watch a short film about the families that lived on the farm, or turn up for a special event like ice cream making in the summer and sleigh rides during the winter months. If there's snow on the ground, you might also want to spend some time on the slopes. Killington Resort (802-422-6200; www.killington.com) in the Green Mountains west of Long Trail is known throughout the Northeast and across the country as a premiere skiing destination. With 140 trails spread out over six peaks, it's the kind of place that can keep downhill lovers happy for days. Back in the other direction, Quechee State Park (802-295-2990; www.vtstateparks.com/htm/quechee.htm) attracts its fair share of visitors as well, many of whom simply want to snap a few pictures of Quechee Gorge, the deepest ravine in the state. To reach the Quechee Gorge Trail, park at the visitor center on Route 4 or the lot on Dewey's Mill Road.

CONTACT

5520 Route 4
Bridgewater Corners, VT 05035
802-672-5011
www.longtrail.com
@LongTrailBeer

TASTING ROOM HOURS:

Daily, 10am-7pm
(Tours are self-guided)

LODGING:

October Country Inn
362 Upper Road
Bridgewater Corners, VT 05035
802-672-3412
www.octobercountryinn.com/

THE NORWICH
INN AND BREWERY

YEAR FOUNDED: 1890 (hotel), 1993 (brewery)

OWNERS:
Joe and Jill Lavin

ANNUAL PRODUCTION:
250 barrels

YEAR-ROUND & SEASONAL BEERS: Piper Patterson's Wee Heavy, Bohemian Pilsner, Ma Walker's Imperial Stout, Whistling Pig Red Ale, Extra Special Bitter, Oh Be Joyful, Old Slipperyskin India Pale Ale, Stackpole Porter, Famous Sidekick, Fuggle & Barleycorn, Another Ale, Private Stock Old Ale, Second Wind Oatmeal Stout, 70 Shilling Scottish Ale, 90 Shilling Scottish Ale, Dark Humour, Light Humour, J & R's Birthday Brown, Perfectly Good Ale, Underground Bitter II, Two Stuck Trucks, Union House Lager, Dunkelweizen, Schwarzpils, Bock From the Trail, 3304 Pale Ale, Fred's Pick, Porch Rocker Red, Kolsch, Norwich Abbey

LOCAL FLAVOR: In July of 1817, President James Monroe stayed at the Norwich Inn, making it the first tavern in Vermont to entertain a chief executive of the United States.

All across New England, colonial inns and country bed and breakfasts beckon travelers to picturesque little towns with village greens, general stores, and pointed white church steeples. The Norwich Inn along the New Hampshire border is one such place, a historic hotel that was the first in Vermont to host a U.S. president. The fact that they brew their own beer sets this inn apart however. They don't do it with much fanfare, and scores of beer pilgrims regularly zip past Norwich on their way to sought-after ales in the north. When Sally and Tim Wilson took over as owners in 1991, Tim decided to add his homebrewed beers to the equation, brewing just five gallons at a time in a cottage converted from a chicken coop behind the inn proper. As demand grew, he scaled up his little operation and turned the livery stable into a brewhouse, pumping his English- and Irish-style beers from the basement across the yard to the Inn, roughly a hundred feet away. Patrick Dakin took over as brewer for a while, and now Jeremy Hebert crafts the beers sold in Jasper Murdock's Alehouse, the pub named for the Dartmouth graduate who established the original hotel in 1797.

The pub at the Norwich Inn keeps six different beers on tap and also mixes a few interesting cocktails like the Lumbahjack: Knob Creek bourbon, sweet vermouth, and Vermont maple syrup ($10). A rectangular room at the back corner of the inn, the pub has a homey vibe with a short little bar by the door and a number of small tables surrounded by ladder-back wicker seat chairs. Plenty of windows, a bright, cheery green coat of paint and leaf-pattern wallpaper, plus the absence of a distracting television, give the space a friendly, welcoming ambience. The

confined brewhouse and Hebert's busy schedule prevent the Inn from offering regular tours, although they do host semi-regular beer events including Brewer's Banquets, beer and cheese pairings, and Bread & Brew Weekends. The latter includes two nights lodging, a brewer's reception and cheese tasting, a hands-on brew day or an optional bread-making class at King Arthur Flour, breakfast, a four-course Brewer's Banquet, a bottle of beer, and a Jasper Murdock glass.

A limited capacity, a one-man brew team, and the decision not to distribute means that Norwich Inn and its Jasper Murdock's Alehouse operate like a brewpub. Guests and passing visitors can purchase select twenty-two-ounce bottles, but the vast majority of the liquid sold here moves through their taps. Beers rotate in and out of the pub with frequency and run the gamut of styles. The one beer that's always available is Whistling Pig (5.6% ABV) a malty, toasty, and well-balanced Irish red ale. Otherwise, you might find the popular Oh Be Joyful (4.8% ABV), a lightly hopped English mild, the pleasantly roasty and decidedly drinkable Stackpole Porter (6% ABV), or Fred's Pick (3.9% ABV), a mild, light-bodied ale with a leafy character provided by fresh hops grown by one of the Inn's servers. In general, the malts and hops Hebert brews with conform to their styles

and traditions of origin: East Kent Golding, Brambling Cross, and Fuggles hops from the United Kingdom for the sessionable English beers, and German ingredients for those influenced by Bavaria's history and culture. A few exceptions do break this mold, however. Norwich Abbey (7.32% ABV) might be best described as a cross between an English brown and a Belgian dubbel; aromas of fruitcake, dates, and brown sugar waft up from a deep brown, near-opaque body with a rich flavor that recalls bread pudding or sticky toffee pudding and malted milk chocolate balls.

The dinner menu at the Norwich Inn isn't particularly lengthy, but it does offer enough variety to please most people. Seating areas include a larger dining room and

an outdoor pub, but choose the pub with its cheery green walls and homey décor to be closest to the six beers on tap. Several of the entrees and appetizers are prepared with Hebert's English-style ales, from the Whistling Pig Wings tossed in a Buffalo sauce made with Whistling Pig Ale, to a venison chili spiked with a liberal splash of beer and served with a side of corn bread. Portions are generous, so a six-ounce filet mignon served with wild mushroom ragout and garlic rosemary whipped potatoes should tide you over until breakfast. Especially when accompanied by a pint of Ma Walkers Imperial Stout (7.17% ABV), a beer named for Mary "Ma" Walker, an innkeeper who allegedly sold bootleg liquor from the basement during Prohibition. Norwich Abbey, meanwhile, a hybrid style with dates and brown sugar in the nose and a sticky toffee pudding flavor, is a rich, full of character beer that can be appreciated on its own as you digest your meal. And while they don't pour Jasper Murdock ales, Seven Barrel Brewery just across the New Hampshire State line in West Lebanon is a fun detour for the beer tourist. Started in 1994 by Greg Noonan, who also opened the state's first brewpub in Burlington, Seven Barrel has eight taps of its own ales as well as mead from New Hampshire's Moonlight Meadery.

From concerts to film festivals, and free lectures to theater performances, the Hopkins Center for the Arts (603-646-2422; www.hop.dartmouth.edu) at Dartmouth College just across the Connecticut River is the closest place to go for an evening of entertainment. Every year more than 300 film screenings, live performances, and other events take place in the main auditorium or one of the two theaters here, in a building designed by the architect of New York City's Lincoln Center. Also on campus, the Hood Museum of Art (603-646-2808; www.hoodmuseum.dartmouth.edu) includes close to 65,000 artifacts and works of art from Africa, Asia, Europe, Oceania, and the Americas. Highlights such as ninth-century BCE Assyrian reliefs, paintings of the American West by Frederick Remington, as well as modern works from Georgia O'Keeffe, Pablo Picasso, and Yves Klein, make a free tour of the Hood's galleries worthwhile. To enjoy some time outdoors, head to the Mink Brook Nature Preserve (603-643-3433; www.hanoverconservancy.org/lands/mink-brook), a 112-acre parcel of wooded land maintained by the Hanover Conservancy. Explore the preserve by following one of five short trails that wind alongside and across Mink Brook and Trout Brook. 🍶

CONTACT

325 Main Street
Norwich, VT 05055
802-649-1143
www.norwichinn.com
@NorwichInn

TASTING ROOM HOURS:

Tue-Sat, 11:30am-Close;
Sun, Noon-Close
(Breakfast hours vary)

ROCK ART
BREWERY

YEAR FOUNDED: 1997

FOUNDERS:
Matt and Renee Nadeau

ANNUAL PRODUCTION:
5,000 barrels

YEAR-ROUND &
SEASONAL BEERS: Ridge Runner, Whitetail Ale, Double IPA, Double Porter, Hells Bock, Golden Tripple, Infusco, American Red, IPA, Midnight Madness, Riddler, Stock Ale, Stump Jumper, Sunny & 75, Vermonster, Black Moon IPA, Belvedere IPA, Jasmine Pale Ale, Magnumus ete Tomahawkus, Vermont Maple Wheat Ale, Vermont Hop Harvest, Pumpkin Imperial Spruce Stout, Mountain Holidays in Vermont

LOCAL FLAVOR: Before building a new brewery on Route 100, Rock Art operated out of a former granite warehouse near Lake Lamoille on the north side of town.

The name and kokopelli logo might suggest the American Southwest, but Rock Art is a decidedly Vermont company, owned and operated by Matt Nadeau and his wife, Renee, two natives of the Green Mountain State. After meeting at Johnson State College, the couple headed west, ending up in Colorado just as the Breckenridge Brewery got off the ground. The timing and location of their move proved influential, and when they moved back to Vermont to get married and start a family, they also began to think seriously about a brewery. Initially running a brewing supply store out of their basement in Johnson, Nadeau developed recipes in his free time and brought his beers to parties where friends would tell him he ought to sell it. So in 1997, the homebrew shop became a brewery, and Rock Art was born. Putting their profits back into the company, the Nadeaus soon reached capacity at their basement brewery and relocated to Morrisville where they could install a larger brewhouse and more tanks. Even after a second move, Rock Art continues to source locally whenever possible, using glassware from Bennington and malt from Montreal.

Now in their third location since starting, the Nadeaus finally have a brewing facility and a visitor center that didn't require any compromises. The brewery itself is impressive in size, with room to grow even more, while the public space, which occupies a former creamery, is big enough to fit a few dozen people without feeling crowded. If it does feel crowded, step out onto the front porch for some mountain air. At the tasting bar, eight taps pour the freshest Rock Art ales and lagers in the state. Sample any four beers for $4 and then head upstairs to the balcony to view the 10,000-square foot brewery. Twice a day the staff also leads brief tours. Growler refills cost between $6 and $10 (plan to pay a little more if you didn't bring one with you). In addition to bottles of their own products, Rock Art's large gift shop also carries apparel, chocolate, cheese, water bottles, and other items from other Vermont businesses, including wood products crafted by Renee's brother, Jason, who also makes their tap handles.

As with many craft brewers, Nadeau began by making the beers he liked to drink himself; he still doesn't do a fruit beer because he doesn't enjoy them. To try to distinguish himself from the numerous pale and amber ales at the time, he released Whitetail Ale (5% ABV), a lighter golden-colored beer with a mellow character, first. Intending to brew a stronger barleywine with Ridge Runner (7.2% ABV), Nadeau discovered that he couldn't get the alcohol level much higher than 7.5% in his basement brewery, and decided to settle on a toned-down version of this English style. Pumpkin Imperial Spruce Stout (8% ABV) is a big beer inspired by colonial brewers who lacked access to malt and supplemented their recipes with other starches. It owes much of its flavor to spruce tips and black strap molasses. Black Moon IPA (10% ABV) is bolder still, pouring with a pitch-black body and a thick brown head of foam. Lots of piney hops and woodsy aromas leap from the glass immediately and the medium-bodied ale delivers plenty of resinous bitterness, followed by a burnt-cookie sweetness and a drying finish.

South of Rock Art, Hen of the Wood (802-244-7300; www.henofthewood.com) in Waterbury began attracting attention soon after opening in a former gristmill built in the nineteenth century. Billed as a celebration of Vermont's farms and named after an edible wild mushroom, this is a restaurant where you can expect to find quail liver pâté or steak from an Angus farm forty miles away. Request a bottle of Ridge Runner, a mild-mannered version of a style that's typically higher in alcohol, and drink it with a selection from their cheese list, preferably a crumbly yet creamy blue like Jasper Hill Farm's Bayley Hazen. Walking distance from the brewery on Morrisville's Main Street, The Bee's Knees (802-888-7889; www.thebeesknees-vt.com) also sources ingredients from local growers and producers, including their own Do Nothing Farm. For something different, try an Asian stir fry over udon noodles with Rock Art's Golden Tripple (8% ABV). The addition of fresh ginger to the kettle during the brewing process makes this semi-dry beer a friend of Asian cuisine, as does its lush, gentle level of carbonation. At Claire's Restaurant and Bar (802-472-7053; www.clairesvt.com) in Hardwick, pair Vermont Maple Wheat Ale (5.4% ABV) with the maple-glazed pork loin.

When the weather in Vermont is agreeable, spend as much time outdoors as your schedule will allow. From November to late April, Stowe Mountain Resort (802-253-3000; www.stowe.com) on Mount Mansfield, the highest point in the state, attracts skiers from across New England and beyond. With more than one hundred trails, terrain parks, and a Nordic skiing center, it's been a popular escape for winter sport enthusiasts since 1937. Sitting between Spruce Peak and Mt. Mansfield, the Stowe Mountain Lodge is also the only place to find Hourglass Ale (6% ABV), a beer made by Rock Art. But there's more to Stowe than the powdery stuff. Golf courses, a climbing wall, a bungee trampoline, and an alpine slide that winds 2,300 feet down Spruce Peak make the resort an appealing stop in the summer, too. Instead of skiing or snowboarding during a winter visit to the area, you can also take a two-hour journey through the backcountry with Stowe Snowmobile Tours (802-253-6221; www.stowesnowmobiletours.com). Or, if you prefer horses to snowmobiles, continue south on Route 100 through Waterbury until you reach the little town of Fayston and the Vermont Icelandic Horse Farm (802-496-7141; www.icelandichorses.com). Reserve a spot on a guided trail ride or a multi-day trek. 🍾

CONTACT
632 Laporte Road/Route 100
Morrisville, VT 05661
802-888-9400
www.rockartbrewery.com/home
@RockArtBrewery

TASTING ROOM HOURS:
Mon-Sat, 9am-6pm (Tours at
2 & 4pm; otherwise self-guided)

LODGING:
Thistledown Inn Bed & Breakfast
201 Park Street
Morrisville, VT 05661
802-279-6120
www.thistledowninn.com

ACKNOWLEDGMENTS

Alison Rohrs, Gayle and Jack Keene, Becky Keene, Rob Tempio, Erin Graham, Caitlin Allen, Chris and Lary Shafer, Mike Wei, Stephanie Jelliffe, Bill Elliston, Lavina Lee, Luke Andrews Hakken, Charlie Rohrs, Grace Labatt, Dennis Pernu, Steve Roth, Maeve Sheridan, Catherine Matthews, Garrett Oliver, Katie and Ben Adams, and Kate McKwean.

BIBLIOGRAPHY

Adamian, John. "Relic Brewery in Plainville Creates Demand for Its Small-Batch Artisanal Beers." *Hartford Advocate*. June 20, 2012.

Asimov, Eric. *How to Love Wine*. New York, NY: HarperCollins, 2012.

Bilger, Burkhard. "A Better Brew." *The New Yorker*. November 24, 2008.

"Born in a Barn: America's Farmhouse Breweries." *Draft*. March/April 2011.

Bostwick, William, and Jessi Rymill. *Beer Craft*. New York, NY: Rodale, 2011.

Burgess, Nathan. "Rock Art Brewery." *Stowe Today*. April 22, 2009.

"The 'Burgh Beer Bible." *Pittsburgh Magazine*. October 2012.

Bryson, Lew. *Pennsylvania Breweries*, 4th ed. Mechanicsburg, PA: Stackpole Books, 2010.

Carter, Spike. "An Interview with Shaun Hill, Brewmaster at Hill Farmstead, the 'Best Brewery in the World'" *Vanity Fair*. April 25, 2013.

Chance Smith, Larissa. "These Buds Make Brews: Chambersburg's Roy Pitz Brewing Company." *Hagerstown*. July/August 2010.

Crouch, Andy. *The Good Beer Guide to New England*. Lebanon, NH: University Press of New England, 2006.

Curtin, Jack. "Different Strokes, Different Coasts: How Craft Brewing Grew on Either Side of the Country." *American Brewer*. Summer 2006.

D'Ambrosio, Dan. "Three Vermont Brewers Taking Beer World by Storm." *Burlington Free Press*. March 1, 2013.

Danehower, Cole. *Essential Wines and Wineries of the Pacific Northwest*. Portland, OR: Timber Press, 2010.

DeBenedetti, Christian. *The Great American Ale Trail*. Philadelphia, PA: Running Press, 2011.

Dresser, Michael. "Belgian-Type Beers From N.Y. Brewery." *The Baltimore Sun*. November 28, 2001.

Dzen, Gary. "Crafting a Better Beer." *The Boston Globe*. April 12, 2013.

Falco, Mat. "A Project of Passion." *Philly Beer Scene*. June/July 2009.

Fleischer, Chris. "On Tap: Larger Brewers Think Small to Keep Innovation Flowing." *Valley News*. April 24, 2013.

Fromson, Daniel. "Craft Brewery with Built-in Dreams." *The Washington Post*. February 19, 2013.

Giuca, Linda. "Something's Brewing." *Hartford Magazine*. October 2012.

Goode, Steve. "New Partner at Right Moment Allows Brewery to Flourish." *Hartford Courant*. January 30, 2011.

Gorelick, Richard. "The 7 Percent Solution." *Baltimore City Paper*. February 25, 2004.

Haiber, Rob. "Belgo-American Brewing." *All About Beer*. January, 2002.

Helterman, Jolyon. "Homegrown: Hill Farmstead Brewery in Vermont." *Yankee*. March 2013.

Hindy, Steve, and Tom Potter. *Beer School*. Hoboken, NJ: Wiley, 2005.

Holl, John, and April Darcy. *Massachusetts Breweries*. Mechanicsburg, PA: Stackpole Books, 2012.

Hop Variety Handbook. Yakima, WA: Hopunion LLC, 2011.

Hughes, Christopher. "Liquid Diet: A Chat with Dogfish Head's Sam Calagione." *Boston Magazine*. February 7, 2013.

Jackson, Michael. *Great Beer Guide*. New York, NY: Dorling Kindersley, 2000.

Jackson, Michael. *The New World Guide to Beer*. Philadelphia, PA: Running Press, 1988.

Johnson, Julie. "Pull Up a Stool with Scott Vaccaro." *All About Beer*. November, 2008.

Johnson, Steve. "Jasper Murdock's Alehouse." *Brew Your Own*. June, 1995.

Kalesse, Rob. "16 Mile: Delaware's Newest Craft Brewery." *Spark 247*. August 11, 2009.

Kasper, Rob. *Baltimore Beer*. Charleston, SC: The History Press, 2012.

Keene, Ben. "Heads Up, Big Boys." *Edible Jersey*. Fall 2011.

Keene, Ben. "Suds and Sand." *Edible East End*. Summer 2010.

Kiriluk-Hill, Renée. "More Beer: River Horse Moving from Lambertville to Bigger Space in Ewing." *Hunterdon County Democrat*. January 11, 2013.

Lamardo, Michael. "Brewery Profile: Fiddlehead Brewing Company." *The Washington Times*. February 15, 2013.

Lawson, Nancy. "New Brew Pub Opening Before the Beer's Ready." *Baltimore Business Journal*. September 16, 1996.

Lewis, Sean. "From the Source: Crossroads Brewing Co." *BeerAdvocate*. June 2012.

Luttrell, Martin. "Ale in the Family." *Worcester Telegram & Gazette*. June 21, 2006.

Magee, Jamie. "Thomas Hooker: Transformed." *Yankee Brew News*. February/March 2011.

Malone, J. D. "Weyerbacher Tripling Capacity at Easton Brewery." *The Morning Call*. February 27, 2012.

Martin, Justin. "A Creepy Sea Hag Legend Sells Beer." *Fortune Small Business*. March 4, 2007.

McCormack, Lisa. "The Art of the Brew." *Stowe Toda*. June 23, 2011.

McMorrow, Paul. "9 Steps to Beerdom: Casey Hughes." *BeerAdvocate*. December 2012.

McMorrow, Paul. "9 Steps to Beerdom: Scott Smith." *BeerAdvocate*. May 2012.

Mosher, Randy. *Tasting Beer*. North Adams, MA: Storey Publishing, 2009.

Oliver, Garrett. *The Brewmaster's Table*. New York, NY: HarperCollins, 2003.

Oliver, Garrett. *The Oxford Companion to Beer*. New York, NY: Oxford University Press, 2011.

Pumphrey, Will. "Coastal Crafting." *Philly Beer Scene*. April/May 2013.

Reed, Brian. "The Church Brew Works." *Craft Pittsburgh*. January–March 2013.

Reid, Peter. "The Art in Brewing." *Modern Brewery Age*. May 8, 2000.

Rhen, Brad. "Beer: A New Aroma in Hershey." *Lebanon Daily News*. January 21, 2012.

Rulison, Larry. "At Long Last, A Dream Is On Tap." *The Times Union*. October 19, 2010.

Schenck, John. "Newport Storm: Days and Nights with Derek Luke." *Edible Rhody*. Winter 2007.

Serpick, Evan. "Baltimore's Beer Renaissance." *Baltimore*. October 2010.

Sharpton, Ale. "Innovators Series: Garrett Oliver." *The Beer Connoisseur*. Spring 2010.

Simmon, Virginia. "Brewing Up a Storm" *Business People-Vermont*. August 2005.

Simpson, Stan. "Serial Entrepreneur Finds Fun, Profit in Brewing Beer." *Hartford Business Journal*. January 7, 2013.

Smith, Peter A. "Rob Tod." *The Maine Magazine*. January/February 2010.

Sopchak, Julie. "Relic Brewing Hops into Town." *The Plainville Citizen*. April 26, 2013.

Trofa, Grace. "Sean Larkin: Inspiration by the Pint in a Job Well Done." *Edible Rhody*. Summer 2008.

Vandenengel, Heather. "Honest Pint: Oxbow Brewing Company." *DigBoston*. August 22, 2012.

Young-Knox, Sara. "Brewery Now on Tap at Woodstock Inn Station." *New Hampshire Union Leader*. February, 9, 2013.

INDEX